L'Hermite de la Tombe Mystérieuse, ou le Fantôme du Vieux Château, anecdote extraite des Annales du Treizième Siècle, par Mme Anne Radcliffe (sic), et traduite sur le Manuscrit anglais par M. E. L. D. L. Paris (Ménard & Desenne), 1816, frontispiece, tome I.

The Gothic Imagination:
Essays in Dark Romanticism

Edited by G. R. Thompson

Washington State University Press

138362

For my parents

Maxine Louise Thompson

Ralph Burton Thompson

Preface

The essays in the present volume are published here for the first time. They were all written expressly for this book, which itself grew out of the informal discussions of a handful of Medieval and Romantic scholars at Washington State University on the general subject of the Dark Tradition in literature, with special reference to Romantic Gothic. At first, we thought to collect a few papers on various aspects of this tradition, from ancient Gnostic rites to alchemy, revenge tragedy, witchcraft, the graveyard school of poetry, and Gothic fiction and poetry of the eighteenth and nineteenth centuries. At my invitation, scholars from five other universities joined us in the venture. Instead of a diversity of loosely related subjects and themes, as we might have expected, we found that we had a volume focused on the religious and meta-physical aspects of "romance" literature of the diabolist strain. This correlation of interests was fortuitous but perhaps inevitable in a curious dialectical way. Until the 1950's, the prevailing critical view of Gothic literature was essentially that of the later nineteenth-century moralists: namely, that the Gothic lacked "high seriousness." Even in a book on the growth of the English novel published not too long ago, we are told that the Gothic "denies the principle of original sin." Both judgments constitute radical misconceptions. And it is the exact converse of such pronouncements that the present volume, despite its genesis as a miscellany, persistently suggests by placing Gothic works in a developing tradition. Some favorite critical generalizations are overturned in this volume, and the moral support for the book has been substantive. I wish here to acknowledge the generous gift of a grant-in-aid from Mrs. Mildred Bissinger. Maurice Lévy made available illustrations from his private collection of frontispieces to French translations of early English Gothic novels. My colleague, Thomas C. Faulkner, gave us access to his extensive collection of photographs of cathedrals and grotesques and has also written brief comments on the plates we were able to use. Encouragement of various kinds came from other colleagues, Virginia M. Hyde, Nicolas K. Kiessling, and particularly John W. Ehrstine; a special debt of gratitude is owed Henry Grosshans, Editor at Washington State University Press, for his unwavering belief in the value of the project. Inclusion of illustrations was made possible by a Shell Companies Foundation faculty development grant. Finally, though it is gratuitous, it would at the same time be remiss not to thank all the scholars whose essays are published here and whose contributions to our understanding of the Gothic imagination will be self-evident.

Pullman, Washington
April 1974

CONTENTS

Introduction:
Romanticism and the Gothic Tradition

G. R. THOMPSON

In art history the word *Gothic* normally refers to various architectural styles of cathedrals built during the Middle Ages. In literature the word refers to the kind of work, usually fiction, that developed during the later eighteenth and earlier nineteenth centuries out of the sentimental romance into the Dark Romantic tale of terror. The word *Romantic* usually evokes an ideal world, infused with internal energy and dynamically evolving toward a yet higher state, in which the single, separate self seeks unity with Nature, itself symbolic of the aesthetic harmony of the cosmos. Adding the adjective *Dark* may evoke an image of the lonely, isolated self, pressing onward despite all obstacles while either indulging or struggling with an internal evil, the very conflict a source of energy. But when the word *Gothic* is applied to literature, it merely evokes images of ghosts, demons, trapdoors, castles. In America, Gothic fiction is frequently associated with the "dime novel," in Britain perhaps more precisely called the "shilling-shocker" or the "penny-dreadful." All three terms point to the origins of the Gothic romance as a popular literature, inexpensively produced for a mass audience, with the consequent implication that it is merely a literature of surfaces and sensations.

This judgment tends to ameliorate somewhat when the ostensible genre of such literature is poetry or drama. In poetry, one has to contend with the names of Byron, Coleridge, and Keats; and in drama, one thinks immediately of the bloody revenge plays of Shakespeare and Webster, replete with ghosts and visions. Certain masterworks of Gothic fiction have been acknowledged— *The Monk, Melmoth the Wanderer, Frankenstein*—but the suspicion persists that these are lesser works than the "standard" classics. And classic works of fiction which employ Gothic conventions and subjects, like *Heart of Darkness,* tend not to be critically examined in the tradition of a developing Gothic mode but in some other, more acceptable tradition of the novel. Thus, although critics will grant that a work like *Wuthering Heights* comes out of the Gothic tradition, it is usually regarded as transcending its surface mode of Gothic.

G. R. THOMPSON, Associate Professor of English at Washington State University, is author of *Poe's Fiction: Romantic Irony in the Gothic Tales* and other works.

The prime example of this critical phenomenon, perhaps, is *Moby-Dick*, for it has seemed to most readers somehow reductive to call Melville's novel a Gothic romance. Yet its very Gothic quality may be what gives such a wild and whirling work as *Moby-Dick* its peculiar excellence.

Indeed, in France the Gothic has long been considered a *genre*, though the French meaning of the word may differ slightly from the English. But a theory of *genre* that precisely defines, analyzes, and distinguishes among themes, subject matters, formal elements, characteristic devices, philosophical concerns, or a developing tradition is yet to be written. The twentieth-century assumption of the essential rightness of dividing literary genres into fiction, poetry, drama, biography, and essay is obviously inadequate for a history of literature. At one time, the principal genres were—in view of what had been written—epic, tragic, and lyric—established forms we still recognize but the precise delimitations of which dissolve the closer we examine them. We have had Henry Fielding's "comic epic in prose," as well as tragic drama, tragic poetry, prose tragedy, lyric drama, dramatic lyrics, and so on; and one may recall Polonius' reading of the players' list of types in *Hamlet*: ". . . tragedy, comedy, history, pastoral, pastoral-comical, historical-pastoral, tragical-historical, tragical-comical-historical-pastoral, scene individable or poem unlimited." The question therefore becomes one of recurrent configurations of concerns, themes, subjects, characters, conflicts, conventions, modes, devices, or images that identify the Gothic as a form. Such a question does not necessarily imply an exclusive differentiation from all other genres. *Moby-Dick*, again, is part narrative, part drama, part poetry, part essay. It is also deeply Gothic throughout.

Although the present volume began as a general collection on the darker side of Romanticism, representing diverse interests and diverse critical approaches, it has taken on surprisingly sharp focus as the parameters of a Dark Romantic genre began to outline themselves. Indeed, it seems to me now a very bold book, in which scholars have been willing to risk their reputations in some unusual speculation. What emerges is an essay toward a definition of the Gothic in literature—an exploration, however tentative, in quest of a Gothic monomyth that explains the curious power of the literature— something beyond the local terrors and horrors of stage villains and trembling heroines and ghostly manifestations. What the essays persistently suggest is that the kind of high Gothic represented by *Melmoth*, or *Moby-Dick*, or *Heart of Darkness* is the embodiment of demonic-quest romance, in which a lonely, self-divided hero embarks on insane pursuit of the Absolute. This self-destructive quest is metaphysical, mythic, and religious, defining the hero's dark or equivocal relationship to the universe. Its imagery characteristically employs an iconography tracing an unbroken tradition to the Age of Faith. Thus the essays collected here explore in one way or another the complex relationship between Medieval origins of Gothic art and the Romantic literary mode of Gothic terror and horror. Diabolist and Paradisaical (Dark and Light) Romanticism are examined with recurrent reference to Medieval antecedents, recognizing not form only but also religious or metaphysical meaning.

The concept of the icon, both verbal and visual, is an important means of illustrating the extent of the continuity of Medieval Gothic and Romantic Gothic, bringing graphic proof to religious claims and religious significance to formalist observations. Medieval images and motifs are used by later writers to define a negative or positive relationship to God. Although not every essay is specifically iconographic, and although not every essay is specifically focused on a Romantic Gothic work, each revolves in some manner around the breakdown of a stable Medieval world order, paralleling the mythic expulsion of man from Eden. Collectively, the essays trace the Romantic Age's fascination with the duality of the Middle Ages. This duality finds expression, on the one hand, in the evocation of the transcendent, upward thrust of Gothic cathedrals and in the "romances" of idealized knights in quest of the Holy Grail; and, on the other hand, in the vision of the dark night of the soul and the nightmare terror of demons Satan-sent from Hell to drag man down. Romantic Gothic deals with the tormented condition of a creature suspended between the extremes of faith and skepticism, beatitude and horror, being and nothingness, love and hate—and anguished by an indefinable guilt for some crime it cannot remember having committed.

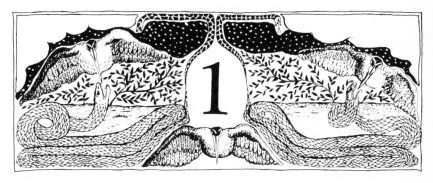

As the foregoing suggests, the phrase "tale of terror" is inadequate to describe the effect of the Gothic romance, for it has a complex rather than a single unified impact—Poe's famous definitions notwithstanding. The chief element of the Gothic romance is not so much terror as, more broadly, dread—whether physical, psychological, or metaphysical, whether of body, mind, or spirit. The Gothic romance seeks to create an atmosphere of dread by combining terror with horror and mystery. *Terror* suggests the frenzy of physical and mental fear of pain, dismemberment, and death. *Horror* suggests the perception of something incredibly evil or morally repellent. *Mystery* suggests something beyond this, the perception of a world that stretches away beyond the range of human intelligence—often morally incomprehensible—and thereby productive of a nameless apprehension that may be called religious dread in the face of the wholly *other*. When in Gothic literature this sense of mystery is joined with terror or horror, the effects of each expand beyond ordinary fear or repugnance. Mrs. Radcliffe suggested as much in her often-misunderstood essay "On the Supernatural in Poetry," wherein she asserts that terror and horror are really "opposite." Terror "expands the soul" and "wakens the faculties to a high degree"; horror "contracts, freezes, and nearly annihilates them." But this is another paradox of Gothic duality; terror and horror represent complementary poles of a single continuum of perception and response. Terror, in her terms, may be seen as coming upon us from without, engulfing

3

us with an aweful sense of the sublime in which sense of self is swallowed in immensity—whereas horror rises up from within, with a vague consciousness of the "dreader evil" sinking downward through levels of subconscious "uncertainty and obscurity" into a vast unconscious reservoir of primitive dread. The central image for these paradoxes in the Gothic is the cathedral itself, for it has both an outward, upward movement toward the heavens, and an inward, downward motion, convoluting in upon itself in labyrinthine passages and dark recesses, descending to catacombs deep in the earth.

But while we conceive of the Gothic romance as evoking that supernatural sense of mystery associated with the dark interior of a cathedral, the earliest meanings of the English word *Gothic* involved an elementary kind of aesthetic and cultural disapproval based on imprecise historical hypotheses. Early eighteenth-century writers used *Gothic* to indicate any architectural structure not in the "classical" style of Greece and Rome; they hypothesized that "Gothic" or other northern barbarians had invaded the Roman empire, wreaking destruction on the true art of the ancient Roman works and replacing them with a "fantastical" manner of building characterized by walls that were too thick, towers that were too tall, arches that were too steeply pointed. This unhappy circumstance was made yet more lamentable in their eyes by subsequent infusions of Arab temple styles during the Moorish invasions of Europe between the twelfth and thirteenth centuries. The effect of such structures on the human mind, they thought, was a barbarous "confusion." In retrospect, however, this eighteenth-century response can be seen as reflective of the consistent duality found also in the Gothic literature of the end of the century: on the one hand, the sublime evoked the thrill of mystery and wonder, the aspiration upward toward God; on the other hand, it evoked a ponderous, depressing sense of somber gloom, as well as terror engendered by such demonic ornamentation as bass figures and gargoyles within and without the cathedral. In 1764-65, Horace Walpole in *The Castle of Otranto,* usually considered the first Gothic romance in English, emphasized the vaults, stained windows, tombs, darkness, and carefully coordinated perspective of Medieval buildings—a perspective that in the cathedral was designed to bring the observer to his knees. Walpole's work effected a shift of meaning in the most common use of the word *Gothic* from the architectural denotation of "Medieval buildings" to the emotional effect of weird, supernatural, fantastic, and terrifying events in a work of literature in which the Medieval cathedral or castle served as a theater for such events.

Between 1750 and 1800, however, a larger reevaluation of the Gothic emphasized the "natural" symbology that man-made cathedrals presented. Edmund Burke in his *Enquiry into The Sublime and Beautiful* (1756-57) observed that a certain "wildness" in nature and art produced the effect of the "sublime" through the evocation of a sense of supernatural mystery. Others observed that the external mass of the cathedral suggested a mountain and that the interior, profuse with grotesque scrollwork around windows and ceilings, suggested branches and groves of trees. By the turn of the century German Romantic writers were contending that Gothic buildings were actually symbols of forests, icons of the primitive, natural, Edenic habitat of man. And by 1825, British and American Romanticists had inverted the equation, as articulated in William Cullen Bryant's "A Forest Hymn":

The groves were God's first temples. Ere man learned
To hew the shaft, and lay the architrave,
And spread the roof above them—ere he framed
The lofty vault, to gather and roll back
The sound of anthems; in the darkling wood,
Amid the cool and silence, he knelt down. . . .

Here we have an expression of a view adopted by many European and American writers of the later eighteenth and earlier nineteenth centuries—namely, transcendental, cosmic optimism—that spiritual and aesthetic faith in a harmoniously integrated, organic universe dynamically evolving toward a yet higher and better state. The overt cultural values of the earlier nineteenth century in Europe and America were, of course, solidly Christian, Enlightenment losses of faith notwithstanding. In one sense, the cosmic optimism of Romantic thinkers was the secularization of a powerful Christian tradition and liturgy into a rhetoric that ostensibly omitted an anthropomorphized God but which still assumed a deific force. This God-force seemed to be dynamically propelling man through a prefigured (though not precisely predestined) pattern of events toward some beneficent end; and the element of God's justified vengeance and wrath upon sinful and fallen man that formed one aspect of Medieval Christian thought was temporarily submerged in the dominance of this optimistic Romanticism. But the apprehension that there was a dark substratum to the rock of Romantic faith obsessed those Romantic writers who turned to the Gothic mode of terror and horror in an effort to express a complex vision of the existential agony confronting man since the Age of Faith.

Fallen man's inability fully to comprehend haunting reminders of another, supernatural realm that yet seemed not to exist, the constant perplexity of inexplicable and vastly metaphysical phenomena, a propensity for seemingly perverse or evil moral choices that had no firm or fixed measure or rule, and a sense of nameless guilt combined with a suspicion that the external world was a delusive projection of the mind—these were major elements in the vision of man that the Dark Romantics opposed to the mainstream of Romantic thought. This vision was reenforced by the recently propounded subjective philosophies of Berkeley, Hume, and Kant in the second half of the eighteenth century. And once the doubt was established in the Dark Romantic mind, it did not matter whether one assumed the world to be objective or subjective, for the same dialectics of agony could apply to either. If one contemplates the world as object, it may be either a structure infused with spirit and supplying neoplatonic symbols of the other dynamic life beyond this one, or mere physical material with no object beyond the immediate fact of existence. If one contemplates the world as subject, then it may either be a dynamic projection of the indwelling spirit of man himself, or a deceptive, arbitrary imposition of idiosyncratic meaning upon Void. Moreover, Medieval antecedents clearly conceive of Void as double. The Void of Plenitude asserted God's immanence in all things; the Void of Nothingness imaged God's absence. The Dark Romantics tended toward an ambiguous midregion of agonized doubt or suspension, believing neither in Plenitude nor in Nothingness—though obsessed with the latter possibility.

In a Romantic context, then, Gothic literature may be seen as expressive of an existential terror generated by a schism between a triumphantly secularized philosophy of evolving good and an abiding obsession with the Medieval conception of guilt-laden, sin-ridden man. In part, Gothic themes represent a quest for a theory adequate to world perceived as mind. In the absence of any satisfactory theory that accounted for the existence of evil and pain, the Gothic tale could at least embody the world felt, if not perceived, as mind. If Romanticism is largely a philosophy of consciousness, Dark Romanticism is the drama of the mind engaged in the quest for metaphysical and moral absolutes in a world that offers shadowy semblances of an occult order but withholds final revelation and illumination. If a distinction between the Romantic Gothic imagination and the Dark Romantic imagination can be made, it is perhaps that the purely Gothic vision ends in despair, pain, and annihilation. The Gothic hero is ultimately torn apart by demons. The Dark Romantic hero, by working in and through evil and darkness, by withholding final investment of belief in either good or evil, by enduring the treachery of his own mind, and by accepting his crucifixion by whatever demonic forces may exist, perhaps attains some Sisyphean or Promethean semblance of victory.

In any event, as dramas of darkness, the literary productions of the Romantic Gothic mind embody this nameless dread in characters of flesh and blood. Whereas transcendental Romantic thought attempted in essence to depersonalize or de-anthropomorphize the traditional Void of Plenitude, in which the God-spirit was imminent but not particularized, the Dark Romantics adapted images of anthropomorphized evil in the form of Satan, devils, ghosts, lamia, incubi, succubi, vampires, and ghouls. While these demonic creatures frequently inhabit an ambiguous landscape of duplicitous imagery, the recurrent images in the literature of terror and horror are yet vivid. The empty seascapes, frozen wastes, bottomless abysses, vast blank landscapes are opposed to images of aspirational height in cathedral vaulting or spires; darkness is opposed to luminous shining forth; a solitary figure edging toward the precipice, surrounded by forked lightning threatening to blast his wracked body, is opposed to the resurrection of the body in full perfection of form, surrounded by the ascending heavenly host. In addition to symbolizing the particular dramatic situation, however, Romantic Gothic imagery employs a rich complex of traditional images—in short a Christian iconography of fallen man. But the difference is that in Romantic Gothic literature man is confronted with an ambiguous world structure rather than the clearcut world of the Middle Ages. Instead, he faces a world that he has no hope of comprehending and in which he cannot make the proper moral choices, even though he is yet held responsible by some occult power for such choices.

Now, by an "iconography" of the Gothic, or more broadly of Dark Romanticism, we should understand several things simultaneously about the literature: the obsessive images and recurring emblematic figures; the recurring religious undercurrent of meaning; and some sort of objective correlative found both in specific works and in the "genre" that co-relates the themes of physical terror, moral horror, and religious mystery with recurring character types and recurring images of desolate landscapes and seascapes, castles and cathedrals, towers and dungeons. As suggested, in a large sense, we are in quest of a Gothic monomyth; but more specifically we are in quest of a verbal icon that brings together the various threads and strands of the Gothic fabric. Here, of course, I borrow a phrase from W. K. Wimsatt's *The Verbal Icon.* In this volume, addressing himself to a theory of verbal meaning, Wimsatt deals with the "interpenetration of abstractly stated meaning and the more concrete, unspecified, and diffusive meaning of metaphors and dramatic structures." In the epigraph to the book as a whole, Wimsatt defines this construct as follows:

The term *icon* is used today by semeiotic writers to refer to a verbal sign which *somehow* shares the properties of, or resembles, the objects which it denotes. The same term in its more usual meaning refers to a visual image and especially to one which is a religious symbol. The verbal image which most fully realizes its verbal capacities is that which is not merely a bright picture (in the usual modern meaning of the term *image*) but also an interpretation of reality in its metaphoric and symbolic dimensions.

The essays in this volume suggest the persistency of Gothic writers in using religious symbols and images as a vehicle for presenting a picture of man as eternal victim—victim of both himself and of something outside himself. The demons, gods, mythic heroes, and other human icons, along with castle, cathedral, manor house, temple, graveyard, churchyard, charnel house, dungeon, labyrinth, cave, icebound seas, high mountain crags, lightning, storms—are all, simultaneously, emblems of supernatural power external to the human mind, and of the agony within the human mind and spirit. They are metaphors of the self and of the nameless other, conjoined for a metaphor of the agonizing duality imbedded deep in the human personality.

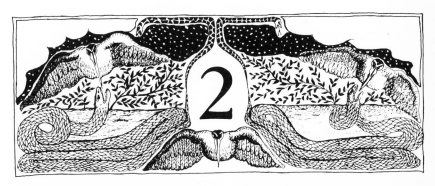

Despite an implied uniformity of theme that emerges from these essays, however, they present no single approach. S. L. Varnado, synthesizing certain theological concepts of Rudolph Otto, keynotes the volume by suggesting that Otto's term "numinous" may explain the profound impact of much Gothic literature. The theological concept of the numinous, with its emphasis on a sense of godlike power and creative consciousness, parallels Romantic concepts of the godlike power of poetic imagination; and in its emphasis on feeling, the idea of the numinous strikes yet another chord with the aesthetics of Romanticism. Varnado details three affective qualities of the numinous: the overpowering religious dread beyond natural fear that Otto designates *tremendum,* the stupefaction or blank astonishment one feels in the presence of the "wholly other" that Otto calls *mysterium,* and the Dionysian allure, transport, and utter ravishment of the experience that Otto calls *fascinosum.* By this radical application of Otto's terms to Gothic literature, Varnado is able to suggest a powerfully felt metaphysical reason for the recurrent subjects and symbols of that literature. The sublime, aweful landscapes, the pre-ternatural events, the iconography of height and depth, of darkness, silence, and emptiness are archetypal embodiments of a moral and ethical perception of an occult, unknowable, sacred power somehow violated by the sinful, pride-ful, profane presence of man.

From a much different approach, Nicolas K. Kiessling conducts by philologi-cal and historical means an exploration into man's preconscious dread of the demonic insofar as its skeletal imprint yet remains on our language. He focuses on one of the most fascinating creatures of man's darker imagination, the legendary figure of the night molester, the haunter of dreams, the Incubus. The relationship of this early mythical bisexual creature to such pagan figures as Dionysus, Pan, and other vegetation and fertility gods, to such Medieval figures as devils and gargoyles which leer down at us from the sculpted vines and grotesque foliage in the cornices and friezes of the great Medieval cathedrals, and to the witches, fatal women, lamias, and vampires of Romantic literature, has never before been delineated. Kiessling not only details the theological agonies of the Church Fathers over the procreant urge, but also shows the larger implications of the Incubus/Succubus figure. The Incubus, he suggests, is a tortured iconographic embodiment of man's desire for re-generation, for reproduction, and of his theological guilt over the very fact that he exists, over his very lust for life. Tracing the transmutations of the figure through three confluent Medieval cultures, Kiessling shows us in the history of the words used to describe the Incubus the vestiges of a mythic embodiment of man's guilty consciousness of himself in an unstable world, haunted as he is by grotesque images of his darkest lusts and fears. By thus conjoining both Freudian and Jungian concepts of the meaning of dreams in a philological and theological context, Kiessling is able to suggest the power-ful impulse behind the tendency of the Romantic imagination to seize upon the Incubus figure as an icon of its troubled sense of its own creative powers.

Joel Porte puts the locus of the Gothic novel in the dual tension of re-ligious terror and love and examines the historical dialectics at work in the superseding of the Medieval world order by a Protestant, and specifically Calvinist, vision of the majority of mankind as unredeemable. In a Protestant world order, he argues, the moral frame of man's world becomes ambiguous; Gothic literature of the Romantic period presents man as a fallen creature seeking to regain entrance into Paradise, but lost in a wasteland and terrified of ultimate damnation—a damnation that he himself creates out of his over-powering sense of guilt over he knows not what. More or less centrally placed in the sequence of essays, Porte's discussion is central to the collective argument of the volume. Thus the next two essays, on Poe and Byron, directly pursue the themes Porte delineates, though in radically different ways. Barton Levi St. Armand, while focusing on Poe, explores the Romantic taste for the "myster-ies" of Egypt. Romantic interest in Egypt was, of course, stimulated by a series of contemporary excavations and by the discovery of the Rosetta Stone; but St. Armand suggests that Egyptian lore also provided Romantic writers with an iconography appropriate to the Gothic genre. Poe, he argues, worked with the Egyptian occult tradition behind Christian myth in full awareness of the conflux of the two cultures. Poe's most famous work, "The Fall of the House of Usher," presents a Faustian quest for initiation into the occult mysteries of forbidden sacred knowledge, derived from the rites of Isis. The novitiate becomes victim when he profanes such mysteries by his presence at the rites. The development in the Middle Ages of the pseudoscience of alchemy represented in part a merging of Egyptian and Christian myth. As the hierarchy of metals became codified in a mystic science representing a quest for ultimate illumination, there developed an iconography suitable for a richly implicative substratum of meaning in the Gothic romance as it matured in the Romantic period. Thus, in Gothic literature, the Isis figure is transmuted into a sinister supernatural presence, the high priest into a mysterious monk or arch-villain heading a secret brotherhood of the illuminati, and the novitiate into a trembling and stupefied victim—while the theater for all this, the temple, becomes a cathedral or castle.

John W. Ehrstine takes up another kind of transmutation in his essay on Byron. In an attempt to define the darker aspects of Byron's mind, he deals with the image of the "Byronic Hero" pervasive in the Romantic Age, not so much as a configuration of Renaissance stage villains embodying Faustian overreaching, but as a tension between Faustian and Promethean (Dark and Light) impulses. Although he notes Byron's Calvinist upbringing, Ehrstine is more interested in linking the recurrent theme of guilt in Byron's Gothic works to what Morse Peckham has called Negative Romanticism, by exploring the suspended moral investment of Byron's later heroic figures. The Negative Romantic is one who has rejected the apparently stable world order of the preceding era and who desires to embrace the world view of the optimistic Romantics, but cannot. Byron's heroes, in their Gothic pursuit of the demonic, finally achieve a detached metaphysic which is, however, not indifferent either to life or death, and which brings to synthesis both the positive and negative aspects of experience; the Byronic hero must finally take on his guilt, whatever it is, whether deserved or not. In such a work as *Cain,* this quest is set forth in specifically Biblical and religious terms, in which Jehovah creates only to annihilate, and Byron's poetic vision is finally the expression of the suspended moral vertigo of one caught between two worlds who yet has somehow to bring them together.

Robert D. Hume, in an essay with broader focus though with special reference to Byron, marks out the quandary of the Romantic Age similarly. He surveys the Gothic literature of the period with reference to the image of Faust the overreacher in what he sees as "three stages" of Negative Romanticism. The basic Negative Romantic vision of the world, he claims, is that of pain, No Exit, damnation. There are two Faustian modifications of this negative vision. One he calls a "low Faust" solution, that of travesty, satire, and irony, as seen in Beckford's *Vathek* and in Byron's *Don Juan.* The opposite mode is the hero's deliberate assumption of the grandeur of pain, a tragic-heroic conception of self-enduring punishment and guilt meted out by some occult providence without reference to whether such punishment is merited.

From this Romantic abyss, we move both forward into the twentieth century and back into the world order of the Middle Ages. Virginia M. Hyde explores in detail the iconographic techniques of Franz Kafka in his two Gothic novels, *The Castle* and *The Trial.* In his presentation of fallen man seeking to regain a stable world order yet somehow guilty of crimes committed in his absence, Kafka seems carefully to have paralleled his narrative technique with the allegory of the Last Judgment depicted on the Western tympanum of Medieval cathedrals. God delivers His judgment from on high, placing the saved on His right hand, the damned on His left. Thus Kafka, with searing irony, employs Christian Medieval iconography, symbolic of a unified and unambiguous moral world, in order to intensify the dilemma of modern man lost between worlds. Cathedral becomes castle, and the Last Judgment dissolves into a bizarre labyrinthine bureaucracy of legalities that leads only to a judgment of death without possibility of redemption. Hyde implies that the entire Gothic Revival in literature may be seen in the line of the Medieval diabolists, that is, oriented toward the left hand of God.

Even in what is a highly specialized bibliography of the impact of the shilling-shocker on the French imagination, Maurice Lévy suggests that one reason for the popularity of English Gothic fiction among French readers of the Revolutionary Period was its fierce anti-Catholicism. Lévy indicates that the Gothic novel sprang from the ambiguous attitudes and divided feelings of the mid-century Gothic revivalists. At the same time that they celebrated the melancholy beauty of some "hallowed fane" or of some "ruin'd abbey's moss-grown piles," they also rejoiced at the decline and fall of the Medieval world order which meant political oppression in the form of the Roman church.

Thus, a backdrop of continuity from before the thirteenth century through the twentieth gives unusual depth to this collection of essays on the literature of "horror" and "terror." The iconographic focus on the left hand of God gives context for the Romantic expressions of the "Gothic" in literature. Although the surface form of Gothic literature seems to have developed from the eighteenth-century sentimental romance, the major Gothic works contain within them mythic sources that account for their hidden power. The Gothic thrusts us forward into an existential void as it simultaneously recalls to us the Age of Faith. Like the Medieval romances of knights in quest of the Holy Grail, the Gothic romance is also a quest literature. But the quest is finally metaphysical rather than purely religious, with destruction rather than redemption, at the end.

The Idea of the Numinous in Gothic Literature

S. L. VARNADO

One of the engaging aspects of modern literary criticism has been the enthusiastic acceptance of aid from nonliterary disciplines. Psychoanalysis, anthropology, sociology, and semantics have undoubtedly enriched our understanding and influenced our critical response to literature.[1] One suspects, however, that such methodologies are best applied to works which are more or less subjective in nature. The Gothic tradition in British and American literature, for instance, offers itself as a prime candidate. Critical appraisal of Gothic literature has sometimes been marked by an ambiguity, as though critics found difficulty in coming to terms with the material. In a well-known pronouncement on Edgar Allan Poe, T. S. Eliot has stated a common attitude toward Gothic fiction: "The forms which his lively curiosity takes are those in which a pre-adolescent mentality delights: wonders of nature and of mechanics and of the supernatural, cryptograms and cyphers, puzzles and labyrinths, mechanical chess-players, and wild flights of speculation. . . . There is just that lacking which gives dignity to the mature man: a consistent view of life. . . ."[2] The Gothic elements in Poe's writings seem to be at the root of Eliot's rejection. On the other hand, a writer whom Eliot admires, Charles Baudelaire, takes a different view toward this same sort of material. For Baudelaire, "what will always make him [Poe] worthy of praise is his preoccupation with all the truly important subjects and those which are *alone* worthy of the attention of a spiritual man: probabilities, mental illnesses, scientific hypotheses, hopes and considerations about a future life, analysis of the eccentrics and pariahs of this world. . . ."[3]

Such an antinomy raises, in fact, the central question about the Gothic spirit as it is reflected in the work of early novelists such as Horace Walpole,

S. L. VARNADO, Associate Professor of American and British Literature at the University of South Alabama, has made many contributions to national reviews and to religious journals.

[1] See Stanley Edgar Hymen, *The Armed Vision, A Study in the Methods of Modern Literary Criticism* (New York: Vintage Books, 1948), p. 3.

[2] "From Poe to Valéry," *Hudson Review*, 2 (1949), 335.

[3] *Baudelaire on Poe*, trans. and ed. Lois and Francis E. Hyslop, Jr. (State College, Pa.: Bald Eagle Press, 1952), p. 151.

11

Ann Radcliffe, and Mary Shelley, as well as later writers like Charlotte Brontë, Edgar Allan Poe, Algernon Blackwood, and Franz Kafka. What, precisely, is the common denominator of a literary tradition that includes such a diverse company, and that has attracted, at least for a time, such dissimilar minds as those of Charles Dickens, Henry James, Joseph Conrad, and William Faulkner? The answer, as suggested, demands in part an analysis by way of nonliterary disciplines, since it is evident that the literary powers of such writers are not in question.

The particular nonliterary discipline that I propose for analyzing the Gothic tradition consists of the impressive body of work left by the late German theologian and philosopher Rudolf Otto (1869-1937). In his major work, *The Idea of the Holy* (1917), Otto attempted to analyze religious experience by means of what he termed the numinous. His central concern in the book is indicated by its subtitle: "The nonrational factor in the idea of the divine and its relation to the rational." The numinous, the word he coined to represent this nonrational factor, is man's underlying sense of supernatural fear, wonder, and delight when he is confronted by the divine. Although the several elements in numinous feeling may be analyzed, the numinous is essentially nonrational—that is, not able to be fully understood conceptually. It is a "feeling" but a feeling that has innate connections with the intellect. The numinous, which in its more primitive forms gives rise to the belief in ghosts and other supernatural fantasies, is still present in purified form in the higher manifestations of religion. This experience, with its associated forms and connections, its dichotomies between "sacred and profane," between "natural and supernatural," "rational and non-rational," and its often fragile but sometimes strong relations to the human sense of the "holy" is, I believe, the essential goal of the Gothic writer, and so far as it is achieved, his central distinction.

Otto's terminology and some of his ideas have appeared in works of literary criticism. There is, for instance, a very sound discussion of Otto's works in Maud Bodkin's *Archetypal Patterns in Poetry*. Both G. Wilson Knight and Walter Kaufman have used Otto's terminology in exploring certain aspects of Shakespeare.[4] But even if the legitimacy of the numinous as a literary concept is granted, the question of relating it to the Gothic tale may appear doubtful. In what sense, it will be asked, does the preternatural element in Gothic fiction enter into the psychology of religious experience? Indeed, it will appear almost paradoxical to attempt to relate the two, since the more evident varieties of religious experience—prayer, contemplation, and mysticism—whether orthodox or otherwise, seem remote from the Gothic experience of Romantic literature.

It is in answer to this problem that the insights of Rudolf Otto are applicable. For Otto was certain that the area of religious experience which he termed the numinous is, in its early stages, closely associated with the preternatural; and that while some religions in their more advanced stages outgrow this association, they still retain vestiges of it. In fact, Otto was convinced that the preternatural as a condition of human consciousness is

---

[4] See Maud Bodkin, *Archetypal Patterns in Poetry* (London: Oxford Univ. Press, 1934), pp. 223, 241; Walter Kaufman, *From Shakespeare to Existentialism* (Boston: Beacon Press, 1949), p. 37; G. Wilson Knight, *The Crown of Life* (London: Methuen, 1947), p. 128.

intimately connected with the whole phenomena of religion.

Otto begins *The Idea of the Holy* by distinguishing conceptual from non-conceptual statements about religion. Theistic religion, he believes, characterizes God by various conceptual statements about his nature, for example, his spirituality, power, and unity. Such conceptual statements Otto terms rational, and he makes it clear that they are of first importance in religious discussion. On the other hand, the nature of God is such that these rational attributes do not fully comprehend Him. "For so far are these 'rational' attributes from exhausting the idea of deity, that they in fact imply a non-rational or supra-rational Subject of which they are predicates." This nonrational element, however, must be apprehended in some way "else absolutely speaking nothing could be asserted of it."[5]

To characterize this nonrational element or "unnamed Something" as he calls it, Otto coins the word *numinous,* from the Latin *numen* (a god or power). "I shall speak, then, of a unique 'numinous' category of value and of a definitely 'numinous' state of mind, which is always found wherever the category is applied. This mental state is perfectly *sui generis* and irreducible to any other; and therefore, like every absolutely primary and elementary datum, while it admits of being discussed, it cannot be strictly defined" (p. 7). But if the numinous cannot be defined it can, nevertheless, be suggested. "We must once again endeavour, by adducing feelings akin to them for the purpose of analogy or contrast and by the use of metaphor and symbolic expressions, to make the states of mind we are investigating ring out, as it were, of themselves" (p. 12).

In attempting to suggest these numinous states of mind, Otto uses as an ideogram the Latin phrase *mysterium tremendum.* "Conceptually *mysterium* is merely that which is hidden and esoteric, that which is beyond conception or understanding, extraordinary and unfamiliar. The term does not define the object more positively in its qualitative character. But though what is enunciated in the word is negative, what is meant is something absolutely and intensely positive. This pure positive we can experience in feelings, feelings which our discussion can help make clear to us, in so far as it arouses them actually in our hearts" (p. 13).

A number of distinct "notes" or feeling-states enter into Otto's analysis of the phrase *mysterium tremendum. Tremor,* for example, is the Latin word for the familiar experience of the natural emotion of fear. However, Otto uses it to suggest "a quite specific kind of emotional response, wholly distinct from that of being afraid. . . . There are in some languages special expressions which denote, either exclusively or in the first instance, this 'fear' that is more than fear proper. The Hebrew *Hiqdīsh* (hallow) is an example. To 'keep a thing holy in the heart' means to mark it off by a feeling of peculiar dread, not to be mistaken for any ordinary dread, that is, to appraise it by the category of the numinous" (p. 13).

The subtle, but distinct, qualitative difference between this feeling and ordinary human fear is suggested by an analysis of the physical reactions that accompany these states.

We say: 'my blood ran icy cold,' and 'my flesh crept.' The 'cold blood' feeling may

---

[5] Rudolf Otto, *The Idea of the Holy,* trans. John W. Harvey (New York: Oxford Univ. Press, 1958), p. 2.

be a symptom of ordinary, natural fear, but there is something non-natural or supernatural about the symptom of 'creeping flesh.' And any one who is capable of more precise introspection must recognize that the distinction between such a 'dread' and natural fear is not simply one of degree and intensity. The awe or 'dread' *may* indeed be so overwhelmingly great that it seems to penetrate to the very marrow, making the man's hair bristle and his limbs quake. But it may also steal upon him almost unobserved as the gentlest of agitations, a mere fleeting shadow passing across his mood. It has therefore nothing to do with intensity, and no natural fear passes over into it merely by being intensified. (p. 16)

The accuracy of Otto's description is attested to by a number of passages from Gothic fiction. Cold blood and creeping flesh are, in fact, staples of Gothic literature, but it is the exceptional reader who has distinguished between "ordinary human fear" and the numinous emotions. A passage from Algernon Blackwood's short story "The Willows" suggests some remarkable parallels with what Otto has to say about numinous awe. In this tale, the narrator and a companion proceed by canoe into the upper reaches of the Danube where, amidst the loneliness of the primitive forest and a rising windstorm, they come upon a remote island entirely covered by small willow trees. They make camp, and as night falls the narrator attempts to analyze the alien emotions aroused in him by the island.

Great revelations of nature, of course, never fail to impress in one way or another, and I was no stranger to moods of the kind. Mountains overawe and oceans terrify, while the mystery of great forests exercises a spell peculiarly its own. But all these, at one point or another, somewhere link on intimately with human life and human experience. They stir comprehensible, even if alarming, emotions. They tend on the whole to exalt.

With this multitude of willows, however, it was something far different, I felt. Some essence emanated from them that besieged the heart. A sense of awe awakened, true, but of awe touched somewhere by a vague terror. Their serried ranks, growing everywhere darker about me as the shadows deepened, moving furiously yet softly in the wind, woke in me the curious and unwelcome suggestion that we had trespassed here upon the borders of an alien world, a world where we were intruders, a world where we were not wanted or invited to remain—where we ran grave risks perhaps![6]

This sense of the "uncanny" or "awesome" does not, however, exhaust the feeling states aroused by the ideogram *tremendum*. Otto perceives another element in it, namely the sense of "might," "power," "absolute overpoweringness," to which he gives the name of *majestas*.

This second element of majesty may continue to be vividly preserved, where the first, that of unapproachability, recedes and dies away, as may be seen for example in mysticism. It is especially in relation to this element of majesty or absolute overpoweringness that the creature-consciousness, of which we have already spoken, comes upon the scene, as a sort of shadow or subjective reflection of it. Thus, in contrast to the 'overpowering' of which we are conscious, as an object over against the self, there is the feeling of one's own submergence, of being but 'dust and ashes' and nothingness. And this forms the numinous raw material for the feeling of religious humility. (p. 20)

Otto's representation of *majestas* must not be confused with the sense of "natural" majesty, although such awareness may be its starting point. This fugitive feeling-state is hard to depict in a single passage of literature. It generally finds its context in a cumulative series of narrations, as in the final

---

[6] Algernon Blackwood, *Tales of Terror and the Unknown* (New York: E. P. Dutton & Co., 1965), pp. 20-21.

chapters of *Moby-Dick*. The emotion does seem well focussed, however, in the description of the first sight of the numinous and nearly supernal whale.

A gentle joyousness—a mighty mildness of repose in swiftness, invested the gliding whale. Not the white bull Jupiter swimming away with ravished Europa clinging to his graceful horns; his lovely, leering eyes sideways intent upon the maid; with smooth bewitching fleetness, rippling straight for the nuptial bower in Crete; not Jove, not that great majesty Supreme! did surpass the glorified White Whale as he so divinely swam.
On each soft side—coincident with the parted swell, that but once leaving him, then flowed so wide away—on each bright side, the whale shed off enticings. No wonder there had been some among the hunters who namelessly transported and allured by all this serenity, had ventured to assail it; but had fatally found that quietude but the vesture of tornadoes. Yet calm, enticing calm, oh, whale! thou glidest on, to all who for the first time eye thee, no matter how many in that same way thou may'st have bejuggled and destroyed before.[7]

A final element suggested by the ideogram *tremendum* is termed by Otto the "urgency" or "energy" of the numinous object. This element is sometimes projected symbolically as the "wrath of God," and in qualities of vitality, passion, emotional temper, will-force, movement, excitement, activity, and impetus. Such a feeling, Otto tells us, makes its appearance in mysticism, especially "voluntaristic" mysticism and "the mysticism of love." It appears in Fichte's speculations on the Absolute as the gigantic, never-resting, active world-stress, and in Schopenhauer's daemonic "Will." In Goethe, too, the same note is sounded in his strange description of the "daemonic."[8] The quality isolated here is prominent in Gothic fiction. Some of it enters into the characterization of Mr. Rochester in *Jane Eyre,* and of the monster in Mary Shelley's *Frankenstein.* It appears in rather melodramatic form in the final chapter of *The Monk* when the fiend carries Ambrosio out of the dungeon and across the mountain peaks. And it certainly contributes to the character of Captain Ahab, the "grand ungodly god-like man" of *Moby-Dick.*

Thus Otto distinguishes three distinct, but related, moments suggested by the ideogram *tremendum*: awfulness, majesty, and energy. He now proceeds to an analysis of the substantive *mysterium,* which stands as the form of the numinous experience. The mental reaction to this "moment" in the numinous consciousness is best described analogically by the word "stupor." "Stupor is plainly a different thing from *tremor;* it signifies blank wonder, an astonishment that strikes us dumb, amazement absolute." Its objective concomitant, the *mysterium,* suggests that which is "wholly other" (*anyad, alienum*) or in other words "that which is quite beyond the sphere of the usual, the intelligible, and the familiar, which therefore falls quite outside the limits of the 'canny' and is contrasted with it, filling the mind with blank wonder and astonishment" (p. 26).

To suggest this sense of the "wholly other" Otto undertakes an analysis of the fear of ghosts—a subject obviously quite germane to the Gothic.

The ghost's real attraction . . . consists in this, that of itself and in an uncommon degree it entices the imagination, awakening strong interest and curiosity; it is the weird thing itself that allures the fancy. But it does this, not because it is 'something

---

[7] Herman Melville, *Moby-Dick,* ed. Charles Feidelson, Jr. (Indianapolis: The Bobbs-Merrill Company, Inc., 1964), p. 690.

[8] As described by Otto, pp. 23-24.

long and white' (as someone once defined a ghost) nor yet through any of the positive conceptual attributes which fancies about ghosts have invented, but because it is a thing that 'doesn't really exist at all,' the 'wholly other,' something which has no place in our scheme of reality but belongs to an absolutely different one and which at the same time arouses an irrepressible interest in the mind. (pp. 28-29)

The accuracy of Rudolf Otto's analysis of such ghostly matters is attested to by a great deal of literature of the supernatural, but no better paradigm is available than Henry James' classic ghost story "The Jolly Corner." The description of Spencer Brydon's encounter with his horrific doppelgänger clearly depicts both the "wholly other" character of the spirit as well as the sense of blank wonder and stupor.

The hands, as he looked, began to move, to open; then, as if deciding in a flash, dropped from the face and left it uncovered and presented. Horror, with the sight, had leaped into Brydon's throat, gasping there in a sound he couldn't utter; for the bared identity was too hideous as *his,* and his glare was the passion of his protest. The face, *that* face, Spencer Brydon's?—he searched it still, but looking away from it in dismay and denial, falling straight from his height of sublimity. It was unknown, inconceivable, awful, disconnected from any possibility—! He had been "sold," he inwardly moaned, stalking such game as this: the presence before him was a presence, the horror within him a horror, but the waste of his nights had been only grotesque and the success of his adventure an irony. Such an identity fitted his at *no* point, made its alternative monstrous. A thousand times yes, as it came upon him nearer now—the face was the face of a stranger. It came upon him nearer now, quite as one of those expanding fantastic images projected by the magic lantern of childhood; for the stranger, whoever he might be, evil, odious, blatant, vulgar, had advanced as for aggression, and he knew himself give ground . . . he felt the whole vision turn to darkness and his very feet give way. His head went round; he was going; he had gone.[9]

In this passage, as in the entire story, the *mysterium* is transformed into and partakes of James' private universe, with all its exquisite values and peculiar defects. No writer could be further, in some ways, from the "average Gothic," and yet the numinous qualities provide a link. The apparition is "unknown, inconceivable, awful, disconnected from any possibility—!" which one takes to be a Jamesian rendition of the "wholly other." In fact, as James himself attests in several of his prefaces, the supernatural tale fascinated him.

It is the sense of fascination that forms the final strand in Otto's analysis of numinous feeling. Having analyzed what might be termed the daunting aspect of the numinous (*mysterium tremendum*), Otto discusses another element that stands at the opposite pole. This element Otto designates by the term *fascinans*, a kind of fascination, attraction, or allurement in the numinous. This *fascinans* is "a bliss which embraces all those blessings that are indicated or suggested in a positive fashion by any 'doctrine of salvation,' and it quickens all of them through and through; but these do not exhaust it. Rather by its all pervading, penetrating glow it makes of these very blessings more than the intellect can conceive in them or affirm of them" (pp. 33-34).

Thus, Otto groups in what he calls a "harmony of contrasts" the various moments in the numinous experience; and these he indicates by the phrase (or ideogram as he terms it) *mysterium tremendum et fascinosum.*

These two qualities, the daunting and the fascinating, now combine in a strange

---

[9] Henry James, *Ghostly Tales of Henry James,* ed. Leon Edel (New York: Grosset & Dunlap, 1963), pp. 427-28.

harmony of contrasts, and the resultant dual character of the numinous consciousness, to which the entire religious development bears witness, at any rate from the level of the 'daemonic dread' onwards, is at once the strangest and the most noteworthy phenomenon in the whole history of religion. The daemonic-divine object may appear to the mind an object of horror and dread, but at the same time it is no less something that allures with a potent charm, and the creature who trembles before it, utterly cowed and cast down, has always at the same time the impulse to turn to it, nay even to make it somehow his own. The 'mystery' is for him not merely something to be wondered at but something that entrances him; and beside that in it which bewilders and confounds, he feels a something that captivates and transports him with a strange ravishment, rising often enough to the pitch of intoxication: it is the Dionysiac-element in the numen. (p. 31)

The peculiar "harmony of contrasts" is a prominent feature in the work of Edgar Allan Poe, who certainly had an intuitive grasp of the numinous consciousness as Otto expounds it, and explains, to some degree, Poe's puzzling ideas concerning "perversity" ("The Imp of the Perverse"), ideas which interested Baudelaire. But on a higher plane this daunting-attracting quality of the numinous infuses most of Poe's tales and poems. A striking example is his tale "A Descent Into the Maelström." As the protagonist finds himself drawn into the immense and terrifying depths of the maelström, his reflections vary from awe and terror before this nearly preternatural manifestation to a strange sense of fascination.

"It may look like boasting—but what I tell you is truth—I began to reflect how magnificent a thing it was to die in such a manner, and how foolish it was in me to think of so paltry a consideration as my own individual life, in view of so wonderful a manifestation of God's power. I do believe that I blushed with shame when this idea crossed my mind. After a little while I became possessed with the keenest curiosity about the whirl itself. I positively felt a *wish* to explore its depths, even at the sacrifice I was going to make; and my principal grief was that I should never be able to tell my old companions on shore about the mysteries I should see."[10]

Throughout his book, Otto continually emphasizes that the numinous is not identical with the fully developed sense of the Holy. The concept of Holiness must of necessity include theological and moral elements. The numinous may thus be seen as bearing intrinsic relationship with and even providing a definition for a number of works, both literary and artistic, which might not generally be termed religious. For what else is one to say of the castles and mountain crags of Mrs. Radcliffe's novels, the glaciers, ice-floes, and desolate Scottish islands of *Frankenstein*, or the spectral sea-scapes of *The Narrative of Arthur Gordon Pym* but that they summon up many of the moods and tones that Otto has analyzed? Thus, by making use of Otto's insights, one is able to sense a new and more profound note in some very good literature of this kind that has sometimes been looked at with bewilderment if not downright condescension by certain critics.

Another fruitful link between the numinous and the Gothic tradition is to be found in Otto's remarks about preternatural events and magic. Preternaturalism has, of course, been a source of annoyance to some critics of the Gothic; and it does, indeed, require a strong palate to accept all the bleeding portraits, animated skeletons, lycanthropes, rattling chains, and vampires that infest Gothic literature, especially the older novels. But the artistic incorpora-

---

[10] Edgar Allan Poe, *The Complete Works of Edgar Allan Poe,* ed. James A. Harrison (New York: Thomas Y. Crowell & Co., 1902), II, 240.

tion of the preternatural into literature should not, in itself, form a barrier to critical appreciation. It is on this point that Otto supplies a strong apologetic. "Now the magical," he says, "is nothing but a suppressed and dimmed form of the numinous, a crude form of it which great art purifies and ennobles." He adds, "To us of the West the Gothic appears as the most numinous of all types of art. This is due in the first place to its sublimity; but Worringer in his *Problem der Ghotik* has done a real service in showing that the peculiar impressiveness of Gothic does not consist in its sublimity alone, but draws upon a strain inherited from primitive magic, of which he tries to show the historical derivation" (pp. 67-68).

The magical or preternatural event, then, if introduced artistically may serve to reinforce the numinous quality of the work. Nathaniel Hawthorne, who was sparing in his use of the preternatural, seems to achieve the proper effect in a passage from *The Marble Faun.* Donatello, Miriam, and Kenyon approach the open bier of a dead monk who lies in the Church of the Capuchins in Rome.

> And now occurred a circumstance that would seem too fantastic to be told, if it had not actually happened, precisely as we set it down. As the three friends stood by the bier, they saw that a little stream of blood had begun to ooze from the dead monk's nostrils; it crept slowly towards the thicket of his beard, where, in the course of a moment or two, it hid itself.
> "How strange!" ejaculated Kenyon. "The monk died of apoplexy, I suppose, or by some sudden accident, and the blood has not yet congealed."
> "Do you consider that a sufficient explanation?" asked Miriam, with a smile from which the sculptor involuntarily turned away his eyes. "Does it satisfy you?"
> "And why not?" he inquired.
> "Of course, you know the old superstition about this phenomenon of blood flowing from a dead body," she rejoined. "How can we tell but that the murderer of this monk (or, possibly, it may be only that privileged murderer, his physician) may have just entered the church?"[11]

The Idea of the Holy contains chapters, of special interest to the literary critic, on the means of arousing the numinous consciousness by artistic works. "Of directer methods our Western art has only two," Otto says, "and they are in a noteworthy way negative, viz. *darkness* and *silence*." His discussion of the artistic use of darkness conjures up many images of the "haunted castle" theme so dear to the tale of terror: "The semi-darkness that glimmers in vaulted halls, or beneath the branches of a lofty forest glade, strangely quickened and stirred by the mysterious play of half-lights, has always spoken eloquently to the soul, and the builders of temples, mosques and churches have made full use of it" (p. 68). Silence is "what corresponds to this in the language of musical sounds. . . . It is a spontaneous reaction to the feeling of the actual *numen praesens*" (pp. 68-69). Both of these "artistic means" are native to Western art; but Oriental art makes continual use of a third, namely, empty distance and emptiness. "Empty distance, remote vacancy, is, as it were, the sublime in the horizontal. The wide-stretching desert, the boundless uniformity of the steppe, have a real sublimity, and even in us Westerners they set vibrating chords of the numinous along with the note of the sublime, according to the principle of the association of feelings" (p. 69).

---

[11] Nathaniel Hawthorne, *The Writings of Nathaniel Hawthorne* (Boston: Houghton Mifflin and Company, 1903), IX, 263.

Perhaps Otto is right in concluding that most Western art has generally failed to make consistent use of emptiness, but the Gothic literary tradition has, indeed, effectively utilized this method as a means to register a sense of the numinous. The vacant loneliness associated with sea, desert, mountain prospects, or the night sky is a constant theme. This characteristic is especially true of Coleridge's *Ancient Mariner* ("Alone, alone, all, all alone/ Alone on a wide wide sea!") and Poe's *Narrative of Arthur Gordon Pym,* as well as of several of Joseph Conrad's novels in which brooding descriptions of the sea stimulate the numinous sense of emptiness and silence. In *Victory,* for instance, a work which contains certain strong numinous elements, the lonely protagonist Heyst is a man who feels this numinous call of the sea.

Like most dreamers, to whom it is given sometimes to hear the music of the spheres, Heyst, the wanderer of the Archipelago, had a taste for silence which he had been able to gratify for years. The islands are very quiet. One sees them lying about, clothed in their dark garments of leaves, in a great hush of silver and azure, where the sea without murmurs meets the sky in a ring of magic stillness. A sort of smiling somnolence broods over them; the very voices of their people are soft and subdued, as if afraid to break some protecting spell.[12]

Thus, it seems clear that Otto's work provides many insights into the spirit of Gothic literature. The mountain gloom, lonely castles, phantom ships, violent storms, and the vastness of sea and polar regions correspond closely with Otto's description of the numinous. Likewise, the preternatural machinery of Gothicism, whether magical lore, apparitions, ghouls, vampires, or revenants, finds its explanation not in an over-ripe fantasy, but in an effort to instill a sense of the numinous.

We have seen several ways in which the numinous plays a part both in background and event in the Gothic tale. But the numinous is not confined to ontological reality; Otto contends that it also has an axiological character. This is to say, the numinous exists as a category of value within its own right; and as a consequence it can be used in analyzing character and moral value.

According to Otto, the numinous experience in itself is not an ethical manifestation and may exist without any relation to morality, as for instance in the case of certain primitive religions. When the numinous is commingled with moral and rational elements it becomes something different—namely *The Holy.* On the other hand, the numinous in its pure form, and without moral connotations, is still permeated by certain axiological elements. The numinous "object" produces in the percipient a sense of "creature feelings"; in fact, this result is one of the essential ways in which it impinges upon the individual consciousness. Out of such a feeling grows the sense of numinous value and of numinous disvalue. In opposition to this sense of "disvalue" or the profane stands the sacred. "This sanctus is not merely 'perfect' or 'beautiful' or 'sublime' or 'good,' though, being like these concepts also a value, objective and ultimate, it has a definite, perceptible analogy with them. It is the positive numinous value or worth, and to it corresponds on the side of the creature a numinous disvalue or 'unworth'" (Otto, p. 51).

The sense of numinous value, the sacred, is recognized as standing outside the sphere of morality as such. "In every highly-developed religion the appreciation of moral obligation and duty, ranking as a claim of the deity upon

---

[12] Joseph Conrad, *Victory* (New York: The Modern Library, 1921), p. 64.

man, has been developed side by side with the religious feeling itself. Nonetheless, a profoundly humble and heartfelt recognition of 'the holy' may occur in particular experiences without being always definitely charged or infused with the sense of moral demands. The 'holy' will then be recognized as that which commands our respect, as that whose real value is to be acknowledged inwardly" (p. 51). Likewise, the opposite pole, the numinous "disvalue" or sense of the profane, is not intrinsically a moral category. "Mere 'unlawfulness' only becomes 'sin,' 'impiety,' 'sacrilege,' when the character of *numinous unworthiness or disvalue* goes on to be transferred to and centered in moral delinquency . . ." (p. 52).

Otto's explanation of numinous value and disvalue, if viewed as a phenomenological description, applies with equal force to many Gothic works which might otherwise appear to be morally neutral and therefore, at best, mere entertainment. There are, it is true, certain patent moral lessons attached to Mary Shelley's *Frankenstein*, but the categories of the sacred and profane, if applied to the hero's unholy experiments, add a new dimension to the story.

To explore this interpretation briefly, we must remember that the story projects a feeling of horror and evil that is disproportionate to the moral framework out of which Mary Shelley worked. The crimes of the monster and the ultimate ruin of his creator Frankenstein are the results of an experiment begun, perhaps, in good conscience. Mary Shelley suggests, in fact, that some of the evil nature of the monster is the result of economic and moral dislocations in society. Then, too, as a rationalist and liberal who followed the views of her father, she would have rejected a belief in the innate evil of man. What then is responsible for the brooding sense of profanity and unhallowed occupation that characterizes the inception of the monster?

Who shall conceive the horrors of my secret toil, as I dabbled among the unhallowed damps of the grave, or tortured the living animal to animate the lifeless clay? My limbs now tremble and my eyes swim with the remembrance; but then a resistless, and almost frantic, impulse urged me forward; I seemed to have lost all soul or sensation but for this one pursuit . . . . I collected bones from charnel-houses, and disturbed, with profane fingers, the tremendous secrets of the human frame. In a solitary chamber, or rather cell, at the top of the house, and separated from all the other apartments by a gallery and staircase, I kept my workshop of filthy creation: my eye-balls were starting from their sockets in attending to the details of my employment.[13]

There is really no "rational" explanation for such feelings, given the moral views of Frankenstein. He feels, rather, the sense of numinous "disvalue" attendant upon his profane experiments, a feeling that Mary Shelley shared despite her liberal and utopian sentiments to the contrary. The famous description of the animation of the monster heightens this sense of profanity.

It was already one in the morning; the rain pattered dismally against the panes, and my candle was nearly burnt out, when, by the glimmer of the half-extinguished light, I saw the dull yellow eye of the creature open; it breathed hard, and a convulsive motion agitated its limbs.

How can I describe my emotions at this catastrophe, or how delineate the wretch whom with such infinite pains and care I had endeavoured to form? His limbs were in proportion, and I had selected his features as beautiful. Beautiful!—Great God! His yellow skin scarcely covered the work of muscles and arteries beneath; his hair was of

13 Mary W. Shelley, *Frankenstein* (London: Everyman's Library, 1963), p. 48.

a lustrous black, and flowing; his teeth of a pearly whiteness; but these luxuriances only formed a more horrid contrast with his watery eyes, that seemed almost of the same colour as the dun white sockets in which they were set, his shrivelled complexion and straight black lips. (p. 51)

The question of Frankenstein's guilt in tampering with the well-springs of life is not treated directly. The consequent crimes and atrocities perpetrated by the monster are the results of "man's inhumanity to man," the evils of society and, to a certain extent, mere chance. Even at the last, Frankenstein absolves himself of direct guilt: "During these last days I have been occupied in examining my past conduct; nor do I find it blameable. In a fit of enthusiatic madness I created a rational creature, and was bound towards him, to assure, as far as was in my power, his happiness and well-being. This was my duty; but there was another still paramount to that. My duties towards the beings of my own species had greater claims to my attention, because they included a greater proportion of happiness or misery" (p. 235). Thus, on the merely rational level, *Frankenstein* expounds some rather patent moral truths which are perhaps most interesting from a historical standpoint. But in a deeper sense, the book portrays the mysterious sense of "profanity" and numinous disvalue which, according to Otto, is part of man's spiritual life.

It is upon such a system of thought, profound and original, that a new survey of Gothic literature may be conducted. Otto's description of the numinous, self-authenticating and convincing, suggests a new dimension to the literature of the preternatural.

Demonic Dread:
The Incubus Figure in British Literature

NICOLAS K. KIESSLING

That monstrous demon of the night, the night "mare" or Incubus, stalked through the dreams of primitive Western man straight into the myths and writings of poets and theologians, proving that the imagination of the dreamer, like that of "the lunatic, the lover and the poet," "apprehend[s] more than cool reason ever comprehends." Down the centuries the Incubus, like "Tiresias throbbing between two lives," has appeared in the form of either sex, and also in many functions and under various names. Thus Chaucer equated it with elves and fairies in the "Wife of Bath's Tale" (D 860-880); Shakespeare identi-fied it with Queen Mab in *Romeo and Juliet* (I.iv.92-4); and Milton, with Baalim and Ashtaroth (*Paradise Lost*, I, 423 ff.). In the Romantic age, Cole-ridge, in "Christabel," and Polidori, in the Gothic tale, *The Vampyre,* pictured it as a vampire, and Keats, in the poem "Lamia," as a serpentine lamia. The Romantics seized upon the concept of the Incubus as a natural metaphor and enlarged it into a symbol of the more overwhelming aspects of life. The omnipresence of the sinister figure prompted one nineteenth-century scholar to suggest that the *Uralptraum* (primordial nightmare) was the father of all mythology.[1] Whatever the validity of such a claim, it is clear that the mythology of the Incubus derived from "such stuff as dreams are made on."

Originally this creature, "half human and half angelic," living, as Geoffrey

NICOLAS K. KIESSLING, Associate Professor of English at Washington State Uni-versity, has written articles on a variety of Medieval and Renaissance topics for such journals as *Modern Philology, Journal of Biblical Literature, Chaucer Review, Studies in English Literature,* and *Shakespeare Quarterly.*

[1] Ludwig Laistner, *Das Rätsel der Sphinx* (Berlin: W. Hertz, 1889); see K. F. S. Kirby, "Brief Mention," *American Journal of Philology,* 22 (1901), 233. Three sources for primary materials on the Incubus, all translated into English, are: Jacob Sprenger and Henry Kramer, *Malleus Maleficarum* (c. 1490), trans. Montague Summers (Lon-don: John Rodker, 1929; rpt. ed., New York: Benjamin Bloom, 1970); Ludovico Maria Sinistrari (d. 1701), *De Demonialitate, et Incubis et Succubis,* trans. Montague Summers, *Demoniality* (London: The Fortune Press, 1927); and Henry C. Lea, *Ma-terials toward a History of Witchcraft,* ed. Arthur C. Howland (Philadelphia: Univer-sity of Pennsylvania Press, 1939). The last includes a vast collection of quotations and summaries, many of which concern the Incubus figure.

of Monmouth described him, in midair "between the moon and our earth,"[2] was conceived as a physical presence—specifically as an "oppressor." The Greek *ephialtes* (and *empusa*), Latin *incubus,* German *Mahr,* Old English *maere,* Old Norse *mara,* and Old Irish *mar/mor* all mean "one who leaps on, oppresses or crushes." He lived up to his name in the popular imagination, for he was often pictured as a sexual molester who operated in the dead of night against helpless victims. Like other demons, he could usually be exorcized by the proper ritual.

The Incubus in English literature derives ultimately from similar figures in three traditions, the Judeo-Christian, the Early Germanic, and the Celtic. These antecedents are generically similar, though each tradition emphasized specific characteristics which are represented in the respective literary forms and types of the creature.

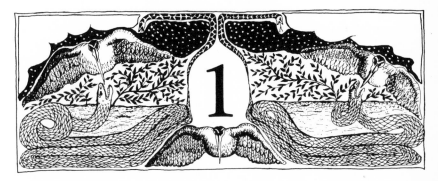

In Judeo-Christian tradition, the ambition of the Incubus creature was to mate with a woman. Yet Asmodeus of the Apocryphal Book of Tobit, who to Milton is "the fleshiest incubus" (*Paradise Regained,* II, 152), never wanted to go beyond adoring Sara, the daughter of Raguel, the object of his passion. "He does no harm to her because he loves her; but as soon as a man tries to approach her he kills him" (Tobit 6.15). The murderous but seemingly chaste Asmodeus had killed seven husbands in Sara's bridal chamber before he was chased away with incense concocted from the heart and liver of a fish by her eighth bridegroom, Tobias. Then Asmodeus was shackled by the angel Raphael. Apart from this notable exception, the intentions of the Incubi in Judeo-Christian traditions were always strictly dishonorable. The earliest Christian commentators, confronted by many stories of the molesting demons from both Classical and local sources, attempted to reconcile these stories with Biblical and Apocryphal truths. They had at hand the Septuagint account of Genesis 6.1-6, which tells how "angels of God [Septuagint: *angeloi;* compare the Vulgate: *filii,* sons] came in unto the daughters of men" and had giant offspring. This union was highly displeasing to God. The Apocryphal Book of Enoch lent additional support to the Genesis passage. It narrates in greater detail the story of the fallen angels and the daughters of men. Their offspring

---

[2] *Historia Regum Britanniae,* 6, 18. Ed. Acton Griscom (London: Longmans, Green & Co., 1929), pp. 381-382.

were the giants. After their deaths, the evil spirits of these giants afflict, oppress, destroy, attack—"rise up against the children of men and against the women . . ." (15.12).[3]

Echoes of both the Genesis and Enoch passages occur in Jude 6-8, 2 Peter 2.4, and the Apocalyptic Book of Jubilees 7.21 ff. and 10.5-10. In all of these accounts the punishment of the fallen angels is alluded to. The later Acts of Thomas (early third century) includes the serpent's version of Genesis 6: "I am he who hurled the angels down from above and bound them in lusts for women. . . ."[4] Justin Martyr (c. 100-165) followed the Biblical and Apocryphal accounts of the origin of giants and further related these creatures to Classical traditions. The angels "transgressed [their] appointment, and were captivated by love of women, and begat children who are those that are called demons." These "evil demons, effecting apparitions of themselves, both defiled women and corrupted boys, and showed . . . fearful sights to men. . . ." To appease these beings men worshipped them as gods until, Justin writes, Socrates had the courage to deny this error. Prominent church fathers, Tertullian (c. 160-220), the authors of the Recognitions of Clement and the Clementine Homilies (second century or later), Athenagoras (second century), Lactantius (c. 240-320), and Sulpicius Severus (c. 363-420), follow this general interpretation of Genesis and Enoch.[5] Lactantius goes into great detail in his account of the Fall, telling how the angels, fallen because of carnal intercourse with women, became satellites and ministers of Satan—beings of a middle nature, neither angels nor men. Classical grammarians and scholars, writes Lactantius, correctly called these creatures *daemones* (Latin, *genii*), "Spirits of the great Zeus." But as Genesis 6 affirms, they are long since fallen into corruption. They wander over the earth seeking to destroy men in whatever way possible. The acceptance of this version of the origin of spirits also led to some bizarre interpretations of New Testament passages. The Apostle Paul, speaking of a woman's headdress in church, states in 1 Corinthians 11.10 that "the woman ought to have power on her head because of the angels." Whatever Paul intended by this passage, writers from Tertullian to William of Auvergne (c. 1180-1249) and the authors of the *Malleus Maleficarum*, a medieval compendium of the evils of witchcraft (c. 1490), interpret it as the fascination that unveiled, long-haired women have for angels, that is, of the Incubus type.[6]

---

[3] The Book of Enoch presents a fuller account of the fall of the angels in chapters 6-10. R. H. Charles, in his edition, *The Apocrypha and Pseudoepigrapha of the Old Testament* (Oxford: Clarendon Press, 1913), gives superb notes to the account, 2, 191-195.

[4] Act 3, par. 32 (Edgar Hennecke, *New Testament Apocrypha*, ed. Wilhelm Schneemelcher, trans. R. McL. Wilson [Philadelphia: The Westminster Press, 1964], 2, 466-469).

[5] For Justin Martyr on the transgressions of the angels, see *Apology*, 2, 5; for comments on Socrates, 1, 5 (The Ante-Nicene Fathers, ed. A. Roberts and J. Donaldson [New York: The Christian Literature Co., 1890], 1, 190 and 1, 164). For Tertullian and Sulpicius Severus, see Lea, 1, 45 and 57. For the opinions of the others, see Oliver F. Emerson, "Legends of Cain, Especially in Old and Middle English," *PMLA*, 21 (1906), 916-925.

[6] For Tertullian, "The Five Books against Marcian," 5, 8 (The Ante-Nicene Fathers, 3, 445). The authors of the *Malleus* approve of the interpretation and cite Bede and William of Paris (Auvergne) (S. Thomas also "speaks of this"), part 1, qn. 3 (p. 25); see also part 2, qn. 2, ch. 1 (p. 166), for more on the attraction of a woman's hair. Lea, 1, 152-153, gives a summary of the views of William of Auvergne.

Contrary interpretations of Genesis 6 prevailed after the fourth century. Chrysostom, Cassian, Bede, and Alcuin, all working from Latin versions of Genesis, asserted that the "filii dei," sons of God, referred to the sons of Seth (or Shem) who mingled with the sons of man—the sons of Cain (or Ham).[7] These views did not detract from the belief in the existence of demons such as the Incubi, but only from the theory that they derived from the union between angels and men. Augustine, for example, wrote in his *De Civitate Dei* that he distrusted the Book of Enoch and was not wholly convinced that the "sons of God" were angels. But he did accept the presence of Incubi: "Silvans, and pans, who are commonly called incubi, had often performed obscenities on women and attacked and sought congress with them. . . . These attacks are affirmed by persons of such indubitable honesty and credit that it would be impudence to deny it" (15.23).

The molesting demons were not only of the male sex. Indeed, one of the most colorful was a female, Lilith. She owes her existence to a single passage in the Bible—Isaiah 34.14—where "lilith" appears in a list of creatures dwelling in the desert. The word is variously translated—Septuagint: *onokentauros* (tailless ape); Jerome's Vulgate: *lamia* (child-devouring female monster); KJV: screech owl; Moffatt: vampire; RSV: night hag; and NEB: nightjar. Whereas the Hebrew word was perhaps only a survival of forgotten Assyrian folklore, rabbinical commentators made a seductress out of this puzzling being. According to one tradition she was Adam's first wife, and the result of that union was a race of demons, spirits, and ghosts. Like the Latin *lamia*, she also devoured children. In a second tradition she, and the Latin *lamia* as well, became a distaff Incubus—later called Succubus—who oppressed men at night.[8] The *lamia* occurs frequently in commentaries and glossaries of church fathers and is usually associated with the *pilosus* (hairy creature), the *satyrus*, *incubus*, and other kinds of demonic monsters (dragons, unicorns, night birds). All inhabited the desolate waste lands and shared similar perverse qualities (see notes 17, 18, 30, 38, and 39).

Numerous faithful Christian women and church fathers of the early centuries of the Christian era, especially those committed to celibacy, were prone to attacks from night demons of the opposite sex. The male creature appears in the Apocryphal Acts of Thomas. A beautiful woman in India pleads with the missionary Thomas for his help against a tormenting adversary. She was committed to virginity, but for five years the demon had been uniting with her "in his foul intercourse." Thomas adjured the demon to leave the woman. He then left, amid fire and smoke, after saying that he would find a victim outside the apostle's jurisdiction.[9] Similar episodes featuring a prurient Incubus are found in the Medieval writings of Gervais of Tilsbury, Caesarius of Heister-

---

[7] For Chrysostom and Cassian, see Lea, 1, 52, 57. For Bede, see *In Pentateuchum Commentarii*, "Genesis," cap. 5 (*Patrologia Latina*, 91, 224); see also *Questionum Super Genesim* (P. L., 93, 297), where Bede, following Jerome, explains the confusion between Ham and Cham. Alcuin, *Opuscula Exegetica*, "Interrationes . . . in Genesim," Interrog. 95-96 (P. L., 100, 526), calls Noah's sons Cham and Sem (ms. readings). These views of Genesis prevailed, but much later, Sinistrari (d. 1701) reasserted the earlier views, p. 26, and the editor of Sinistrari's work, Summers (1929), approves of Sinistrari's argument, pp. xlii-xliii.

[8] Lea, 1, 145-147, cites several early Jewish traditions.

[9] Act 3, pars. 42-47 (Hennecke, 2, 466-469).

bach, Johannes Nider, and in the *Malleus Maleficarum.*[10]

The female creature later to be known as the Succubus appears in Athanasius' "Life of St. Anthony" (c. 356). Here a devil assumes the form of a woman and attacks the youthful Anthony "in the navel of the belly." The ascetic managed to keep his thoughts on Christ and escaped.[11] St. Anthony was not spared by the Incubus either. In a second biography, by Jerome, the aged Anthony encounters in a desert a small man with budding horns on his forehead, a hooked nose, and the feet of a goat. The creature seeks to disarm Anthony by confessing that he is one of those worshipped by deluded Gentiles as "fauns, satyrs, and incubi." Anthony is not quite sure what to make of the creature, but his words about the saving grace of Christ cause the monster to fly away as if on wings.[12]

Thus the existence of molesting demons suggested by Biblical and Apocryphal writings was made concrete in the commentaries and biographies of early church fathers. Later Christian scholars and commentators then drew upon this sizable literature and perpetuated the myth of the specific demon called Incubus. Gregory (540-604) relates the outcast monsters of the Old Testament to Classical demons as did his great predecessors, Augustine and Jerome. In his popular *Moralia on Job* (7.18) he quotes Isaiah 34.14 and elaborates upon the beasts in that passage. The *pilosi* of the desert lands are, according to him, what the Greeks call Pans and the Latins, *incubi*. They have human forms which end in beastly extremities and symbolize *gula* (gluttony).[13] About the same time that Gregory was writing, Isidore of Seville (c. 560-636) recorded a similar entry in his encyclopedic *Etymologiae.* He there equated the *incubi* with the standard Classical demons and also with the Gallic *Dusii* and the Latin *fauni ficari* (fig tree fauns). He almost quotes Augustine when he lists the essential characteristics of the Incubus in Latin Christian tradition: "They often appear immorally to women, and accomplish intercourse with them."[14]

Three of the sources cited above, Augustine's *De Civitate Dei,* Gregory's *Moralia on Job,* and Isidore's *Etymologiae,* were among the most popular works in the early Middle Ages. They served as authoritative reference works in England from the time of Aldhelm and Bede (d. 706 and 735) and on the continent wherever good libraries existed. Hence we find the expositions of haunting demons rarely depart from the standard definitions found in Augustine, Isidore, and Gregory. In the *Glossa Ordinaria,* formerly attributed to Walafrid Strabo (c. 808-849), the *pilosi* of Isaiah 13.21 are "incubi, satyrs, or kinds of

---

[10] Lea points out the similarity between the demon in the Thomas story and the one in the medieval *Vita S. Bernardi* 1, 149. For Gervais and Nider, see Lea, 1, 173-174, and 264. Caesarius, *Dialogue on Miracles,* 3, 6-12 (trans. H. von E. Scott and C. C. Swinton Bland [London: G. Routledge, 1929], 1, 130-139). In *Malleus,* pt. 2, qn. 2, ch. 1 (p. 164-166), the story by Caesarius is also retold.

[11] "Life of St. Anthony," ch. 5 (trans. Sister Mary Emily Keenan, *The Fathers of the Church,* ed. Roy J. Deferrari [Fathers of the Church, Inc., 1952], 15, 138-139).

[12] "Life of St. Paul, the First Hermit," ch. 8 (trans. Sister Marie Liguori Ewald, *The Fathers of the Church,* 15, 230-231). The story of St. Anthony was widely disseminated. The English *Marvels of the East* (Bodl. 614, fol. 50b, par. 48) includes a reference to satyrs—"just as St. Anthony, in his solitude, saw." Ed. M. R. James (Oxford: John Johnson, University Press, 1929), p. 24.

[13] *Moralia,* cap. 28, vers. 18, par. 34 (*P. L.,* 75, 786).

[14] *Etymologiae sive Origines,* lib. 8, cap. 11, par. 103-104. Ed. W. M. Lindsay (Oxford: Clarendon Press, 1911).

demons."[15] To the German theologian Haymo of Halberstadt (c. 778-853), the *lamia* of Isaiah 34.14 is a "monster having the face and body of a beautiful woman but feet of a horse."[16] A more secular work, the *Liber Monstrorum,* an assemblage of monsters and beasts, includes this paragraph: "Likewise satyrs and incubi are called men of the forest. The upper parts of their bodies are depicted as human, but the lower parts as in the manner of wild animals and fauns."[17] Carvings of grotesque monsters of this type at Cluny prompted St. Bernard of Clairvaux to make scathing remarks against anthropomorphic and zoomorphic imagery. What purpose, he asked, did such "ridiculous monsters" serve in a sanctuary for the Lord.

Discussion of the Incubi became more popular among clerics especially in the Germanic and Celtic countries of the North, where local customs and folklore concerning similar demons made the topic relevant. As a result, questions concerning their origin were again posed. Aquinas, for one, accepted the interpretation that the sons of God (Genesis 6) were spirits or demons.[18] The authors of the *Malleus Maleficarum* state that "giants were created not by some incredible act of men, but by certain devils, which are shameless toward women." They go even further: "The Scripture speaks of Incubi and Succubi lusting after women. . . ."[19] Some scholars did not think that spirits could copulate with humans, but the Genesis story, the testimony of the church fathers, and numerous Medieval commentaries, lives, and stories provided massive evidence to the contrary.

One of the oddest questions posed in the discussions is whether the Incubi and Succubi could cause conception. Walter Map (1140-c.1210) told several stories of fruitful intercourse between men and wood and water nymphs.[20] In traditional sources the Huns were represented as offspring of demons, and the most famous magician of the Medieval world, Merlin, was the son of an Incubus. Caesarius of Heisterbach (c. 1230) staged a lengthy debate between a monk and a novice on the topic. The novice posed the crucial question whether these creatures could cause conception, and the monk replied: "I know nothing which can answer this question of yours."[21]

William of Auvergne (c. 1180-1249) suggested that the spirit could blow

---

[15] *Glossa Ordinaria, Liber Isaiae,* cap. 13, vers. 21 (*P. L.,* 113, 1252).

[16] *Commentarium in Isaiam,* cap. 34 (*P. L.,* 116, 893). Haymo gives here the standard definitions of *pilosi* as well. See also cap. 13 (*P. L.,* 116, 789). These definitions were picked up by later literary artists. See John Lydgate, *Troy Book,* 2, 7700-7703. Ed. Henry Bergen, EETS, ES, 97 (London: Kegan Paul, 1906), p. 364.

[17] *Liber Monstrorum,* 49. Ed. Douglas R. Burtorff as "The Monsters and the Scholar: An Edition and Critical Study of the *Liber Monstrorum*" (Diss. University of Illinois 1968), p. 73.

[18] Lea, 1, 155-156. See also Sinistrari, note 7, above.

[19] Pt. 1, qn. 3 (p. 23); pt. 1, qn. 4 (pp. 29-30). Perhaps in opposition to this idea in the popular *Malleus,* Thomas Ady, in his *A Candle in the Dark* (1655), pointed out that there is no Biblical authority for the Incubus and Succubus; see K. M. Briggs, *Pale Hecate's Team* (London: Routledge and Kegan Paul, 1962), p. 25.

[20] Lea, 1, 149-150.

[21] Caesarius tells the story of the Huns and of Merlin, "a reasonable man and a Christian," *The Dialogue on Miracles,* 3, 12 (1, 139); for the debate as well as for several stories about Incubi, see 3, 6-10 (1, 130-139). Sinistrari lists numerous such offspring, such as Romulus and Remus, Servius Tullius, Plato, Alexander, down to Martin Luther, p. 22.

the seed into the womb.[22] Other writers, including Thomas of Cantimpré, Aquinas, and the authors of the *Malleus Maleficarum*, presented what was to become a standard opinion. Spirits as such cannot procreate, but by acting alternately as Succubi and Incubi they can gather seed and impregnate. Human children could then result.[23] Other questions were posed: Did the demons copulate for pleasure or to bring humans closer to hell? The answers were various, but the prevailing opinion was that demons performed only to bring humans closer to hell.[24] Did copulation result in damnation? Evidently not; many were forgiven. The "witch bull" of Innocent VIII (1484) reveals the Pope's horror that so many German laymen should be so forgetful of their soul's salvation as to have commerce with Incubi and Succubi.[25] Repentance would seem to wash away past indiscretions. Why were women oppressed more than men? The "weaker vessels" owed their origin to Eve, made from a "crooked rib," and were more easily overcome, according to the authors of *Malleus Maleficarum*. They also give the etymology of *femina* as *fe - minus*: less faith.[26] These questions arose because of the pervasiveness of the belief in demons in the early Middle Ages, and even though men from Tertullian to William of Auvergne did agree that many of the so-called appearances may have been illusions caused by dreams,[27] this pervasiveness can hardly be over-emphasized. Figures of grotesque creatures became staple ornaments in the interiors of churches, but with the first Gothic cathedrals these figures were removed because of their incompatibility with sacred experience. The profane figures were then banished to roofs, archivolts, and buttresses where they stood as terrifying reminders of demonic perversion. In later, more lax times, they again were installed in church interiors.

---

22 Lea, 1, 153.

23 For the opinions of Thomas of Cantimpré, Aquinas, and others, see Lea, 1, 154-156. For the *Malleus*, see pt. 3, qn. 3 (pp. 21-28, esp. p. 26), where the question is discussed in great detail. Reginald Scot, *The Discoverie of Witchcraft* (1584), Booke 4, ch. 2 (Carbondale: Southern Illinois University Press, 1964), pp. 81-82, scoffs at the opinions in the *Malleus*. Generally the offspring of Incubi and Succubi were monsters, witches, fairies, magicians, or changelings (false pregnancies, too, resulted from such unions).

24 See Lea, 1, 149, 153, 156, and Rossell Hope Robbins, *The Encyclopedia of Witchcraft and Demonology* (New York: Crown Publishers, Inc., 1959), p. 257.

25 This bull was included in the second edition of the *Malleus Maleficarum* (see pp. xliii-xlv).

26 Pt. 1, qn. 6 (pp. 41-47).

27 Tertullian, "De Anima," ch. 45, par. 4 (trans. Edwin A. Quain, *Fathers of the Church*, 10, 280-281). Tertullian would not blame a man "for a rape committed in a dream." For William of Auvergne, see Lea, 1, 154. For similar views of classical physicians, see Wilhelm H. Roscher, *Ephialtes, Abhandlungen der königlich sächsischen Gesellschaft der Wissenschaften,* phil.-hist. Classe, 20.2 (Leipzig: Teubner, 1903), esp. 18 ff. For a historical development of the modern view, see Ernest Jones, *Nightmare, Witches, and Devils* (New York: Norton, 1931). The influential *Canon Episcopi* (c. 900) also dismisses witches and night demons as "illusions and phantasms . . . dreams." See Joseph Hansen, *Zauberwahn, Inquisition und Hexenprozess im Mittelalter* (München & Leipzig: Oldenbourg, 1900), pp. 78-95.

The nightmare monster, however, was not exclusively the product of Classical and Judeo-Christian cultures. As the church expanded into Germanic and Celtic territories, clerics learned that similar types of creatures existed in the North. They found it necessary to explain these creatures by equating them with more familiar monsters. In Germanic areas this practice can be seen most obviously in Old English and Old High German glosses, where Old English *maere* (mare, compare nightmare) is equated with *incubus, satyrus, monstrum,* or *pilosus,* and Old High German words for the wood hag, water sprite, witch, and masked spirit (for example, *holzvrowe, waltminne, mermine minie, striga,* and *masca*) are equated with *lamia.*[28] In literature, this practice of linking northern and southern creatures had two important results. First, the local demon generally became broader in scope, having added to its native physical, mental, and symbolic characteristics those of its southern counterparts (the latter were already extended, representing the amalgamation of the Hebrew and the Classical conceptions). Second, the strength of the local tradition in which the demon figured was reinforced by giving it Scriptural antecedents and analogues.

The best early example of such amalgamation is found in the Old English poem *Beowulf.* The poem was clearly put into its present form by a Christian author who yoked the northern and southern traditions in a masterly fashion. The Grendel kin of *Beowulf,* in contrast to the relatively colorless and weakly outlined trolls of Scandinavian analogues, are vibrant and pathetic creatures with a heritage of outlawry going back to the Biblical Cain. With this background, the acts of Grendel and especially of his mother take on meaning, and their suffering, poignancy. They are the last survivors of an underworld kingdom, ostracized Cainites who numbered as their compatriots monsters, elves, demons, and giants (lines 101-113, 1261-2). They are called "scuccum ond scinnum" (demons and evil spirits, line 939) by Hrothgar (see *Christ and Satan,* line 72, where *scinna* = fallen angels) and are included among the *helrunan* (spirits of hell, line 163), a word equated with witches and sorceresses in glosses. There is some evidence that Grendel himself, the "dark death shadow" (line 160), is an early form of the northern mare, for Old English *maere* is twice

---

[28] See my article, "Grendel: A New Aspect," *Modern Philology,* 65 (1968), 194-195.

used to describe him.[29] His mother, the *merewif,* sea woman (line 1519), is conceptually similar to the Old English *meremenin,* sea sprite, the gloss to Latin *Sirena,* and to the Old High German words for sea sprite, forest hag, and witch (for example, *mermine minie, waltminne, holzvrowe,* and *strigae*). These Old High German words in turn are glosses to Latin *lamia.*[30] All are destroyers of men. In sum, the northern and southern concepts are intertwined in the depictions of the Grendel kin. The monsters possess the horrifying physical appearance of both their northern and southern counterparts; their minds are warped in the manner appropriate both to underworld giants of Germanic lore and to the descendants of Cain. They share a symbolic significance with types common in the South, for Grendel and his dam are to some extent metaphoric representations of the evils that plague the kingdom of the Healfdanes, with its aged leader Hrothgar, its culpable counsellor Unferth, and its dependency upon heathen gods.

Thus, though the *Beowulf* monsters were not Incubi in the technical sense, they illustrate the process of combination and metamorphosis that made the Classical-Biblical monsters denizens of the spirit world of the North. A more purely northern demon called *mara* is found in Snorri Sturluson's *Heimskringla.* As the story goes, the Finnish princess Driva was angered because her husband Vanlande had left her to visit Sweden for ten years. Since he had promised to return in three, she bribed the witch-wife Huld to bewitch Vanlande to return or else to kill him. Vanlande's companions feared that his sudden urge to return to Finland was brought about by witchcraft and would not let him return, so Huld began to crush him. He called out, saying that the mare rode him, but his men were helpless: "When they took hold of his head the mare trod on his legs so that they nearly broke; and when they seized his feet it pressed down on his head so that he died." In a brief poem following the prose story, the *mara* is called a *trollkund,* troll woman.[31] The mare in this story is a destroyer, though she does not seem to share the sexual perversion of the southern Incubus.

A poem in the Old English *Lacnunga,* a book of medical remedies dating from about 1000, mentions the pre-Christian dwarf which resembles both the *mara* and the Incubus. A description of this night oppressor is given along with a remedy to free one from its nightly visits:

Here came stalking in a creature all swathed [or spider-like or hostile].
He had his bridle in his hand; said that thou wert his steed;
Laid his bonds on thy neck; they began to move from the land.[32]

They flew until Eastre, the goddess of the dawn, came. The metaphor of the dwarf-mare as a rider and the man as the horse in time became reversed. Because of the eventual semantic configuration between *mearh* (horse) and *maere* (mare), the night-mare was sometimes described as a female horse.

---

[29] "Grendel," pp. 194-195.

[30] "Grendel," p. 195.

[31] *Heimskringla,* trans. Lee M. Hollander (Austin: University of Texas Press, 1964), pp. 16-17.

[32] *Lacnunga,* no. 93. Ed. J. H. G. Grattan and Charles Singer in *Anglo-Saxon Magic and Medicine* (London: Oxford Univ. Press, 1952), pp. 162-163. For another interpretation see G. Storms, *Anglo-Saxon Magic* (The Hague: Nijhoff, 1948), pp. 168-173.

Shakespeare speaks of the nightmare and her nine fold (foals) (*Lear* III.4. 121),[33] and throughout later literature, folklore, and art, the mare is frequently pictured as a ghostly horse which treads on the sleeper.

In the Old English *Leechbook* dating from roughly the end of the tenth century, we find that the mare is more clearly a sexual offender. Specific remedies are prescribed for both men and women to relieve them from attacks by the "mare," "night stalker," "elf disease" (nightmare), and the nightly "temptations of the enemy."[34] The northern mare, then, performs acts similar to those of the southern Incubus, and, indeed, the mare and Incubus become synonymous. The northern night monster seems to have assumed the characteristics of a sexual molester from its southern counterparts, and with the passing of time, the northern *mara* becomes more a sexual offender and less a night destroyer.

A similar merging of concepts is observable in early Celtic literature. One of a trinity of sinister and ferocious Celtic war goddesses was called Morrígan, queen of demons (*mor*, demon—compare Old English *maere*, *incubus*, or less likely, *mor*, great; and *rígan*, queen).[35] Sometimes the name Morrígan was applied collectively to all three goddesses. The Romans referred to these goddesses as *lamia* from ancient times. In a subterranean level of a Romano-Celtic temple in Benwell, the inscription "lamiis tribus" is found.[36] In an early Irish Vulgate (A.D. 876 or 877), a Christian cleric glossed the *lamia* of Is. 34.14 with "monstru[m] in femine figura .i. morgain,"[37] and Cormac equates the Macha, one of the three war goddesses, with *lamia*. The Morrígan

---

[33] See the comments of George I. Duthie and John D. Wilson in their edition of *Lear* (Cambridge: University Press, 1968), p. 214.

[34] On the date, see Oswald Cockayne, ed., *Leechdoms, Wortcunning and Starcraft of Early England* (London: Longman, 1865), 2, xxiv. For night attackers, see *Leechbook*, 1, 64 (Cockayne, *Leechdoms*, pp. 140-141); 2, 65 (pp. 296-297); 3, 1 (pp. 306-307); 3, 54 (pp. 342-343), 3, 58 (pp. 342-343); 3, 61 (pp. 344-345).

[35] *Contributions to a Dictionary of the Irish Language*, arr. Maud Joynt (Dublin: Hodge, Figgis & Co., n. d.), M., p. 173.

[36] Anne Ross, *Pagan Celtic Britain: Studies in Iconography and Tradition* (London: Routledge, 1967), p. 223.

[37] *Thesaurus Palaeohibernicus*, eds. Whitley Stokes and John Strachan (Cambridge: University Press, 1903), 1, 2, line 6. See also Whitley Stokes, ed., "The Second Battle of Moytura," *Revue Celtique*, 12 (1891), 128, where the *morrígan* is defined.

was also a shape-shifting goddess of fertility. She usually appeared as a raven, a young woman, or an old hag. In the form of a beautiful woman she attempted to seduce the Celtic hero, Cú Chulain, and in the form of an old hag, she deceived him into granting her three blessings. Her cave was at one of the entrances to the underworld. Along with the other war goddesses who also appear throughout the earliest stratum of Old Irish mythology, she guards wells, haunts mountain paths, drives deer over hills, blesses or harms humans, influences the outcome of battles by magic or terror, and at times has intercourse with tribal deities or heroes.[38] The Morrígan, therefore, shared enough crucial characteristics with the Classical-Christian *lamia* to make the identification of the two plausible. Both engaged in sexual relations with men, were destructive, and came from the world of spirits. Thus, the *lamia,* already linked to the *incubus* in Latin Christian sources and the female counterpart to the *maere* in Germanic-Latin glosses, is here linked to the *morrígan* in Celtic-Latin glosses and in early Celtic literary sources. *Lamia, incubus, maere,* and *morrígan,* then, were diverse male and female manifestations of a similar type of underworld creature.

The differences between the *lamia* and *morrígan* reveal in general terms the new dimension that Celtic mythology and folklore have added to the later English traditions of otherworldly creatures. The *morrígan,* as other fundamentally Celtic spirits, is at times either beneficent or destructive, and if destructive, she is not necessarily demonic. Certainly the supernatural figures of Celtic myth and folklore could become aligned with the Satanic, especially by Christian authors, but they generally are of a neutral sort, as the following examples will show.

Geoffrey of Monmouth, in his *Historia Regum Britanniae* (c. 1135), and Wace and Layamon, in their successive renditions (1155 and c. 1200), all tell the story of the miraculous conception of Merlin.[39] Geoffrey was a well-educated Christian writer and seems to have retold a genuine Celtic story, even though he gives Classical-Christian color to certain features. As his story goes, a handsome young man regularly appeared to a nun and, after making love to her, would disappear. From that union Merlin was born. A sage explained the nature of the phantom man: "In the books written by our wise men and in many historical works, I have discovered that many men have been born in this way." He then relates this spirit-man to the Latin *incubus*: "As Apuleius states in the *De Deo Socratis,* between the moon and the earth live spirits which we call incubi demons." These creatures, part men and part angels, assume mortal shapes and have intercourse with women. For this reason Merlin had something supernatural about him. But he is not at all an evil creature, like Cain's demonic descendants who also have spirit

---

[38] See *Contributions to Irish Language,* M., p. 173, and Ross, pp. 219-223, 233, 244.

[39] For Geoffrey, see note 2, above. A translation of the Welsh manuscript, by Robert Ellis Jones, is on the same pages. In this version, a bishop explains the nun's conception in a quaint way: "When Lyssyffer and the evil angels who sinned with him, fell, in the places and in the forms under which they were when God bade them cease, in those places they are to this day, and some of them are able to assume the forms of women, some of men; and thus perhaps was this boy begotten." For Wace's *Le Roman de Brut,* 5, 7439-7456, see the edition by Ivor Arnold, SATF (Paris: SATF Publications, 1938-1940), 1, 394-395. For Layamon's *Brut,* lines 7872-7881, see the edition by G. L. Brook and R. F. Leslie, EETS, 250 (London: Oxford University Press, 1963), 1, 408-409.

parentage, and he intends to bring about good. Thus the Celtic tradition represents a significant departure from the Latin-Christian view that all copulating spirits were demons from hell and that their offspring by human partners could hardly be better.

The Welsh churchman, Walter Map (1140-c. 1210), relates several Celtic stories of fruitful unions between men and spirits. These spirits he calls "daemones incubos et succubos," thereby also making the equation between Celtic fairies and the Latin *incubi*. Being a Christian scholar, he understandably reports that the progeny of such unions was usually unfortunate. He tells an early version of the Orfeo story in which a knight recovers his buried wife from among a band of spirits and subsequently has children by her.[40] Fairies of the Incubus type that appear in the lay of *Sir Orfeo* again illustrate the difference between Christian and Celtic creatures. They dwell in the kingdom of death. Their king abducts Orfeo's beloved bride, Heurodis, and takes her to his abode in a cave, where she becomes one of his train of captive ladies. He seems to represent only death and is no sexual offender. He is also honorable and keeps his word when Orfeo, disguised as a humble but talented harpist, obtains from him the promise of whatever boon he desires. Orfeo asks for Heurodis and is allowed to leave with her. Thus the Celtic fairy king, a spirit of the underworld somewhat akin to and often identified with the Latin-Christian Incubus, is not unequivocally evil as he would have been in a purely Christian tradition. Rather, he shared the neutral disposition of most other Celtic spirits. Evidently clerics saw no reason to consign these Celtic creatures of the underworld to the Christian Hell or to equate them with demons of horrifying Gothic dimensions, as Latin church missionaries had done when confronted by the evil chaos of the Germanic pantheon.

Celtic fairies of the more benign type continued to appear in early Middle English literature. This persistence is revealed nowhere more eloquently than in the romance *Sir Gawain and the Green Knight*, which dates from the later part of the fourteenth century. *Sir Gawain* presents three important supernatural creatures: the host, Sir Bertilak, who doubles as the elfish Green Knight; Morgan le Fay, the mistress of Merlin; and the seductress wife of the host.[41] The last two are traditional Celtic figures of the Succubus-Lamia type and are distinguished from any Latin-Christian counterparts by their relative neutrality. While they threaten to humiliate the complacent court of King Arthur, they do not damn souls into perdition. The defender of courtly honor, Sir Gawain, proves superior to most of the challenges, but he cannot escape all the subtle nets woven by his supernatural hosts and for his one indiscretion receives a small nick on the neck from the axe of the elf man, the Green Knight. His reputation is slightly marred. Even if Gawain had

---

[40] A. J. Bliss, ed., *Sir Orfeo*, 2nd ed. (Oxford: Clarendon Press, 1966), pp. xxxii-xxxiii. Obviously the author merged Celtic and Classical traditions. This practice was not uncommon, see, for example, Chaucer's "Merchant's Tale."

[41] I assume that the Green Knight and his "wife" are also supernatural creatures, see line 2361. On the relationship between Morgne la Faye and the Old Irish Morrígan (Morrígain), there has been much discussion and no firm conclusion. See J. R. R. Tolkien and E. V. Gordon, eds., *Sir Gawain and the Green Knight*, 2nd ed., rev. Norman Davis (Oxford: Clarendon Press, 1967), p. 129. The Green Knight is thought to be related to an early Celtic vegetation demon and as such would be related to the later dwarfish Green Men who decorate numerous churches in England.

An Incubus figure appearing in English folk tradition is commonly known as the Green Man. English Green Men are manifestations of the various forms of wood deities or vegetation gods found in European folk tradition. The size of these figures varies from dwarf to giant, and they are frequently dressed in green and have green skin and hair. They often have ivy or tree branches twisted about their bodies and may carry an uprooted tree as a staff or walking stick. Like all vegetation gods or demons, they have associations in classical myth with Pan, Dionysus, Satyrs, and Centaurs and usually have the ability to metamorphose from an anthropomorphic form into a tree or bush. As is common with vegetation gods, they can revive after being killed.

It is probable that the multiplicities of carvings of masks and human heads surrounded by leaves and branches in English churches are representations of Green Men. The dwarf form is most common and frequently occurs on misericord seats, roof bosses, and stone moldings and as tympanum decoration. Sometimes the foliage surrounds the head but more frequently sprouts from the mouth. (Thomas C. Faulkner)

---

succumbed to the temptation of the supposed young wife, he would have been punished only for violating a code of proper conduct—seducing the wife of his host. So also, if he had not offered the Green Knight a retaliatory stroke at his own head, according to the bargain, he would have probably suffered only earthly ignominy, not death. Ultimate issues are clearly not at stake. The mirth and laughter at the court of Arthur, and the humor and irony in the accounts of the various episodes in the castle, also emphasize that point. Even the Christian elements in the romance fail to imbue it with a tragic eschatological quality, though they do encourage the "enlightened" reader or listener to view the whole matter from a different perspective, to see that the challenge by the supernatural creatures of Celtic lore concerns merely secular and transitory values.

Sir Gawain and the Green Knight demonstrates the strength of the indigenous Celtic tradition long after it had come in contact with that of Latin-Christian origin. Christianity had prevailed at an early date in Celtic lands, and it may have been on that account that native Christian authors did not always deem it necessary to demote Celtic supernatural beings by associating them with Biblical demons, as was done with the monsters of the Germanic tradition, for instance, when the *Beowulf* poet traced Grendel's pedigree back to the primal murderer Cain. That British authors tacitly accepted the Celtic fairy kingdom and considered it a third path into the other world may be gathered from the ballad "Thomas Rhymer," in which the Queen of Elfland shows Thomas the "path of righteousness" and the "path of wickedness," and then takes him down the "road to fair elfland."[42] So also in *Sir Gawain* a third world, that of the supernatural fairies independent of Heaven and Hell, is allowed to exist.

Occasionally the Celtic elf was identified with a hellish creature. The "Incubus" in the ballad "The Daemon Lover" carries the unfaithful wife to a place that resembles Hell more than Elfland, and Malory writes in *Le Morte D'Arthur* that one of the damsels of the lake called Nimue "was aferde of hym [Merlin] for cause he was a devyls son."[43] The most important bequest of Celtic myths and folktales to later English literature, however, was the concept of the neutral, benign or comic fairy Incubus—a playful counterpart to the malign Incubus of the Latin-Christian and Germanic world.

In *Sir Gawain* we have a relatively comic set of underworld creatures— a knight who carries his severed head in his arms, and a lady who bestows negotiable kisses and a green girdle on a non-cooperating knight. About the same time, Chaucer gave a comic twist to Celtic mythology when he had his Wife of Bath explain that the elves and fairies who once walked the land do so no more. As a result women can go safely "up and doun," for "ther is noon oother incubus but he [the friar],/ And he ne wol doon hem but dishonour." She means that whereas the fairy Incubus was likely to rape or abduct, the friar—and she has Friar Hubert in mind—would only seduce with smiles, double talk, and an ingratiating lisp—he will do "but dishonour."[44] In this relatively minor passage Chaucer utilized underworld creatures for a purely comic effect, a practice which became increasingly popular. Writers now had at their disposal a whole spectrum of figurative entities ranging from malevolent demons of Hell to beneficent fairies of the upper air—the latter being part of the Celtic heritage.

During the late Medieval and early Renaissance periods, skepticism concerning the Incubus figures did not hinder the increasing use of them as artistic devices. The renewed interest in Classical literature, especially in Ovid's *Metamorphoses*, all the more encouraged the use of a grand spectrum of supernatural creatures. The dramatists Marlowe, Middleton, and Shakespeare seem to have catered to tastes of the general public by including traditional "English" as well as the "newer" Classical figures in their plays—sometimes in combination. Marlowe shows Faustus enraptured by the Succubus spirit, Helen of Troy: "Her lips suck forth my soul: see where it flies!"[45] Middle-

---

[42] Child, no. 37, versions A and C. Francis James Child, ed., *The English and Scottish Popular Ballads* (Boston: Houghton Mifflin, 1892), vol. 1, pt. 2, pp. 317-329.

[43] "The Daemon Lover," Child, no. 243, versions A, E, and F, vol. 4, pt. 2, pp. 362-369. Eugène Vinaver, ed., *The Works of Sir Thomas Malory*, 2nd ed. (Oxford: Clarendon Press, 1967), 1, 126, lines 20-21.

[44] See my note supporting this point, "The Wife of Bath's Tale: D. 878-881," *The Chaucer Review*, 7 (1972), 113-117.

[45] For influential Classical works in Renaissance times, see Briggs, *Pale.Hecate's Team*, pp. 9-10. *Doctor Faustus*, 18. 102 (5. 1. 1877). John D. Jump, in his edition (Cambridge: Harvard Univ. Press, 1962), p. lvi, states: "Faustus in embracing her commits the sin of demoniality, or bodily intercourse with demons. The Old Man, learning this, concludes that he can now do nothing for Faustus." However, one could be forgiven for this sin, see note 27, above.

ton's *The Witch* includes a traditional and grotesque Succubus-Incubus team, Heccat and her son Firestone. Heccat has "had him [Almachaldes, a fantastical gentleman] thrice in *Incubus* already," and Firestone wishes to "ramble abroad tonight, with the Night-Mare; for I have a great mind to overlay a fat parson's daughter."[46] Shakespeare refers to the night-mare Incubus only three times,[47] but he uses "elves of hills, brooks, standing lakes, and groves," and other types too, for every kind of effect. This quotation from *The Tempest* (V.1.33) is derived from Ovid's *Metamorphoses* and there described as evil maleficent creatures. But Shakespeare describes an opposite type—beneficent, prankish fairies of English heritage. These give an airy lightness to *Midsummer Night's Dream* and to the major part of *The Tempest,* while the foul Calaban, the son of Sycorax and an Incubus, casts a somber, frightening shadow over some portions of the latter play (I.2.321).

A book that furnished material for both Shakespeare and Middleton was written by an earlier contemporary of theirs, Reginald Scot, who in his *Discoverie of Witchcraft* (1584) made a supreme effort to refute the irrational but deep-rooted belief in Incubi and demons. His aim was to prevent the persecution of innocent persons for witchcraft by exposing the impostures and the credulity that supported the belief.[48] But his efforts fell on deaf ears, calling forth even the counterblast of a king, James VI of Scotland (later James I of England), in his *Daemonologie* (1597). James supported the traditional arguments of earlier demonologists such as Johannes Nider, Henry Kramer and Jacob Sprenger (who compiled the *Malleus Maleficarum*), and Jean Bodin. James' mouthpiece in the *Daemonologie,* Epistemon, states that the Incubi were real and present, especially in the northern lands "where the Devil finds greatest ignorance and barbarity."[49]

In the succeeding centuries, the Incubus and other demonic figures thrived as literary entities. They tended to represent absolutes—fallen angels who were damned and who tempted humans to mortal sins. The fallen angels in Milton's *Paradise Lost* and *Paradise Regained* are of this type, and though the greatest of these, Satan, is grandly delineated, he remains throughout the story a victim of self-deception. The minor angels whom Milton portrays specifically as types of Incubi-Succubi, such as Baalim and Ashtaroth, are more obviously fallen creatures of passion (*Paradise Lost,* I, 422-431; see also Asmodeus, *Paradise Lost,* IV, 168 ff. and *Paradise Regained,* II, 152). In the eighteenth century Alexander Pope employed several kinds of supernatural creatures, all transformed souls of dead women: sylphs, salamanders, nymphs, and a gnome, in the "heroi-comical" *Rape of the Lock,* but these are derived, as Pope himself says, from Rosicrucian lore.[50]

---

[46] 1 (sc. 2). 396-398 and 1 (sc. 2). 283-285. Ed. F. P. Wilson, Malone Society Reprints (Oxford: Univ. Press, 1948, rpt. 1963), pp. 17, 12.

[47] *King Lear,* 3. 4. 121; *2 Henry IV,* 2. 1. 77-78; *Romeo and Juliet,* 1. 4. 92. In the last reference, the hag that presses is Queen Mab, and her victims, maids.

[48] Scot was well versed in native and classical lore. For passages on the Incubus, see Booke 4, chs. 1-2 (pp. 80-82), and elsewhere.

[49] Bk. 3, ch. 3 ed. G. B. Harrison (London: The Bodley Head, Ltd., 1922-1926; rpt. ed., New York: Barnes and Noble, 1966), pp. 66-69.

[50] In his "Epistle" preceding the poem, Pope discusses the "Rosicrucian Doctrine of Spirits," and the "best Account" he knows of, *Le Comte de Gabalis.* According to the Rosicrucians, "the four Elements are inhabited by Spirits, which they call Sylphs, Gnomes, Nymphs, and Salamanders, . . ." *The Rape of the Lock* (1714; facsimile rpt., Menston, England: The Scholar Press, 1969), p. A 4-5.

Within the Incubus-Succubus tradition, an important alteration of meaning occurs in the Romantic age. The major poets began to use these figures to symbolize both the temptations and aspirations of man in terms of his underlying sense of supernatural fear or wonder at his ability to transcend his condition or transform it. Thus the dark figures in the Romantic period take on more complex meanings. No longer are they mere absolutes—whether magical fairies or agents of Satan bound to destroy man—but more ambiguous, more ominously ambivalent figures. In the poetry of Coleridge, for example, they can become symbols of imaginative currents too mysterious for even the poet to comprehend; in the drama of Byron, they promise fulfillment of emotional and religious aspirations to the person who is profoundly dissatisfied with the ordinary; and in the poetry of Keats, they personify aspects of the imagination too awesome, sublime, and urgent to be understood in profane, rational, and natural imagery.

Each of these poets, Coleridge, Byron, and Keats, relied on traditional sources in his depiction of the dark figures. Coleridge's interest in the demon lover and vampire at the time he wrote "Kubla Khan" and "Christabel" is amply documented by John Livingston Lowes and Arthur H. Nethercot.[51] Byron very clearly returned to traditional conceptions of the Satanic figures who appear to men when he composed his "speculative quartet": *Manfred, Cain: A Mystery, Heaven and Earth: A Mystery,* and *The Deformed Transformed.* Both *Cain* and *Heaven and Earth* are "mysteries" in the Medieval sense, being based on Biblical subject matter, and the latter owes its inspiration in part to the Book of Enoch and its stories of angels of God who unite with daughters of men.[52] All four plays feature Faustian and Promethean characters who at times echo Milton's Satan, the archetypal, and to Romantics, heroic overreacher. Keats turned to saint's legend, traditional ballad sources, and classical myth (via Robert Burton) in his "The Eve of St. Agnes," "La

---

[51] Lowes, *The Road to Xanadu* (Cambridge, Mass.: The Riverside Press, 1927), pp. 233-241. Nethercot, *The Road to Tryermaine* (Chicago: Univ. of Chicago Press, 1939), pp. 80-105.

[52] Ernest Hartley Coleridge, *The Works of Lord Byron* (New York: Scribner's, 1905), 5, 280-281, cites the publication in 1821 of the complete *Book of Enoch,* translated by Richard Laurence.

Belle Dame sans Merci," and "Lamia." Yet each of these poets superimposes upon the traditional dark figures new Romantic values which mirror the artist's imaginative experience. This experience, while it may allow a mystical vision of the ultimate reality, is also potentially dangerous, for the vision can destroy as well as enlighten.

Coleridge stated his well-known purpose in dealing with the supernatural shortly before he wrote "Christabel" and "Kubla Khan." He would direct his attention to "persons and characters supernatural, or at least romantic; yet so as to transfer from our inward nature a human interest and a semblance of truth sufficient to procure for these shadows of imagination that willing suspension of disbelief for the moment, which constitutes poetic faith. . . ."[53] Thus the shadow of imagination, which represents an inner truth and reality, is translated into "persons and characters supernatural." Geraldine, then, seems in general terms a manifestation of a potentially destructive truth of man's "inner nature" and seems a threat to Christabel after she had "dreams all yesternight of her own betrothed knight" and presently "in the midnight wood will pray" for her lover's weal. At such an hour, in the silent forest, the vampirish Geraldine moans from the other side of the "huge oak tree" at which Christabel kneels to pray. It is not altogether clear whether Geraldine is a benign or malign answer to Christabel's prayer—she is, in flashes, good as well as bad—and Coleridge himself could not finish the poem and resolve the ambivalence of Geraldine.

This same mysterious ambivalence is also part of the fabric of "Kubla Khan," which Coleridge wrote after he had begun "Christabel." The dream fragment includes a brief allusion to:

> . . . that deep romantic chasm which slanted
> Down the green hill athwart a cedarn cover!
> A savage place! as holy and enchanted
> As e'er beneath a waning moon was haunted
> By woman wailing for her demon-lover!

If "Kubla Khan" is a poem about poetry, as some critics believe, the holy and enchanted place where the woman wails for her demon lover describes a sacred altar at which a communion, not necessarily sacrilegious, with a divinity takes place. The simile then describes in brief the larger ambivalent experience of the poem. The concept of the beneficent "Incubus" is not without precedent, as we have seen in Celtic and Arthurian literature of the later Middle Ages. Also, an Italian theologian, Ludovico Sinistrari, sometime before his death in 1701, presented in *De Daemonialitate, et Incubis et Succubis* the positive aspects of a union with Incubi: "When having intercourse with an Incubus, man does not degrade, but rather dignifies, his nature . . ." (p. 88). This book was not published until 1875, and it is highly doubtful that Coleridge knew of it. I cite Sinistrari only to demonstrate that there were alternative sources—Celtic as well as Catholic—which argued the potentially edifying aspects of a union with an Incubus. Whatever Coleridge's source in depicting the demon lover, we know that Byron was impressed by the line from "Kubla Khan": "And woman wailing for her

---

[53] *Biographia Literaria,* chapter XIV. Ed. J. Shawcross (Oxford: Clarendon Press, 1907), 2, 6.

demon lover" [sic], for he chose it to serve as the motto of his mystery, *Heaven and Earth.*

All four of Byron's plays include supernatural creatures. In *Manfred,* spirits abound, but one with the familiar name of Astarte represents Manfred's ultimate goal and what he is unable to attain. In *Cain,* Lucifer represents almost a wish fulfillment of the hero, Cain, when he ponders his No Exit situation. In *The Deformed Transformed,* an unfinished play, the very spirit who killed the seven husbands of the bride of Tobias is fostering the aspiring hopes of a lowly hunchback, Arnold, called by his own mother, "Thou Incubus! Thou nightmare." *Heaven and Earth: A Mystery* was written as a successor to *Cain* and includes several spirits of the traditional Incubus type. This play, too, presents the most positive—and improbable—solution for the rebels at the end of the play. In both *Cain* and *Manfred,* the heroes rise in anger against their limitations, but must suffer for their resistance. Cain kills his brother, albeit unintentionally, and is ostracized; Manfred must die, even though he does not give in to the demonic figures who cry for his life. In *Heaven and Earth,* on the contrary, the rebellious daughters of Cain reject compromise, spurn possible salvation on the ark, and still can fly away with their angelic seraphs to "some untroubled star, . . . whence we cannot be driven." Thus the metaphor of the otherworldly spirits who prompt the rebellious hero to seek a life unbounded by limitations of god or man becomes a stark reality in this play. Both the daughters of Cain and the angels attain their vision by flight to a new world. The real hero of this mystery, it might be argued, is the rejected lover, Japhet. At the end of the play he stands alone about to be picked up by the already floating ark. He has had a glimpse of another life, of love, beauty, and fulfillment, and is sensitive enough to understand what will never be his. He therefore mourns his loss and wishes for death:

To die! in youth to die!
And happier in that doom,
Than to behold the universal tomb,
      Which I
Am thus condemned to weep above in vain.
Why, when all perish, why must I remain?

In due time, Japhet will become a Cain, Manfred, or Arnold, but he will have no escape as did the daughters of Cain.

The motif of the demon lover appears nowhere so poignantly as in the poems of Keats. He employed this motif with the understanding that it represented a most intense variety of experience. In that respect it would parallel the awesome, sublime, and urgent inspiration of a creative vision. Thus the metaphor and the message in Keats' three poems written between January and August, 1819, dovetail. The most brief, the ballad "La Belle Dame sans Merci," is the story of a knight who has met a beautful "lady in the meads," "a faery's child" with long hair, light foot, wild eyes, faery song and a strange language in which she professes: "I love thee true." Such a creature one follows anywhere, even to a weird "elfin grot." After the climactic moment—"there I shut her wild, wild eyes/ With kisses four,"—she lulls the knight to sleep. When he awakens, the vision has dissipated, as happens so frequently in fairy tales. But the memories of the inimitable vision remain to haunt the knight-narrator as it has haunted others before him. He will wait on the cold hill's side "Alone and palely loitering" until the end of time. The ballad begs to be interpreted as a metaphor of an artist who sees into the depths of things and then, wakened out of his vision, loses the perception. As in "Kubla Khan," the faery lover, the traditional demon lover, serves as an appropriate metaphor of one who grants an awesome, sublime, and urgent vision.

"The Eve of St. Agnes" is a much more complex and ambiguous poem, but when juxtaposed to "La Belle Dame sans Merci," it, too, can be seen as a poem about the duality of inspiration. The Gothic setting greatly affects the mood of the poem. The Baron's ancient castle in the midst of the moors has a gloomy frozen chapel, a dark cobwebbed tunnel, a moonlight room "pale, lattic'd, chill, and silent as a tomb." Darkness and silence reign at the midnight bell, but outside a supernatural storm rages. References to faery fancy, fays, elves, phantoms, witches, demons, and old legend and romance are numerous and provide the magical background for the supernatural vision on the Eve of St. Agnes. Madeline goes through elaborate rituals to insure the "sweetest of all dreams" and "visions of delight" at the middle of the night. As she closes the door to her room, "she panted, all akin/ To spirits of the air, and visions wide." The vision that appears to her is her lover Porphyro, who has been helped into the bedroom by Angela, an ancient beldame. Porphyro then "into her dream . . . melted." The two quickly resolve to fly away into the dark "flaw-blown sleet"; they hurry past all the "sleeping dragons" and glide "like phantoms" through the hall. The inmates of the castle had nightmares as the two fled, though only the Beadsman, who died that evening, was transported out of the castle, as in a different sense was Madeline. The poem does not describe a totally positive experience. Madeline's vision seems exquisite and eternal, and she is taken by her lover on a wished-for journey to a new land. But the Gothic setting and references to the magical and supernatural belie such an interpretation. Porphyro is closely akin to the traditional dark figure of the night—the demon lover— who comes to a receptive maiden at her weakest moment and carries her away. They go together into the "elfin storm from faery land/ Of haggard seeming, but a boon indeed," as he tells Madeline. The experience is fraught with ambiguity.

Keats' "Lamia" also features a supernatural creature of the Incubus-Succubus classification. The traditional Lamia is related to Lilith and to the wild supernatural demons in Classical, Germanic, and Celtic literature. According to this poem she was originally a woman but through metamorphosis became a serpent. Hermes then, in exchange for a favor, allowed her to assume the form of a female spirit. In this form Lamia is free to pursue her lover Lycius and is capable of transporting him into a realm of imagination and beauty. She might have succeeded, for Lycius is initially enthralled by Lamia and indeed will marry her. Yet Lamia is no more than a vision, just as are her tents, musicians, and Dionysian wine bearers. Only the sage philosopher, Apollonius, can see through the vision: "Do not all charms fly/ At the mere touch of cold philosophy?" Apollonius can destroy her and does, when Lycius stands by ineffectual, unable to synthesize reason with imagination. Lamia then disappears, and Lycius himself, devoid of happiness, expires that very evening. The petulant Lycius seems to be a victim of

Lamia only in an ironic sense, since the reader's sympathy is with her through-out. He does not really deserve what Lamia can offer, and his mentor, the frigid Apollonius, forebodes doom. If Lycius had, like Madeline in "The Eve of St. Agnes," flown with his Lamia, we are tempted to think that all the delights of the imaginative world would have been his. But the death of Lycius suggests that his involvement with Lamia, even momentary, has darker, more sinister implications. He had committed himself deeply enough to en-twine his very existence into her own. When she disappears, his own life ebbs. Hence the Lamia, like the faery in "La Belle Dame sans Merci," offers a vision which is potentially dangerous and can destroy as well as enlighten. Thus we see a complication and convolution of meaning in the tradition of the dark figure of the Incubus-Succubus type when it becomes a metaphor for man's creative drive or for his ambition to transcend his limited earthly condition.

The foregoing interpretation of the Incubus-Succubus as a metaphor of man's creative drive does not rule out their basic demonic natures. Indeed, it was this very aspect that seems to have attracted the Romantic poets. After all, as we have seen, the Incubus was a composite creature—the synthesis of the demon-spawned sexual molester of the Judeo-Christian tradition, the violent destroyer of the Germanic tradition, and the unpredictably malign or beneficent, or even comic, fairy of the Celtic tradition. Over the centuries he has appeared in many forms and combinations in English literature, some-times representing single, but more often multiple, traits that were developed in the mythologies of three great cultures. More deeply, as his mythological embodiment in these cultures suggests, the Incubus was a primordial arche-type of man's darkest lusts and fears. As such, he became a natural symbol or icon for the Romantic imagination at a time when the springs of imagi-nation were troubled.

In the Hands of an Angry God: Religious Terror in Gothic Fiction

JOEL PORTE

Efforts to isolate a major underlying interest or concern in serious fiction of the so-called "Gothic" school have not been notably successful, and one is tempted—in imitation of Arthur Lovejoy's famous essay on the multiplexity of "Romanticisms"—to write simply "On the Discrimination of Gothicisms." Basic problems of classification face us at the start. Gothic novels, as we all know, come in various vintages—Early (Walpole, Beckford), Middle (Radcliffe, Lewis), and Late (Maturin, Mary Shelley)—and flavors (Terror Gothic, Horror Gothic, Historical Gothic, *Tendenz-Romanen* masquerading as Gothic, and so on). And the question of whether to include the American school or treat it as separatist has been a lively one for a long time. The most extended recent study of English Gothic fiction, for example, Maurice Lévy's *Le Roman "Gothique" Anglais 1764-1824,* limits itself to the "onirique" and excludes from its purview at the outset such works as *Vathek* (too much irony), *Caleb Williams* (too much social criticism), and *Frankenstein* (too forward-looking and science-fiction oriented). We are faced, then, with such a bewildering variety of designs and intents in a literary fashion which was indulged in for almost a century (if we include Poe), that the critic searching for something like a unified field theory of Gothic fiction will certainly be tempted to throw down his pen in despair.

Some help is afforded, however, by Lévy himself who, in a long chapter entitled "Structures Profondes," speculates suggestively on the underpinnings of Gothic fiction. Reflecting on the broadly Marxian analysis of the genre advanced by André Breton and other Surrealists (*"le genre noir* must be considered as a symptom of the enormous social disorder that took possession of Europe at the end of the eighteenth century"), Lévy notes that the connection between political Terror, particularly in France, and the novel of Terror was repeatedly insisted on by contemporary commentators (the Marquis de Sade among them) and has been suggested as an etiology of *le genre noir* by even

JOEL PORTE, Professor of English and American Literature at Harvard University, has published widely on nineteenth-century literature. His latest book is *The Romance in America: Studies in Cooper, Poe, Hawthorne, Melville, and James.*

non-Marxist critics in our own time.[1] It is important to remember that *The Mysteries of Udolpho* was published in 1794, as was *Caleb Williams, The Monk* in 1796, and that both Radcliffe and Lewis were enormously popular in France at the height of Jacobin fury. But Lévy insists, crucially, that we not think of the Gothic novel of the 1790's and beyond as in any way "a direct transcription of revolutionary horrors, but rather as an expression of the anguish provoked by them." In short, the Revolution only tapped, for authors and readers alike, a fund of deep-seated anxiety and anguish which, in the specifically English context, Lévy tends to associate more with the political and, especially, religio-intellectual upheavals of 1688 and after—a Glorious Revolution which left to the eighteenth century an uncomfortable legacy of scientific rationalism, on the one hand, and religious reform, and uncertainty, on the other. What such an analysis reduces to for Lévy, in a literary context, is the notion that "in some sense the fantastic is a compensation that man provides for himself, at the level of the imagination, for what he has lost at the level of faith." Viewing Gothic mystery thus, as a substitute for discredited religious mystery, we may consent to recognize that, despite its wild extravagances and puerile heresies, *le genre noir* represented for its producers and consumers alike a genuine expression of profound religious malaise. No less notable an atheist than Shelley, the *cor cordium* of his age, had this to say:

> We talk of ghosts; neither Lord Byron nor Monk G. Lewis seem to believe in them, and they both agree, in the very face of reason, that none could believe in ghosts without also believing in God. I do not think that all the persons who profess to discredit those visitations really do discredit them, or if they do in the daylight, are not admonished by the approach of loneliness and midnight to think more respectfully of the world of shadows.[2]

It is surprising, particularly in view of the evidence that lies readily to hand, how little systematic consideration has been given to Gothic fiction as the expression of a fundamentally Protestant theological or religious disquietude. Beginning in 1756, when Burke published his *Philosophical Inquiry into the Origin of Our Ideas of the Sublime and Beautiful,* it became commonplace among both writers and readers to consider the emotions of terror and awe as sources of "the Sublime"—a ready conduit to ideas of Divinity, Omnipotence, and all Final Things. Mrs. Radcliffe, for example, had conned her Burke and knew that the proper business of the orthodox novel of Terror was to expand the soul religiously. So, in the very first chapter of *The Mysteries of Udolpho,* and interminably thereafter, the impeccably well-instructed Emily St. Aubert is sent off, as to a sylvan Sunday school, not into "the soft and glowing landscape," but to "the wild wood-walks, that skirted the mountain; and still more the mountain's stupendous recesses, where the silence and gran-

---

[1] Maurice Lévy, *Le Roman "Gothique" Anglais 1764-1824* (Toulouse: Association des publications de la Faculté des lettres et sciences humaines de Toulouse, 1968). This and subsequent quotations are from Chapter X, "Structures Profondes" (translations are supplied). Since I shall be arguing for the importance, in Gothic fiction, of Protestant —indeed Calvinist—religious motifs, it is worth noting here that the Revolutionary Terror in France has also been analyzed in these terms. Crane Brinton, for example, discusses the parallel between Calvinist and Robespierrean "theology" in *A Decade of Revolution 1789-1799* (New York: Harper & Brothers, 1934), pp. 158 ff. ("The Theory of the Terror").

[2] Cited in Eino Railo, *The Haunted Castle* (New York: E. P. Dutton, 1927), pp. 116-117.

deur of solitude impressed a sacred awe upon her heart, and lifted her thoughts to the GOD OF HEAVEN AND EARTH."[3]

So far as serious religious ideas or emotions are concerned, *Udolpho* does not often get beyond such simple exercises in majuscular Sublimity. One possible exception, but an important one in this context, concerns the shadowy and pathetically mad Sister Agnes, who is finally revealed to be none other than Signora Laurentini di Udolpho, the passion-crazed destroyer of Emily's aunt (the Marchioness de Villeroi) whose story contains the central mystery of the book. In a frightening interview with the dying nun, the *aes triplex* of Emily's innocence is subjected to its most profound threat—intimations of universal sinfulness and the reality of damnation. Asserting that the guilty forfeit the protection of God, Agnes both unburdens herself and moralizes at large:

"Yet who is he, that shall dare to call himself innocent!—all earthly innocence is but comparative. Yet still how wide asunder are the extremes of guilt, and to what an horrible depth may we fall! Oh!"—

The nun, as she concluded, uttered a shuddering sigh, that startled Emily, who, looking up, perceived the eyes of Agnes fixed on hers, after which the sister rose, took her hand, gazed earnestly upon her countenance, for some moments, in silence, and then said,

"You are young—you are innocent! I mean you are yet innocent of any great crime!—But you have passions in your heart,—scorpions; they sleep now—beware how you awaken them!—they will sting you, even unto death!"

Emily, affected by these words and by the solemnity, with which they were delivered, could not suppress her tears.

"Ah! is it so?" exclaimed Agnes, her countenance softening from its sternness— "so young, and so unfortunate! We are sisters, then indeed. Yet, there is no bond of kindness among the guilty," she added, while her eyes resumed their wild expression, "no gentleness,—no peace, no hope! I knew them all once—my eyes could weep—but now they burn, for now, my soul is fixed, and fearless!—I lament no more!"

Here, in a scene that probably influenced Hawthorne's treatment of the Miriam-Hilda relationship in *The Marble Faun,* Mrs. Radcliffe modulates, though only briefly, to that somber key of psychological-cum-moral ambiguity and anxiety which is fundamental to the most affecting Gothic writing. The crucial "characteristic of the Gothic novel is not its devices," notes Robert D. Hume, "but its atmosphere . . . of evil and brooding terror."

---

[3] Even (should we not say especially?) in the wilds of the New World, and without benefit of Burke's theories, the young Jonathan Edwards knew that "being alone in the mountains, or some solitary wilderness, far from all mankind," perhaps "on the banks of Hudson's River, at some distance from the city," he could commune with Godhead best through the medium of Sublimity:

. . . scarce anything, among all the works of nature, was so sweet to me as thunder and lightning; formerly [before his conversion], nothing had been so terrible to me. Before, I used to be uncommonly terrified with thunder, and to be struck with terror when I saw a thunder storm rising; but now, on the contrary, it rejoiced me. I felt God, so to speak, at the first appearance of a thunder storm; and used to take the opportunity, at such times, to fix myself in order to view the clouds, and see the lightnings play, and hear the majestic and awful voice of God's thunder . . . .

Rejoicing in his sanctified state, the believer now recognizes that his former terror was nothing less than the awful voice of God reaching out to his unconverted soul. Had the young sinner been born late enough in the century to peruse *The Mysteries of Udolpho,* however, he would have understood immediately that his fearful emotions experienced in sublime nature were the authentic mark of nascent yearnings toward God.

That terror, I want to insist, is usually at bottom theological, so that I fear Hume only muddies his argument when he goes on to say that "ruined abbeys, and the like, were merely a convenient convention, a standardized method of achieving the desired atmosphere."[4] We have long since learned, I hope, to be wary of distorting or even losing the message by overlooking the significance of the medium; and in serious Romantic fiction, *a fortiori,* the manipulation of convention is often a key to meaning. Surely the iniquitous convents and monasteries, the moldering catacombs and graveyards, of high Gothic writing represent more than a congeries of discardable props or the simple anticlericalism of Protestant authors. Although the action is so often displaced to a Catholic setting (and that fact of displacement is worth attention), what is represented with great force and conviction is a religious drama, the dark rites of sin, guilt, and damnation: Ambrosio's horrific destruction at the hands of his sexual devils in *The Monk;* or the incredibly affecting rendition of Alonzo de Monçada's persecution by the Inquisition in *Melmoth the Wanderer.*[5] Lévy underlines, throughout his massive study, the singular importance of Gothic architecture, both as fact and as symbol. It provided par excellence that dim religious atmosphere where the union of Terror and Sublimity which was alone considered capable of transporting the soul beyond reason and decorum to the very confines of Being itself could be achieved. If the Gothic setting per se is attenuated or eliminated, as so often in the works of Godwin, the Shelleys, and Charles Brockden Brown and the American school generally, it is because the atmosphere of psychological or theological distress has become so pervasive and profound that it scarcely needs to be reinforced by the overt presence of a ruined abbey; like the pestilence, it can be tasted in the surrounding air itself. What I shall attempt, in fact, to demonstrate here is that much Anglo-American *genre noir* fiction from Godwin to Poe owes its gloomy "Gothic" *ambiance* to a brooding sense of religious terror which is notably Protestant in its origin and bearing.

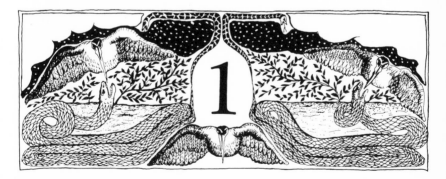

The Wizard Priest and the Witch, a Romance, by Quintin Poynet, is the only book cited for 1822 in Maurice Lévy's chronological listing of some 350 Gothic

---

[4] Robert D. Hume, "Gothic Versus Romantic: A Revaluation of the Gothic Novel," *PMLA,* 84 (1969), 286.

[5] This part of Maturin's book, it seems to me, and not the tedious Byronic posturing of Melmoth or the maunderings of Immalee, is what contains its most profound Gothic vision.

The parish church of Fotheringhay in Northamptonshire. This photograph shows the tower as seen from the lane leading to the north entrance, framed by the branches of newly pruned trees which capture the resemblance between Gothic architecture and the organic forms of nature: here trees and Gothic tower form an ensemble thrusting upward in a striking visual metaphor of the spiritual quest for heaven. (Thomas C. Faulkner)

novels, but another publication of that year, Thomas De Quincey's *Confessions of an English Opium-Eater,* may have greater claim on the attention of a student of the genre. Although I hesitate to call De Quincey's *Confessions* a Gothic novel outright (rated as a fiction, it is a mediocre one, since its drama is blunted by poor organization and the author's rambling, desultory manner), it is unquestionably a work of the English-Gothic imagination, or rather of a mind steeped in the motifs and themes of serious Gothic writing, and it throws into high relief some of the underlying concerns of the genre. As with the inset tales found in *Udolpho, The Monk,* and *Melmoth,* De Quincey's mode, like that of Godwin, Mary Shelley, and Charles Brockden Brown, is the personal narrative of sin, guilt, and retribution. As such, it represents a kind of religious confession or exploration.[6]

Despite De Quincey's curious equivocations as to the true subject of his narrative (himself? opium? dreams?), it is manifestly the tale—which he, like the Ancient Mariner, is driven to recapitulate obsessively—of his fall from grace and subsequent pursuit by demons. De Quincey's story, the principal paradigm of which is *Paradise Lost* (quoted incessantly), concerns his fearfully passionate attachment as a little boy to an elder sister, whose death in De Quincey's seventh year constitutes the fundamental and decisive tragedy of his life. Overwhelmed by grief, the boy is likened by De Quincey in the intensity of his feeling to an Adam bereft of his Eve. But shame (covertly) and rage (overtly) are strongly intermixed with his sorrow. "Where my sister was, there was paradise; no matter whether in heaven above, or on the earth beneath," and the boy is incensed that the priest of God should justify, indeed almost condone, this bitter stroke: "and he had taken her away, cruel priest! of his *'great* mercy!'" Thus De Quincey (who tells us elsewhere in the book that he is most moved by "the great harmonies of the Satanic speeches in *Paradise Regained,* when read aloud by myself") represents the tremendous loss suffered by this diminutive heretic as a Luciferian descent:

"Into what depth thou seest,
From what height fallen."

For, as he avows, "the terrific grief which I passed through drove a shaft for me into the worlds of death and darkness which never again closed."

But perhaps a more startling, and revealing, identification is that made by De Quincey between his bewildering punishment and that of the guilt-driven outcast, alternately a criminal and a martyr, whose figure and fate teased, indeed tortured, the Gothic and Romantic imagination endlessly:[7] "O, Ahasuerus, everlasting Jew! fable or not a fable, thou when first starting on thy endless pilgrimage of woe,—thou when first flying through the gates of Jerusalem, and vainly yearning to leave the pursuing curse behind thee,—couldst not more

---

[6] Although my own interest and emphasis are somewhat different, I have been greatly stimulated by J. Hillis Miller's fine discussion of De Quincey in *The Disappearance of God* (Cambridge: Harvard Univ. Press, 1963).

[7] See Miller, *The Disappearance of God,* pp. 25 ff. On this subject the most thorough study in English is now George K. Anderson, *The Legend of the Wandering Jew* (Providence: Brown Univ. Press, 1965). In a specifically Gothic and Romantic context see also Edgar Rosenberg, *From Shylock to Svengali: Jewish Stereotypes in English Fiction* (Stanford: Stanford Univ. Press, 1960), pp. 187-233, and Railo's *The Haunted Castle,* pp. 191-217.

certainly read thy doom of sorrow in the misgivings of thy troubled brain than I when passing forever from my sister's room." Whether the boy's "sin" here is meant to bear an analogy to the wandering Jew's denial of Christ, or to hint darkly at some taint of that *Geschwisterinzest* so dear to all Gothicists (the boy has just, we are told, "kissed the lips that I should kiss no more, and slunk like a guilty thing with stealthy steps from the room"), is left vague by De Quincey. What matters, at all events, is that, like Ahasuerus, De Quincey receives a kind of compensation for his loss in an *elixir vitae* (of the sort which the *Ewige Jude* Zampieri possesses in Godwin's *St. Leon*)— a "celestial drug" that holds out "the keys of Paradise" to this fallen angel:

> O just, subtile, and mighty opium! that to the hearts of poor and rich alike, for the wounds that will never heal, and for 'the pangs that tempt the spirit to rebel,' bringest an assuaging balm;—eloquent opium! that with thy potent rhetoric stealest away the purposes of wrath, and, to the guilty man, for one night givest back the hopes of his youth, and hands washed pure from blood. . . .

Like the short-lived ecstasy that the Monk Ambrosio finds in the bosom of his prodigious Matilda, De Quincey's regained paradise is of course illusory, for there are devils at work beneath his feet. Although we need not rehearse the full catalogue of nightmares to which he is exposed, it is worth noting just how Gothic is De Quincey's chamber of horrors. He writes, for example, in a famous passage of the ghastly form of architectural sublimity into which his disordered dreams shaped themselves:

> Many years ago, when I was looking over Piranesi's Antiquities of Rome, Mr. Coleridge, who was standing by, described to me a set of plates by that artist, called his *Dreams,* and which record the scenery of his own visions during the delirium of a fever. Some of them (I describe only from memory of Mr. Coleridge's account) represented vast Gothic halls; on the floor of which stood all sorts of engines and machinery, wheels, cables, pulleys, levers, catapults, &c., expressive of enormous power put forth, and resistance overcome. Creeping along the sides of the walls, you perceived a staircase; and upon it, groping his way upwards, was Piranesi himself. Follow the stairs a little further, and you perceive it to come to a sudden, abrupt termination, without any balustrade, and allowing no step onwards to him who had reached the extremity, except into the depths below. Whatever is to become of poor Piranesi, you suppose, at least, that his labors must in some way terminate here. But raise your eyes, and behold a second flight of stairs still higher; on which again Piranesi is perceived, by this time standing on the very brink of the abyss. Again elevate your eye, and a still more aerial flight of stairs is beheld; and again is poor Piranesi busy on his aspiring labors; and so on, until the unfinished stairs and Piranesi both are lost in the upper gloom of the hall. With the same power of endless growth and self-reproduction did my architecture proceed in dreams.

These seem to be Piranesi's *Carceri d'Invenzione,* which (resembling the dreamlike prison of the Inquisition in Poe's "The Pit and the Pendulum") are in Professor Lévy's words "the mysterious place of inextricable passages, the place of interminable descents, made at a dizzying pitch in the stealthy and anguished steps of dream, down along the spiral of the Self."[8] In this characteristic Gothic nightmare the way up and the way down are the same. "I seemed every night to descend," says De Quincey, "not metaphorically, but literally to descend—into chasms and sunless abysses, depths below depths, from which it seemed hopeless that I could ever reascend."

---

[8] *Le Roman "Gothique" Anglais 1764-1824,* p. 637. On Piranesi, De Quincey, and the Romantic imagination, see Luzius Keller, *Piranèse et Les Romantiques Français* (Paris: J. Corti, 1966). Cf. Miller, *The Disappearance of God,* pp. 67 ff.

Reascend, in terms of overcoming his habit, De Quincey did—twice; but only, he tells us, to sink horribly in a "third prostration before the Dark Idol" that seemed truly without remedy. To express his ghastly "sudden revelation that *all is lost*" De Quincey bethinks himself of "a modern novel" in which "a lady abbess of a convent, herself suspected of Protestant leanings," tries to save one of her nuns who, though innocent, has been condemned to live burial:

At midnight, when all is hushed in the convent, the lady traverses the passages which lead to the cells of prisoners. She bears a master-key under her professional habit. As this will open every door in every corridor, already, by anticipation, she feels the luxury of holding her emancipated friend within her arms. Suddenly she has reached the door; she descries a dusky object; she raises her lamp, and, ranged within the recess of the entrance, she beholds the funeral banner of the holy office, and the black robes of its inexorable officials.

Perhaps here, in this Radcliffean episode, De Quincey has found a way to figure to himself how those "Protestant leanings" of his own led to utter and eternal damnation in the terrors of opium. But his *Confessions* contain in fact an even more potent and profoundly Gothic representation of the scourging of this fallen angel by the avenging powers of an offended Omnipotence.

In 1816, he tells us, there appeared unaccountably at the door of his cottage in Grasmere a Malay, of "sallow and bilious skin," with "small, fierce, restless eyes" and "thin lips." When he departed, De Quincey—impulsively, it would seem—presented the Malay with a largish quantity of opium which, to the Englishman's consternation and distress, the Malay bolted altogether as he left. Thereafter, De Quincey was haunted by the guilty fear that he had killed the man, or at least made him terribly ill. The episode is dropped, and the obvious question is left hanging in air, unasked: was this some sort of moral test or trap which tripped the author? The unarticulated question is answered, presumably, by the "world of troubles" which the Malay brings, as a kind of recompense for the "elixir," in the form of De Quincey's most impressively terrible opium dreams. The Malay becomes the "fearful enemy" who transports De Quincey nightly to a place of inquisition more horrible and madness-producing than any other the author can imagine: Southern Asia. This, for De Quincey, is the home of the gods, "the seat of awful images and associations," to which he always connects "a dim and reverential feeling." More productive of Burkean terror than Mrs. Radcliffe's Alps or the catacombs of Monk Lewis are "the ancient, monumental, cruel, and elaborate religions of Indostan, &c." De Quincey is overpowered by the "antiquity of Asiatic things, of their institutions, histories, modes of faith"; he shudders "at the mystic sublimity of *castes*"; he is "awed by the names of the Ganges, or the Euphrates."

Here then, in this place of total "sublimity," the guilt-racked opium-eater is subjected to the "unimaginable horror" of being pursued by all creation, trapped, mocked, and tortured by the ultimate demon-gods:

I was stared at, hooted at, grinned at, chattered at, by monkeys, by paroquets, by cockatoos. I ran into pagodas, and was fixed, for centuries, at the summit, or in secret rooms: I was the idol; I was the priest; I was worshipped; I was sacrificed. I fled from the wrath of Brama through all the forests of Asia: Vishnu hated me; Seeva laid wait for me. I came suddenly upon Isis and Osiris: I had done a deed, they said, which the ibis and the crocodile trembled at. I was buried, for a thousand years, in stone coffins, with mummies and sphinxes, in narrow chambers at the heart of eternal pyramids.

These visions, De Quincey insists, left him, "not so much in terror, as in hatred and abomination" of what he saw. "Over every form, and threat, and punishment, and dim sightless incarceration, brooded a sense of eternity and infinity that drove me into an oppression as of madness." Assuming that the exhausted and nearly insane sinner is capable of any emotion at all, he can have only feelings of rage and disgust toward the pitiless and inscrutable divinity who has damned him to all eternity without hope of relief or mitigation. De Quincey's Gothic-Oriental nightmare has culminated, we should note, in a form of anguish that seems surprisingly Presbyterian.

The archetypal figures with whom De Quincey identifies in his *Confessions*— Satan and Ahasuerus—were, of course, the common property of Gothic and Romantic writers alike, and, conflated with other mythical celebrities—Cain, Prometheus, Faust—helped to form a type of hero familiar in the literature of the period. Lowry Nelson, Jr. suggests indeed that the Gothic novel "derives most from the enormous interest around the turn of the century in the solitary eccentric, the misfit, the social outcast, or, to use the handy phrase, the guilt-haunted wanderer. In the romantic transvaluation of values Cain becomes a sympathetic figure, unjustly cursed by a vengeful God and incapable of purging his guilt."[9] What should be stressed, I believe, is that this guilty and outcast wanderer so central to the Gothic imagination did not make his appearance accidentally, as it were, because a motley collection of stock figures were conveniently at hand. Each of the figures mentioned above is at the center of a theological fable—a fable of inexpiable guilt and unremitting punishment—in which many Gothic writers saw an image of their own condition and fate. Moreover, the peculiarly Protestant form toward which this fable tended to gravitate in Anglo-American Gothic writing is strikingly Calvinistic, and nowhere more so than in the productions of Godwin, Mary Shelley, and Charles Brockden Brown. It has often been asserted that these writers are dubiously "Gothic," I think, only because the Calvinist fable alluded to here has not been generally noticed in their work and recognized as the underlying mythos of much serious *genre noir* fiction. This school of Gothicists distilled the pure essence of a tradition of religious terror which was to

---

[9] Lowry Nelson, Jr., "Night Thoughts on the Gothic Novel," *Yale Review*, 52 (1962), 237.

find its true culmination in the theologically obsessed romances of Hawthorne, Melville, and Poe.

I speak of the Godwin-Shelley-Brown "school" because the literary inter-relations and interpenetrations of this group make such a term seem inevitable. It is well known that the publication of *Caleb Williams* in 1794 impelled Brown to begin his own career as a writer of fiction. The Mervyn-Welbeck relationship in *Arthur Mervyn* (1799-1800) obviously owes a great debt to the Williams-Falkland opposition in *Caleb Williams*; and, in a much more profound sense, Brown's *Wieland* (1798) is thoroughly permeated with the brooding atmosphere of relentless determinism which informs Godwin's book. For his part, Godwin acknowledged in the preface to his *Mandeville: A Tale of the Seventeenth Century in England* (1817) that he had been much stimulated by a reading of *Wieland*.[10] Margaret Fuller summed up perfectly the complex nature of this intellectual inter-indebtedness when she wrote, in 1846: "It has been the custom to liken Brown to Godwin. But there was no imitation, no second hand in the matter. They were congenial natures, and whichever had come first might have lent an impulse to the other."[11]

Both, as it turned out, lent an impulse to the work of the Shelleys. Percy Shelley's early writing, especially *St. Irvyne* and *The Wandering Jew*, owes a good deal to *St. Leon* (1799), but his general intellectual debt to Godwin is much more broadly diffused throughout his life and thought.[12] As for the American author, Thomas Love Peacock reported long ago in his *Memoirs of Shelley* that the four major romances of Brown (all published between 1798 and 1800) were a major influence on the poet.[13] Mary Shelley was, of course, raised in the Godwin tradition and the shadow of her father's powerful mind and spirit is everywhere visible in her work.[14] The "pre-history" of *Frankenstein* (1818), as Harold Bloom remarks, begins with *Caleb Williams*.[15] Percy Shelley himself pointed out that "the encounter and argument between Frankenstein and the Being on the sea of ice, almost approaches, in effect, to the expostulation of Caleb Williams with Falkland. It reminds us, indeed, somewhat of the style and character of that admirable writer, to whom the author has dedicated his work [*Frankenstein* is dedicated to Godwin], and whose productions he seems to have studied."[16] Brockden Brown's work was naturally a subject of discussion in the Shelley circle, and *Wieland*, which Mary read with interest in 1815, clearly contributed to the compo-

---

[10] Cited in Elton Edward Smith and Esther Greenwell Smith, *William Godwin* (New York: Twayne Publishers, 1965), pp. 102-103.

[11] *Margaret Fuller: American Romantic*, edited by Perry Miller (Garden City, N.Y.: Doubleday Anchor Books, 1963), pp. 223-224.

[12] On Godwin and Shelley, see James Rieger, *The Mutiny Within: The Heresies of Percy Bysshe Shelley* (New York: George Braziller, 1967).

[13] "The superstitious terror of romance could scarcely be more strongly excited than by the perusal of *Wieland* . . . . Brown's four novels, Schiller's *Robbers*, and Goethe's *Faust*, were, of all the works with which he [Shelley] was familiar, those which took the deepest root in his mind, and had the strongest influence in the formation of his character." *Memoirs of Shelley*, ed. H. F. B. Brett-Smith (London: H. Frowde, 1909), pp. 35-37.

[14] See Jean de Palacio, *Mary Shelley dans son oeuvre* (Paris: Klincksieck, 1969), especially pp. 95 ff., and elsewhere.

[15] "Afterword" to *Frankenstein* (New York: Signet Classics, 1965), p. 215.

[16] Cited in Rieger, *The Mutiny Within*, p. 255.

sition of *Frankenstein*.[17]   Mary Shelley also praised "the masterly delineations of the author of Arthur Mervyn" in her powerful romance of pestilential apocalypse, *The Last Man* (1826).   This rehearsal of intellectual cross-pollination is meant, of course, to have more than simply circumstantial interest. Uniting these authors is a deep imaginative affinity of religious proportions whose somber presence in *Caleb Williams, Wieland, Frankenstein,* and *The Last Man* belies both the rationalistic utopianism usually associated with the names Godwin and Shelley, and the Franklinesque air of success which dispels the darkness in *Arthur Mervyn*.[18]

That the same William Godwin who was raised on the stern dicta of John Calvin gravitated to the even harsher doctrines of Sandemanianism, and believed until his twenty-sixth year that the "majority of mankind were objects of divine condemnation, and that their punishment would be everlasting"[19]— that such a man should become an utter atheist is perhaps no more surprising than that his last publication should be *The Lives of the Necromancers*.   An odor of paradox more powerful than any odor of heresy surrounds this author of *Political Justice*, whose *Caleb Williams*, presumably written as a monitory and possibly reformatory description of man's inhumanity to man, dramatizes instead the ineluctable necessity of sin and damnation.   It is hard to see, now, how anyone could mistake the massive tendency of Godwin's novel.   As James Rieger has demonstrated brilliantly, "the reader senses a mythic dimension in *Caleb Williams* because the narrative persona, Caleb himself, orders his world within the framework of a secularized Calvinism. . . . Caleb's character is rotted away by a conviction of merited and universal persecution; he may be crudely labeled Prometheus-as-Protestant."[20]

Godwin himself provides a sufficient hint to the frame of mind that shaped his tale when he remarks, in some prefatory material, that in preparation for composing his book he "read over a little old book, entitled 'The Adventures of Mademoiselle de St. Phale,' a French Protestant in the times of the fiercest persecution of the Huguenots, who fled through France in the utmost terror . . . scarcely . . . finding a moment's interval of security," and turned "the pages of a tremendous compilation entitled 'God's Revenge against Murder,' where the beam of the eye of Omniscience was represented as perpetually pursuing the guilty."   That godlike omnipotence and omniscient eye belong to Caleb's relentless master, Falkland, whose "superhuman power . . . of bringing the object of his persecution within the sphere of his authority" was a perpetual astonishment to Caleb.   "Did his power reach through all space, and his eye penetrate every concealment?"   Apparently, for Caleb

---

17 See F. C. Prescott, "Wieland and Frankenstein," *American Literature*, 2 (1930), 172-173.

18 Cf., for example, Larzer Ziff's remark: "Beginning consciously in the camp of the benevolent Philadelphian of the American Philosophical Society (just as he began with the sentimental tradition), Brown ends his journey through the mind by approaching the outskirts of Edwards' camp." See "A Reading of *Wieland*," *PMLA*, 77 (1962), 54.

19 Cited in Smith and Smith, *William Godwin*, pp. 56-57. Cf. Patrick Cruttwell, "On *Caleb Williams*," *Hudson Review*, 11 (1958), 95: "Though [Godwin's] orthodoxy went early, he did not lose without difficulty—and we may suspect he never completely lost—his Calvinist fatalism. 'All my enquiries,' he says of his early studies, 'terminated in Calvinism.' "

20 *The Mutiny Within*, p. 37.

"could move neither to the right nor the left, but the eye of [his] keeper was upon [him]." "You little suspect the extent of my power," exclaims Falkland to a terrorized Caleb who is quivering with just such a suspicion; "You might as well think of escaping from the power of the omnipresent God, as from mine!"

The fable underlying *Caleb Williams* is the familiar Miltonic one that we have already noticed in De Quincey's *Confessions*. What is remarkable here, however, is the exacerbated Calvinist framework in which Godwin explicitly enacts his story. Caleb may well ask, with the Adam quoted on the titlepage of *Frankenstein*:

Did I request thee, Maker, from my clay
To mould me Man, did I solicit thee
From darkness to promote me?

Godwin's hero, promoted not so much from cosmic darkness as from the common clay of an obscure peasant background, forms "golden visions" of his new station as Falkland's Man-Friday. But what Caleb considers to be election proves only an opportunity for damnation: "I little suspected, that the gaiety and lightness of heart I had hitherto enjoyed were upon the point of leaving me for ever, and that the rest of my days were devoted to misery and alarm." Did Caleb ask to be placed in a situation where he would be subject to the overwhelming temptation of his master's guilty secret? Falkland was "an object of wonder" to the imagination of his servant, and Caleb did not intend to harm, offend, or dishonor his master; "No spark of malignity had harboured in my soul. I had always reverenced the sublime mind of Mr. Falkland; I reverenced it still. My offence had merely been a mistaken thirst of knowledge."

Tremendous primal sin! In Falkland's scheme of things it seems to Caleb to admit "neither of forgiveness nor remission." But this "beneficent divinity," distinguished for his "humanity and general kindness," now shows himself to be "impenetrable" and "entirely arbitrary" in his ways. He decides to exhibit "unmerited goodness" toward the vile sinner whom he had previously raised up. "I smile at his malice, and resolve to spare him," Falkland declares. He establishes the terms of his Covenant Theology:

"Do you know what it is you have done? To gratify a foolishly inquisitive humour you have sold yourself. You shall continue in my service, but you can never share in my affection. I will benefit you in respect of fortune, but I shall always hate you. If ever an unguarded word escape from your lips, if ever you excite my jealousy or suspicion, expect to pay for it by your death or worse. It is a dear bargain you have made. But it is too late to look back. I charge and adjure you by every thing that is sacred and that is tremendous, preserve your faith!"

"Expect to pay for it by your death *or worse*." Caleb is threatened darkly with some form of unending punishment. And since he is finally adjudged to be a "miscreant," a "serpent," a "reptile," a "monster of depravity," sentence is pronounced: "you are the abhorrence of nature, the opprobrium of the human species, and the earth can only be freed from an insupportable burthen, by your being exterminated!"

The attempted extermination proceeds inexorably, and in a predictably Gothic fashion, at the commands of this harsh divinity who "preferred to govern . . . by terror." Caleb "envied the victim of the inquisition in the midst of his torture" because his own doom was surely fated to be worse. Led back to Falkland's estate after one of his numerous escapes, Caleb "seemed as if conducting to one of those fortresses, famed in the history of despotism, from which the wretched victim is never known to come forth alive." His master announces: "I have dug a pit for you; and, whichever way you move, backward or forward, to the right or the left, it is ready to swallow you"; and the prison in which Caleb is finally immured presents "a lively idea of the regions of the damned" to the despairing sinner. In the course of his unremitting persecution Caleb's beloved England becomes itself a claustrophobic torture-cell from which he is never allowed to flee, followed as he is by the ever-watchful eye of the "infernal Gines," a devilish criminal whom Falkland hires as his henchman. Caleb finds, incredibly, that he has been "blasted and branded in the face of the whole world," literally forced to play the part of the archetypal fugitive and vagabond: "My heart burned with universal fury. . . . I cursed the whole system of human existence. I said, 'Here I am, an outcast, destined to perish with hunger and cold. All men desert me. All men hate me. I am driven with mortal threats from the sources of comfort and existence. Accursed world!'" We learn with little surprise that "the exterior" which Caleb "was now induced to assume was that of a Jew." Reduced by a vengeful omnipotence to the position of ultimate scapegoat, Caleb discovers that the role of Ahasuerus fits him as naturally as that of Cain.

But we should notice that, unlike the corresponding figures in the poetry of Shelley, for example, whose final victory resides in their heroic defiance of the despicable tyrant who rules, Godwin's martyr-scapegoat is robbed utterly of any satisfaction and plunged into his deepest degradation in a startling volte-face at the end of the book. Having managed to vindicate himself and destroy the brutal master who has pursued him so mercilessly throughout the course of the narrative, Caleb is stricken with terrible remorse and reviles himself as an "atrocious, execrable wretch"! Guilt and innocence have changed places; the evil "other" is oneself. Perhaps indeed this is the ghastly fate worse than death which Caleb was promised: that he should succeed only in proving to himself ultimately that he is precisely the "monster of depravity" whom he had been represented as being all along. "Prometheus-as-Protestant" concludes his solipsistic career self-condemned and self-punished; "he, like Adam," as Lowry Nelson, Jr., says of Frankenstein's creature, "is very much his own Satan and his own vengeful God."[21]

We may therefore view Godwin's system in *Caleb Williams* not so much as a "secularized Calvinism," in Rieger's formulation, the odd result perhaps of Godwin's "hangover of religious paranoia,"[22] but rather as an internalized Calvinism which Godwin, along with other writers, pressed naturally into the service of a common Gothic fable of total decay. Both master and servant are locked into a system of universal guilt and suffering from which there is absolutely no issue, no catharsis, no hope of redemption. The Gothic "ruin" in the tale is thus felt as a generalized atmosphere of moral entropy. Victimizer and victim are alike "depraved," and the "rank and rotten soil" in which they are set, as Caleb says at the end, is "the corrupt wilderness of

---

[21] "Night Thoughts on the Gothic Novel," p. 247.
[22] *The Mutiny Within*, p. 37.

human society." With such a dour view of "Things as They Are," the author may very well have believed that the extermination promised to Caleb was the best that could be expected. Godwin's daughter, Mary, at all events, was to create just such an apocalyptic vision after many re-readings of her father's famous novel.

Someone coming to Mary Shelley's *The Last Man* after a reading of *Franken-stein* may be surprised to note that the science-fiction aspects—indeed all futuristic aspects—of this book set in the twenty-first century are totally neglected. English republicanism has advanced no further than the replacement of the King by a "Lord Protector," flying is still in the gentle stage of short excursions by balloon, and preventive medicine in this plague-blasted world remains positively Medieval. But the time-setting in *The Last Man* represents little more than the sort of distancing device familiar to readers of romance, as in Shakespeare's seacoast of Bohemia. Otherwise, the ambiance of this book is strictly that of the anxiety-ridden *genre noir* in general and of *Frankenstein* in particular.

The latter, to divert briefly, is an impressive example of the pattern we have been tracing. *Frankenstein* might with more justice be subtitled "A Tale of Geneva" rather than "The Modern Prometheus," for the Genevese protagonist of the book, Victor Frankenstein, is presented as a guilt-ridden sinner-God whose damnable career involves, not benefaction, but death and destruction for himself and those around him. No literary-minded reader could overlook the pervasive presence of Milton in this book, for *Paradise Lost*, which the "monster" (prodigiously Protestant autodidact that he is) reads early in life and accepts "as a true history," is Mary Shelley's central paradigm. But let us observe what a darkly Calvinist version of Milton's fable *Frankenstein* is based on: the creator, though presumably "his heart overflowed with kindness and the love of virtue," commits a deed "of mischief beyond description horrible" by bringing forth a creature who fills his heart with "breathless horror and disgust." Predictably enraged at the "vile insect" ("abhorred monster," "fiend," "wretched devil") whom he has created, Frankenstein easily adopts the rhetoric of an offended Jehovah: "Do you dare approach me? And do not you fear the vengeance of my arm wreaked on your miserable head?" But the creature, no mere puppy in theological disputation, manages to frame the central question of Calvinist man, alternately bewildered and angered at being accused of innate and total depravity by the very God who made him: "Accursed creator! Why did you form a monster so hideous that even *you* turned from me in disgust?" Undermined by such fervent arguments, Frankenstein is forced to reconsider the logic and justice of his position: "I felt what the duties of a creator towards his creature were, and that I ought to render him happy before I complained of his wickedness." But, although the possibility of a *détente* seems to be implied in such a concession, in reality there can be no relaxation of the struggle between creature and creator. Men, as Jonathan Edwards says, are naturally God's enemies. Victor Frankenstein and his "monster" (Caleb Williams, we should recall, is repeatedly called a "monster of depravity"—in the Calvinist system, all unregenerate men are monsters) are conjointly bound, by their antipathy, to a horror-filled flight and pursuit which can end only in mutual destruction.

That inevitable and ghastly conclusion to all things human is imaged in Mary Shelley's eschatological fantasy, *The Last Man*. Here, the concept of the "guilt-haunted wanderer" has swelled to include the whole human race— or rather, a dying remnant thereof which frantically drives itself over the face of the earth in a delusive search for health and life. Like *Frankenstein*, *The Last Man* bears an epigraph from *Paradise Lost*; this time, however, we are faced not with the defiant question "why was I born?" but rather with an ominous assertion about the horrible ineluctability of man's fate:

> Let no man seek
> Henceforth to be foretold what shall befall
> Him or his children.

The nature of that dark destiny is suggested in the part of the passage that Mary Shelley does not quote, as well as in her own book:

> evil he may be sure,
> Which neither his foreknowing can prevent,
> And hee the future evil shall no less
> In apprehension than in substance feel
> Grievous to bear. . . . (XI, 772-6)

That "evil," as painful for the brooding mind as for the afflicted body, is man's own fault, the working out of his self-willed Calvinist doom; for as Michael explains to Adam, "all shall turn degenerate, all deprav'd."

Lionel Verney, Mary Shelley's narrator and sole survivor in *The Last Man*, defines life in the world as "that labyrinth of evil, that scheme of mutual torture." And when Adrian (a rendition of Percy Shelley) hopefully predicts the coming of a new paradise, he is cut short by Ryland (presumably patterned after William Cobbett), who dourly affirms "that earth is not, nor ever can be heaven, while the seeds of hell are natives of her soil." Perhaps the most telling episode in the book, in this connection, concerns the fanatical charlatan who, raised on the "pernicious doctrines of election and special grace" by his Methodist-preacher father, gains tremendous power at the height of the plague by proclaiming hell-fire and damnation for all but the elect members of his sect. Although he is exposed as a fraud and a murderer, his symbolic importance as a representative of the mood of sin and retribution central to the book is not diminished; indeed, his own egregious depravity seems only a special and particularly monitory example of a spirit shared by all. Verney revealingly speaks of "the pestilential atmosphere which adhered to his [the charlatan's] demoniac nature." We recognize at once here an explanation of the book's controlling metaphor: the plague and man's corrupt spirit are equivalent. When the narrator is oppressed by "a sense of degradation," he puzzles over man's value in the divine eye: "Did God create man, merely in the end to become dead earth in the midst of healthful vegetating nature? Was he of no more account to his Maker, than a field of corn blighted in the ear?" Verney's "internal voice, articulate and clear," provides him with his own predestinarian answer: "Thus from eternity, it was decreed: the steeds that bear Time onwards had this hour and this fulfilment enchained to them, since the void brought forth its burthen. Would you read backwards the unchangeable laws of Necessity?" Whatever Mary Shelley herself might have felt on this issue, her narrative voice at least is not inclined to protest, for he grows surprisingly into a mood of patient orthodoxy ("truly we were not born to enjoy, but to submit, and to hope") which may alone explain his survival. To the reader, presumably, is left the implicit and crucial theological question posed by the book: what sort of deity would foredoom his own creature to this end "full of strange horror and gloomy misery"?[23]

---

[23] With surprising oversight, Robert D. Hume remarks that "Mary Shelley, her mother's daughter, largely ignores religion" ("Gothic Versus Romantic," p. 287). Mary Wollstonecraft, who died when her daughter was ten days old, undoubtedly left her legacy; but who can forget that Mary Shelley was also the daughter of William Godwin? Jean de Palacio's summary of Mary Shelley's religious attitudes deserves quotation at length: "The opposition between true and false religion, between the religion of the priests and the religion of the heart, was not only a polemical matter. Without ever having concerned herself with the major dogmas of Christianity, Mary Shelley found herself in the grips of a very old problem, that of reconciling the providential goodness of God with the existence of evil in the world. We have seen her objecting, as much by temperament as by rational argument, to the cruel and omnipotent God of the Methodists. But did not just such a God manifest his irrefutable reality in the spectacle of plagues that ravaged the world and of human corruption generally? Universal cataclysms and private catastrophes seemed to justify belief in the existence of an evil God, or at least to force recognition that the powers of evil in the world operate with His permission. For a universe subject to the caprice of a divine despot, there was no way out . . . . Mary sometimes moved in a curious way toward these pessimistic views: in *The Last Man*, for example, she turned the world into a devastated anthill where one sees man, like an insect, trying to struggle out from amidst all the rubble. Made aware of these menaces by the series of tragic events that marked her own life, living in perpetual fear of losing the only son who remained to her, Mary Shelley, though refusing to believe in the maleficence of God, often demonstrated how overwhelming misfortune could lead man to the confines of doubt and despair." *Mary Shelley dans son oeuvre*, pp. 286-287; translation supplied.

This last phrase could serve as a fair description of Charles Brockden Brown's *Wieland; or the Transformation*, which, along with *Caleb Williams*, seems to have exercised a major influence on Mary Shelley's fictions. Carwin, for example, Brown's mysterious biloquist, bears a certain resemblance to Frankenstein's creature: considered a "monster" of malignant intention, he is in fact a kind of outcast fallen angel who, like the *Ewige Jude*, wanders pathetically in search of love and fellowship (indeed, Carwin's ventriloquism may be seen as a twisted attempt to supply the society that he otherwise lacks).[24] But there are perhaps more important similarities between *Wieland* and *The Last Man* (nor should one overlook the instructive parallel here to Hawthorne's *The Marble Faun*, entitled *Transformation* in England).[25] In each case four central protagonists, two couples, are transformed from relatively innocent creatures into men and women of sorrow presumably through the agency of an alien or outside source of evil (Carwin; the plague; Miriam's Model). In the end, however, the seeds of disaster are shown to lie closer to home: in the guilt-racked and corruptible heart of man, who is internally bound to an ineluctably dark fate. All three books are suffused with an oppressive atmosphere of religious anxiety or positive terror which is more or less Calvinist in bearing.

In the case of *Wieland*, the Calvinist setting is manifest and crucial; indeed, it forms literally the uncertain ground on which the protagonists stand.

---

[24] It is suggestive, I think, to compare the physical descriptions of Carwin and the "monster." First, Brown's biloquist:

> His cheeks were pallid and lank, his eyes sunken, his forehead overshadowed by coarse straggling hairs, his teeth large and irregular, though sound and brilliantly white, and his chin discoloured by a tetter. His skin was of coarse grain and sallow hue. Every feature was wide of beauty, and the outline of his face reminded you of an inverted cone.

Now, the Creature:

> His limbs were in proportion, and I had selected his features as beautiful. Beautiful! Great God! His yellow skin scarcely covered the work of muscles and arteries beneath; his hair was of a lustrous black and flowing; his teeth of a pearly whiteness; but these luxuriances only formed a more horrid contrast with his watery eyes, that seemed almost of the same colour as the dun-white sockets in which they were set, his shrivelled complexion and straight black lips.

[25] On the theme of "transformation" or "metamorphosis" in Brown see Marisa Bulgheroni, *La Tentazione della Chimera* (Roma: Edizioni di storia e letteratura, 1965), pp. 155-156. This is a valuable study of Brown and the Anglo-American Gothic tradition.

Theodore Wieland, his sister Clara, his wife Catharine Pleyel, and her brother Henry (Clara's admirer) enjoy what is apparently a quasi-paradisiacal life of music and literature in the "pure and rapturous" atmosphere of their cultural "fane" on the Schuylkill. The arrival of Carwin, we are led to believe, transforms all this innocent joy to "horror" and "pollution." But the reader has already been told, in lurid detail at the start of the story, that this "summer-house" of delight was originally the gruesome temple where twice daily Wieland *père* used to offer anguished prayers to the most terrible of Calvinist deities, and where he was finally blasted by a species of deadly divine lightning that carried him off. This elder Wieland, who in life "laboured to keep alive a sentiment of fear, and a belief of the awe-creating presence of the Deity," whose features "a sadness perpetually overspread," whose days ended in "gloomy anticipations and unconquerable anxiety" because of his belief that he had committed some offense "incapable of expiation"—this is the Wieland patriarch whose unspeakable legacy of theological *Angst* palpitates beneath the enlightened pleasures of his charming offspring. Not Carwin, but a kind of biological predisposition to religious terror and madness undermines Theodore and Clara; for the son bears an "obvious resemblance" to his father in the cast of his mind and builds his life on the props of "moral necessity and Calvinistic inspiration"; and the daughter is inclined to see in her father's death and subsequent events "the penalty of disobedience . . . the stroke of a vindictive and invisible hand."[26]

The manifestly ambivalent relationship of brother and sister which is central to *Wieland* draws the reader at once back to the Falkland-Williams pairing in Godwin's book and forward to Poe's Roderick and Madeline Usher. As in "The Fall of the House of Usher," Theodore and Clara live in a fearful and morbid atmosphere which derives from a family curse or fault, and they are involved in an oneiric or hypnagogic struggle which hints at *Geschwisterinzest* and lurches dizzily toward mutual destruction at the end. But Brown's narrative method, his religious framework, and the curious peripeteia toward which his tale moves suggest Godwin more than Poe. In *Wieland*, as in *Caleb Williams*, the narrative is related by the intended victim herself, who is accused of monstrous profligacy and depravity by one man (Pleyel) and "hunted to death" by another (Theodore) who considers himself appointed to act as the scourge of an avenging deity. But, *mirabile dictu*, Clara has scarcely escaped from the deadly clutches of her delirious brother when, reflecting that she had merely meditated defending herself against him with a penknife, she, like Caleb Williams after the death of Falkland, suffers a complete reversal of sentiment toward her murderous persecutor and takes all the blame upon herself:

I estimate my own deservings; a hatred, immortal and inexorable, is my due. I listen to my own pleas, and find them empty and false: yes, I acknowledge that my guilt sur-

---

[26] Cf. Bulgheroni, p. 157: "Clara falls short of the perfection which others admire in her because she is vulnerable precisely where she is believed most secure. Clara is disposed, or predisposed, to horror. The enigmatic death of the father who tried to realize in America a tormented religious vocation cast on her childhood the shadow of mystery. The fascination of her personality derives from this contradiction between her intellectual and moral lucidity, on the one hand, and her predisposition to terror, on the other—a predisposition unknown even to herself and hidden from the gaze of others like an invisible fault in a perfect vase."

passes that of mankind; I confess that the curses of a world and the frowns of a Deity are inadequate to my demerits. Is there a thing in the world worthy of infinite abhorrence? It is I.

All this for thinking of self-defense! But, of course, Clara's assumption of the role of archetypal criminal represents not simply a monstrous case of over-reaction, but rather the expression of a fund of deep-seated religious guilt and self-loathing which lies at the bottom of *Wieland*. It amounts to a vision of universal culpability in which victim and victimizer cannot be distinguished; for, as Clara argues in her conclusion, the "frailty" of the one only seconds or abets the evil "efforts" of the other. As with the elder Wieland, whose "own belief of rectitude was the foundation of his happiness," the other characters in this book, along with Caleb Williams and Falkland, must learn that this belief is "destined to find an end." Although Clara does not quote the book of Micah, she might well have done so, for its mood is her very own: "The good man is perished out of the earth; and there is none upright among men."

That Brown, by tradition and upbringing a Quaker, should have chosen an explicitly Calvinist framework for *Wieland* seems to Larzer Ziff to demonstrate Brown's recognition of "the claims which Calvinism makes on the American character."[27] Such a remark would perhaps bear more pointed application to Hawthorne publishing *The Scarlet Letter* in 1850, when those claims really needed to be recognized; but the Calvinist tradition was still sufficiently alive in the America of 1798 to make Brown's choice appear natural, if not even inevitable. We should remember, however, that the elder Wieland was born in Germany and self-educated in London, where he lighted on the writings of Albigensians and Camisards. If we are to ascribe the Calvinist setting of *Wieland* to anything more than the gloomy cast of Brown's imagination, it might make most sense to look culturally toward that same England which nurtured Wieland *père* and which provided, in the writings of Godwin and other Gothicists, abundant examples of the general relevance of Calvinist doctrine and terminology to that "illustration of some important branches of the moral constitution of man" which was Brown's avowed purpose as a writer of fiction.

---

[27] "A Reading of *Wieland*," p. 51.

Francis Thompson, though of course not a Protestant, was English, and thoroughly steeped in the literary culture of his century. It therefore seems peculiarly indicative of the pervasiveness of religiously charged Gothic motifs that his "Hound of Heaven" should begin by sounding the authentic note of *le genre noir*. But his master, one should note, is not so much Mrs. Radcliffe, or Charles Maturin, or even Godwin, as it is Edgar Allan Poe. Pursued inexorably by the divine chastener, the soul flees through the "arches" of time and "down the labyrinthine ways" of his inner being. He is treated to "vistaed hopes" and then, tremendously, in the very accents of Poe, cast "Adown Titanic glooms of chasmed fears." The voice that exclaims, mysteriously, with such insistent force, "All things betray thee, who betrayest Me," could change places with the scourge of William Wilson, who cries out at the end with heightened force, "In me didst thou exist—and, in my death, see by this image, which is thine own, how utterly thou hast murdered thyself."[28]

Poe's "William Wilson" (1839) may serve as one final, cisatlantic demonstration of the persistent conjunction of Gothic terror and Calvinist theology in Anglo-American writing. This tale might—with a justifiable pun and a nod in the direction of Jonathan Edwards—be called "Poe on the Will," for it is an all but patent allegory describing how the perverse Will of fallen man, which is the degenerate offspring of the Divine Will, is pursued relentlessly by the righteous Hound of Heaven—that *other* Will the Son of Will. The narrator begins his story by saying, "Let me call myself, for the present, William Wilson." As with Melville's Ishmael, we are offered a name which is not "real" but is nonetheless significant of reality; it is "a fictitious title not dissimilar to the real." This emblematic name, to which the narrator "had always felt aversion," which was indeed "venom in [his] ears," goes to the very heart of his struggle with the scourging *Doppelgänger*. For this "self-willed" young man of "evil propensities," who at an early age "was left to the guidance of [his] own will," finds himself faced with a twin who not only refuses "implicit belief in [his] assertions, and submission to [his] will," but actually offers "frequent officious interference with [his]

---

28 For evidence of Thompson's interest in Poe's writing see his *Literary Criticisms*, ed. Rev. Terence L. Connolly, S. J. (New York: E. P. Dutton, 1948), pp. 317-322.

will," and finally forces the narrator into "bitterly reluctant submission to his [that is, the other William Wilson's] arbitrary will."

Like Milton's Satan, the narrator—this "outcast of all outcasts" who is guilty of "unpardonable crime"—began his career in a kind of Calvinist heaven, the "dream-like and spirit-soothing" school-prison-church of the Reverend Dr. Bransby. The "ponderous wall" surrounding the school sported an even "more ponderous gate," which "was riveted and studded with iron bolts, and surmounted with jagged iron spikes," and inspired in the boy "impressions of deep awe." On the rare occasions when it opened, he found "in every creak of its mighty hinges . . . a plenitude of mystery—a world of matter for solemn remark, or for more solemn meditation." The building itself, a "palace of enchantment," with its "innumerable-inconceivable" turnings and twistings, suggested ideas "not very far different from those with which we pondered upon infinity"; and the school-room, "the largest in the house—I could not help thinking, in the world," had "pointed Gothic windows" and a "remote and terror-inspiring angle" in which was located "the *sanctum*" of Dr. Bransby. This old gentleman is an impressive and bewildering figure in the pulpit:

With how deep a spirit of wonder and perplexity was I wont to regard him from our remote pew in the gallery, as, with step solemn and slow, he ascended the pulpit! This reverend man, with countenance so demurely benign, with robes so glossy and so clerically flowing, with wig so minutely powdered, so rigid and so vast,—could this be he who, of late, with sour visage, and in snuffy habiliments, administered, ferule in hand, the Draconian laws of the academy? Oh, gigantic paradox, too utterly monstrous for solution!

One could, with justice, accuse Poe of a certain conscious humor here in thus archly describing the paradox of a Jehovah who is at once so awesome in his divine benignity and so small-minded and mean in his petty exactions.

Subjected to "continual anxiety" by the superior "moral sense" and "intolerable spirit of contradiction" possessed by the other William Wilson, the narrator finally flees "awe-stricken" from his youthful paradise and embarks on a career of depravity unparalleled, he tells us, in the history of the race. But his heavenly scourge, the other William Wilson, is never far behind and enforces a flight which Poe has his narrator describe in terms strongly reminiscent of Godwin and Mary Shelley:[29]

I fled in vain. My evil destiny pursued me as if in exultation, and proved, indeed, that the exercise of its mysterious dominion had as yet only begun. Scarcely had I set foot in Paris, ere I had fresh evidence of the detestable interest taken by this Wilson in my concerns. Years flew, while I experienced no relief. Villain!—at Rome, with how untimely, yet with how spectral an officiousness, stepped he in between me and my ambition! at Vienna, too—at Berlin—and at Moscow! Where, in truth, had I *not* bitter cause to curse him within my heart? From his inscrutable tyranny did I at length flee, panic-stricken, as from a pestilence; and to the very ends of the earth *I fled in vain.*

That Poe is here suggesting an antagonism more theological than human— the pursuit of the unregenerate sinner by his predestinated agent of damnation—is made utterly clear on the next page as the language assumes fully a familiar Calvinistic tone:

---

[29] For a discussion of the possible influence of Godwin and Mary Shelley on Poe, see Burton R. Pollin, *Discoveries in Poe* (Notre Dame: Univ. of Notre Dame Press, 1970).

The sentiment of deep awe with which I habitually regarded the elevated character, the majestic wisdom, the apparent omnipresence and omnipotence of Wilson, added to a feeling of even terror, with which certain other traits in his nature and assumptions inspired me, had operated hitherto, to impress me with an idea of my own utter weakness and helplessness, and to suggest an implicit, although bitterly reluctant submission to his arbitrary will.

The drama hastens to its disastrous conclusion: in a kind of reversal, the would-be victim turns aggressor and manages to "kill" the spectral William Wilson, whereupon the narrator is informed that he has murdered himself. Once again, the identity of pursuer and pursued is emphasized, and the tale ends on a note of general gloom and damnation. But the real significance of "William Wilson," and a curious confirmation of its religious bearing, is suggested by a resemblance between this story and the conclusion to Poe's theodicy, *Eureka*. There, Poe writes of "dim but ever present *Memories*," by which we are surrounded in this life, "of a Destiny more vast—very distant in the bygone time, and infinitely awful." The narrator's *Doppelgänger* in "William Wilson" is associated with just such memories: "I discovered, or fancied I discovered, in his accents, in his air, and general appearance, a something which first startled, and then deeply interested me, by bringing to mind dim visions of my earliest infancy—wild, confused and thronging memories of a time when memory herself was yet unborn." In addition, much is made of the fact that the specter speaks in "*a very low whisper*." Here is the relevant passage at the end of *Eureka*: "I have spoken of Memories that haunt us during our youth. They sometimes pursue us even into our Manhood; assume gradually less and less indefinite shapes; now and then speak to us with low voices. . . ." There seems to be little doubt that the other William Wilson is intended to represent one of these haunting and pursuing memories which deliver, internally as it were, important truths. In *Eureka*, as in "William Wilson," the voice tells us that the "Heart Divine . . . *is our own* . . . that man . . . ceasing imperceptibly to feel himself Man, will at length attain that awfully triumphant epoch when he shall recognize his existence as that of Jehovah." Victim and victimizer, hound and hare, the terror-stricken sinner and his awful deity, are one because they represent the divided halves of what was once a primal moral unity from which things have sadly and perversely declined. The ruined world of Gothic fiction is a dramatization of this separation, of the sinner in flight from his God-consciousness, or—as Jung might say—of man pursued by his soul. But on the other side of Gothic terror and disorder, Poe seems to insist, beyond the dark night of this struggle, lie peace and reunion.

Although the provenance of Poe's "William Wilson" was long ago assigned by one scholar to E. T. A. Hoffmann's *Elixiere des Teufels*,[30] the Calvinist slant of Poe's tale might suggest as a likelier source that egregiously Scotch-Presbyterian *Doppelgänger* story, James Hogg's *The Private Memoirs and Confessions of a Justified Sinner* (1824). Indeed, there would seem to be even biographical justification for such an identification in the fact that both Poe's father and stepfather derived from the same Scottish background. But, again, one need not really look beyond the literary tradition that we have been tracing, for Poe himself, as Burton Pollin recently pointed

---

[30] See Palmer Cobb, *The Influence of E. T. A. Hoffmann on the Tales of Edgar Allan Poe* (Chapel Hill: Univ. of North Carolina Press, 1908), pp. 31-48.

out, quoted with apparent approval the remark of a contemporary scholar that "William Wilson, by Mr. Poe, reminds us of Godwin and Brockden Brown."[31] Although Poe makes no specific reference to theological questions in his various remarks on Brown and Godwin, they are several times linked as examples of powerful literary minds, and *Caleb Williams* remained for Poe the standard of serious writing. Nor was Poe alone, it seems. Another great American romancer, Herman Melville, obtained a copy of Godwin's book in 1849, and the impression it made apparently lasted to the end of Melville's life—or at least until the composition of *Billy Budd*.[32] Here, too, we have a theological drama involving "depravity according to nature" and a "mystery of iniquity," fit "for psychological theologians to discuss," which—Melville claims—contains more real mystery than Ann Radcliffe could devise; a drama in which victim and persecutor, angel and devil, are both fated to die according to the baffling decrees of an inscrutable divinity.[33]

We need not, of course, make any specific claims for Melville's adherence to Godwin in particular or to the larger English-Gothic tradition of religious terror which we have examined here. It is sufficient to remember that, in his impassioned reaction to Hawthorne's *Mosses from an Old Manse*, Melville insisted, with an extravagance that may not now seem misplaced, on the general appeal and applicability of "that Calvinistic sense of Innate Depravity and Original Sin, from whose visitations, in some shape or other, no deeply thinking mind is always and wholly free."

---

[31] Cited in *Discoveries in Poe*, p. 264.

[32] See Roland A. Duerksen, "Caleb Williams, Political Justice, *and* Billy Budd," *American Literature,* 38 (1966), 372-376.

[33] In connection with the parallels among Revolutionary Terror, Calvinism, and Gothicism drawn earlier, let us recall that Melville pointedly set *Billy Budd* in 1797, the year of the "Great Mutiny." It was the year, as Benjamin Péret remarks, when *"The Monk* and four of Anne Radcliffe's novels were being published in Paris . . . while Baboeuf was mounting the guillotine." Cited by Maurice Lévy in *Le Roman "Gothique" Anglais 1764-1824,* p. 608.

The "Mysteries" of Edgar Poe: The Quest for a Monomyth in Gothic Literature

BARTON LEVI ST. ARMAND

In exploring the mysteries of Gothic taste, it is easy for the critic to forget that the whole genre was, first and foremost, a fashion, a style, and a mode of interior decoration. That the particular interior being redecorated was human consciousness itself is ancillary to the nature of Gothic as primarily an aesthetic revival which somehow managed to provide Romanticism with its first full set of swaddling clothes. The remarkable thing about this taste is that we can chart its serpentine course almost from work to work in terms of the development of theme, character, and popularity of novel modes and means of decoration. The Wandering Jew, who plays only a minor walk-on part in Lewis' *The Monk*, for example, emerges as the main character type of Maturin's *Melmoth*. Mrs. Radcliffe's Appenines somehow contribute both to Shelley's *Mont Blanc* and to the frozen Arctic landscapes of his wife's *Frankenstein*. The Venetian segment of *The Mysteries of Udolpho* becomes the whole focus of a tale like Poe's deliberately Byronic "The Assignation"; we cannot fully understand the rationale of its conclusion or the presence of "the cracked and blackened goblet" clutched in the marble hand of Poe's dead voluptuary unless we know that Radcliffe's hero-villain Montoni avoided death by using a special type of Venetian glass which splintered and bubbled when poison was poured into it. In such ways, both major and minor, one can chart the growth of Gothic romance from the first appearance of the species in the *Otranto* of 1764 to such late examples as Faulkner's *Absalom, Absalom!*

Yet, even considering Gothicism as a particular formal structure or burgeoning type, the extreme left-wing or avant-garde of Romanticism, with a curious organic vitality seemingly built into it, certain problems arise. These problems are those continuing ones of device and depth, control and connotation, adaptability and meaning. A mode can evolve so fast that, in an attempt to utilize the best of what the recent past has been as well as what the present

---

BARTON LEVI ST. ARMAND, Associate Professor of English and American Studies at Brown University, has published a number of articles on American writers and is author of *The Roots of Horror in the Fiction of H. P. Lovecraft*.

is still yearning to be, it reaches a point of critical mass which collapses from within and leaves only an empty eclecticism. In the case of the Gothic genre, in all its manifestations—architectural and social as well as literary—this circumstance becomes doubly true. For the Gothic was an alien revival which took root in an age devoted to one supreme mode—that of Classicism, with its fidelity to decorum, uniformity, and the rule of law. To preserve its vitality, the Gothic always needed some new exotic quality, some as-yet-untapped antiquarian element, to grow and to flourish. Hence its frank sensationalism, its fantastic "outreaching comprehensiveness of sweep," to quote the American Gothicist, Herman Melville. The Gothic was nothing if not new and varied; yet at the same time, there was an unexpected mental growth as well, a dimensional growth in acuity of intelligence and refinement of consciousness. The problem was to impose or synthesize a style which would control, deepen, and extend the mode's previous line of development. In specific literary terms, it was the same process which led William Blake to purify the experimental chaos of the *Poetical Sketches* by utilizing the ingenuous hymns of Dr. Watts and so produce at last the *Songs of Innocence* and the *Songs of Experience*. Later, Blake was similarly to transmute the pseudo-Celtic meters of James Macpherson's *Ossian* (1762) into the bardic thunder of the *Prophetic Books*, proving that the mode, the style, the species bred in the unlikeliest places and consorted with the most disreputable models in order to bring forth a superior type.

In our own century, William Butler Yeats, emerging from that same Celtic twilight and its peculiar conjunctions of primal myth and Romantic fustian, of Blake and Macpherson, was to speak of "masterful images" that grew out of pure mind yet began in a "mound of refuse or the sweepings of a street."[1] What remains important, however, is the fact that the Celtic and the Druidical were both manifestations of the taste for barbaric revivals which was to become known generally as "Gothic." The variety and adaptability of the style, from William Beckford's Oriental Gothic in *Vathek* to Herman Melville's remarkable cetological sub-species in *Moby-Dick*, masked an underlying search for a monomyth which could exploit the possibilities of this fanciful interior decoration while it unified Romantic multiplicity and became at the same time a paradigm for expressing fundamental human experience. The nature of this experience was in most cases (surprisingly enough given the Gothic's stiff anti-clerical and anti-Catholic bias) profoundly inward, even "religious" in the broadest sense. It may have begun in Walpole's antiquarian fascination with a lost world of Medieval superstition as a means of relieving the boredom of eighteenth-century social realities, but the religious impulse in Gothicism soon galloped from a concern with talking pictures and bleeding nuns to a consideration of man's position in a terrifying and inscrutable universe, an obsession with individual destiny and damnation, and a determined exploration of the mysteries of the soul itself.

"Mystery" is a word which we automatically associate with the Gothic genre since it found its way over and over again into so many Gothic titles, the most famous, of course, being *The Mysteries of Udolpho* (1794) by Ann Radcliffe. But the dimensions of the idea of Gothic mystery can lead us into

---

[1] William Butler Yeats, "The Circus Animals' Desertion," in *Selected Poems,* ed. by M. L. Rosenthal (New York: Collier Books, 1962), p. 185.

a consideration of just what the control of the genre by an underlying mono-myth entails. At the primary level, for example, the "mysteries" of Udolpho are common detective-story mysteries involving the solution of a contrived puzzle: what was the hideous thing behind the black veil which caused the sensitive Emily to swoon so plaintively and so frequently during her incarceration within the dark battlements of Udolpho? It was, we discover at the end of this monumental romance, only a Medieval remnant of monkish superstition, a waxen votary object left as a penance by a long-vanished ancestor of the House of Udolpho. Yet Emily's timid lifting of the black veil has much deeper psychic resonances when, in later Romantic fiction, that veil becomes the Veil of Isis which, as Esther Harding explains, is also "the ever-changing form of nature, whose beauty and tragedy veil the spirit from our eyes. . . ."[2] Shelley develops this symbol in his "A Defense of Poetry" and deepens the connotations of the metaphor even further when he remarks that "Poetry lifts the veil from the hidden beauty of the world, and makes familiar objects be as if they were not familiar." Similarly, it is not Mrs. Radcliffe's invention of a trick ending to the Gothic tale which insures her a place in the larger chronicles of literary culture and the history of Romanticism in particular. To be sure, the wild voices heard in the night are found to be the wind whipping through eroded battlements and the mysterious nocturnal melodies are always traced to a very real but concealed musician; yet this is not what caused De Quincey to call her a "great enchantress" or Keats to acknowledge her as "Mother Radcliffe." Rather, to paraphrase Poe, Radcliffe's terror is not of Italy but of the soul, and her horror is only a small part of the larger landscape of sensibility—of limitless spiritual and psychological "mystery"—which she was the first to enter and explore. Through her heroine Emily, Mrs. Radcliffe helped to spread suddenly open the gorgeous fan of the Romantic consciousness and accomplish what Wordsworth called "widening the sphere of human sensibility." Emily's voyage through the Alps and Appenines toward Udolpho becomes, then, another metaphor for that quest which the Romantics themselves cultivated and often internalized.[3] This was a journey on which the Neo-Classic sensibility was unwilling to embark, as it kept strictly within the limits of a Reason which feared excesses of the imagination and an over-stimulation of the faculties of the soul. Indeed, Emily's unfortunate father, M. St. Aubert, a figure of melancholy common sense who warns Emily about the "evils of susceptibility" at the beginning of the *Mysteries,* actually has to alight from the coach when it pauses on its magic journey in order to renew his contact with the earth. Ostensibly, he crawls so intently over the landscape because, as a typical rationalist, he has a botanical passion for classifying (and so limiting the possibilities of) natural phenomena. Eventually, however, St. Aubert dies of the effects of the journey itself, a journey in which as it continues "the mountains seemed to multiply, as they went, and what was the summit of one eminence proved to be only the base of another," or, "the scene seemed perpetually changing, and its features to assume new forms, as the winding road brought them to the eye in different attitudes while the

---

[2] M. Esther Harding, *Woman's Mysteries: Ancient and Modern* (1935; rpt. ed., New York: G. P. Putnam's Sons, 1971), p. 181.

[3] Cf. Harold Bloom, "The Internalization of Quest-Romance," in *Romanticism and Consciousness: Essays in Criticism,* ed. by H. Bloom (New York: W. W. Norton, 1970), pp. 3-24.

shifting vapours, now partially concealing their minuter beauties and now illuminating them with splendid tints, assisted in the illusions of the sight."[4] It is of this constantly shifting confusion of the real and the ideal, of noumena and phenomena, of the dazzle of the veil, that M. St. Aubert finally expires, and, in truth, it can be said that he died, like the Age of Reason itself, of an overexposure to Romanticism. What Mrs. Radcliffe has done, with her pages and pages of landscape description which never seem to end (in which more and more sublime vistas continue to unveil themselves through the rolling mists and rainbow fogs), is to make the momentous connection between the life of nature and the life of the mind which made Romanticism itself into a true revolution of the human consciousness. Emily does not merely contemplate these sublime scenes, but she actually helps to create, through the ever-expansive faculties of her Romantic imagination, the mountains beyond mountains and the plains behind plains. Her mediumistic powers of reverie and feminine weaving of the warp of landscape with the woof of dreamscape are halted only by a traumatic confrontation with the dark and limiting male reality of Udolpho itself:

> Emily gazed with melancholy awe upon the castle, which she understood to be Montoni's; for, though it was now lighted up by the setting sun, the gothic greatness of its features, and its mouldering walls of dark grey stone, rendered it a gloomy and sublime object. As she gazed, the light died away on its walls, leaving a melancholy purple tint, which spread deeper and deeper, as the thin vapour crept up the mountain, while the battlements above were still tipped with splendour. From these, too, the rays soon faded, and the whole edifice was invested with the solemn duskiness of evening. Silent, lonely and sublime, it seemed to stand the sovereign of the scene, and to frown defiance upon all, who dared to invade its solitary reign. As the twilight deepened, its features became more awful in obscurity, and Emily continued to gaze, till its clustering towers were alone seen, rising over the tops of the woods, beneath whose thick shade the carriages soon after began to ascend. (*Mysteries of Udolpho*, pp. 226-227)

From a conveniently modern Jungian perspective, we could say that the Anima has here met the Shadow. Yet it was not for Mrs. Radcliffe to follow the profound implications of her method, for those implications were at once too dangerous and disturbing for her own retiring sensibility to sustain. Rather, it was for others, like Edgar Allan Poe (who, in his tale "The Oval Portrait," described the chateau to which the wounded narrator is brought as "one of those piles of commingled gloom and grandeur which have so long frowned among the Appenines, not less in fact than in the fancy of Mrs. Radcliffe"[5]) to explore fully those novel elements implicit in *Udolpho*, which were in fact the mysteries of the progress, experience, and destiny of the Romantic soul. In undertaking this quest, Poe also had to solve the problem which had eluded Mrs. Radcliffe in her own attempt to embody such a pilgrimage, for finally *The Mysteries of Udolpho* is subverted by its own freedom and eclecticism. The romance disintegrates from and succumbs to an imitative fallacy, an overindulgence in openness and limitlessness, as Emily becomes supplanted by another heroine, the Lady Blanche, and Mrs. Radcliffe's own interests turn from the adventures offered by a

---

[4] Ann Radcliffe, *The Mysteries of Udolpho*, ed. by Bonamy Dobrée (London: Oxford Univ. Press, 1966), p. 226.

[5] Edgar Allan Poe, "The Oval Portrait," *The Complete Works*, ed. by James A. Harrison (New York: Thomas Y. Crowell, 1902), IV, 245. Hereafter, all references to Poe's works will appear in the text.

picaresque travel narrative to the more genteel enchantments of a sentimental and well-bred fairy tale. This eclecticism and lack of definition, springing from the eternal process of Romantic reverie, was to plague as well such artists as Shelley, whose conflict of Demogorgon and Jupiter in *Prometheus Unbound* is a similar struggle of freedom with tyranny, as is the opposition between the Los and Urizen of Blake's late epics. The common Romantic problem remained the synthesis of an archetypal monomyth which would not destroy the surface mix and float of those novel elements which preserved the beauty and majesty of the free Romantic temperament. In specifically Gothic works of a less epic character, the further dilemma was to preserve the novelty, variety, and dark sensationalism which composed the fabric of the genre while also suggesting a profound spiritual and emotional depth. This is the enigma which challenged Poe when, in describing the effect of the sight of the House of Usher upon the narrator of his most famous tale, he wrote that, "It was a mystery all insoluble; nor could I grapple with the shadowy fancies that crowded upon me as I pondered" (*Works*, III, 274).

Poe confronted this mystery in a typically "Gothic" way; that is, in spite of the fact that, as an anatomist of the imagination, he had mastered all of the genre's obvious popular elements and even felt some condescension toward it as a set of counters which he could manipulate at will, he decided to utilize in "The Fall of the House of Usher" its most radical manifestation for his own particular purposes. The most avant-garde of the Romantic revivals when he was writing the tale in 1839 was the Egyptian mode, and it is my contention that, in experimenting with a daring mixture of the Gothic and the Egyptian, Poe managed to create a work of art which fulfilled the search of the Romantics for a monomyth which functions at two distinct levels: the surface level of the picturesque, or the decorative, and the subterranean level of the subliminal and the archetypal. For, in resurrecting the Egyptian mode as part of the dramatic stage setting of his tale, Poe also revived the pattern of initiation ritual which underlaid the symbols of the Egyptian Mysteries, the Mysteries of Isis and Osiris, as they were understood by his own age. That ritual had already found its way into the ceremonies of the countless secret societies (such as the Masons and the Odd Fellows) which abounded in the America of the early nineteenth century. In *The Modern Eleusinia, or The Principles of Odd Fellowship Explained by a Brother of the Order* (published in Nashua, New Hampshire, in 1844) the anonymous author, speaking of the Eleusinian Mysteries, expresses both a Romantic eclecticism and the fascination of his age at all levels with these "secrets of the soul":

Their object seemed to be to teach the doctrine of one God, the resurrection of the good to eternal life, the dignity of the human soul, and to lead the people to see the Shadow of the Deity, in the beauty, magnificence, and splendour of the universe. The Mysteries of Isis . . . varied in some of their forms, from the Eleusinian, yet they all had one common design; namely, by the most solemn and impressive ceremonies, to lead the minds of the Neophytes, to meditate, seriously, the great problems of human duty and destiny, to imbue them with a living sense of the vanity and brevity of life, and of the certainty of a future state of retribution, to set forth, in marked contrast, the beauty of Virtue and Truth, and the deep bitterness, and tormenting darkness of Vice and Error;—and, lastly, to enjoin on them, by the most binding obligations, charity, brotherly love, and inflexible honor, as the greatest of all duties, the most beneficial to the world, and the most pleasing to the Gods. By their rites, many of which we should now think rude and childish, rites commencing in gloom and sorrow, and ending in light and glory,—they dimly shadowed forth, the transition of man from the savage to the civilized state, from ignorance to science, and his constant progress, onward and upward through the Ages, to still sublimer revelations. By them, they also signified, that the soul's exaltation, and highest good, were to be approached, only by the way of tears, and sacrifice, and toil.[6]

Here we have, optimistically and floridly, the outline of the same mono-myth which is being enacted in the cavernous glooms of "The House of Usher." As Kathleen Raine notes in her *Blake and Tradition*, "The Eleusinian Mysteries were in fashion in and about 1790,"[7] and they soon merged with a general interest in things Eastern, Oriental, and especially Egyptian.

Little of the physical evidence of this Egyptian Revival remains with us today, though there were famous architectural examples such as "The Tombs" (a New York prison in Egyptian style in which Melville's Bartleby found his undeserved end) and we still have the towering obelisk of the Washington Monument as a witness to its brief but powerful influence on public taste. A popular interest in Egyptology had been spurred with the finding of the Rosetta Stone in 1799 by Napoleon's armies, and, after its cession to the British in 1801, it became, along with other Egyptian antiquities, almost as curious and sensational an exhibit as the Elgin Marbles were to be in 1807. The deciphering of hieroglyphics became the rage among antiquarians, and researches were carried on by a host of eminent scholars. Besides prison buildings, cemetery gates and entrances were done in a pylonic form copied from Nile temples, for, while the Gothic style of architecture was naturally associated with religious ideas of spiritual aspiration (hence its use for ec-clesiastical and college buildings), the Egyptian mode was considered to be more suited for the contemplation of darker, more impenetrable mysteries. As Frances Lichten writes of this revival:

The first decorative inspirations derived from the contemplation of these archeological wonders seem weighted with immense solemnity—the Victorian architect, if not the Victorian designer, was sensitive to the portentousness of Egyptian art and used it for equally serious purposes, calculated to move the beholder to thoughts of death. Nor did he miss the correspondence of catacombs with the idea of prisons; therefore prisons styled in the Egyptian manner breathed forth their gloomy implications, even in the United States.[8]

In American literature, as in American art and architecture, the Egyptian Revival produced no really lasting monuments and so always remained some-thing of an underground style. But the Egyptian mode carried with it, as we have seen, a whole host of complex and intricate mythic associations, and it is my contention, to repeat, that many of these associations inform and help to shape the over-all design of the Gothic castle or manor house of literature, which, like much of the architecture of its time, mixes Gothic arches with Egyptian obelisks. The haunted castles and mansions of such

---

[6] Anonymous, *The Modern Eleusinia, or The Principles of Odd Fellowship Explained by a Brother of the Order* (Nashua, New Hampshire: Murray and Kimball, 1844), pp. 29-30.

[7] Kathleen Raine, *Blake and Tradition* (Princeton, New Jersey: Princeton Univ. Press, 1968), I, p. 124.

[8] Frances Lichten, *Decorative Art of Victoria's Era* (New York: Bonanza Books, 1950), p. 71.

tales as Poe's "The Fall of the House of Usher" are, I believe, eclectic structures in which a Gothic frame is supported by a basically Egyptian foundation, and the mystery all insoluble of their effect has a direct relation to the larger Mysteries of Initiation into temple secrets concerned with the exaltation of the soul and its torturous rebirth.

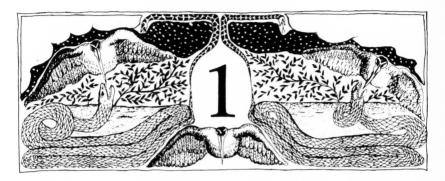

The exact nature of these Egyptian Mysteries, meant to be imparted in the labyrinths of temple and pyramid, springs from the ancient religion which was practiced in Dynastic Egypt from an almost immemorial time until it was adopted, first by the Greeks, and then by the Romans. Finally, it reached an apex in the cult of Isis, which flourished in the world capitals of the early Christian era. Alexandria (the site of the Great Library whose volumes of sacred lore were later used by Arab invaders to fire the waters of the public bath) became the center for this mystery cult and the perpetuation of its ritual, as the sun god, Osiris, sacred to the Pharohs, was transformed into the more cosmopolitan and eclectic deity, Serapis. As Harold Willoughby summarizes in his study of Mystery initiations in the Graeco-Roman world, *Pagan Regeneration*:

The ancient system had centered in the god, Osiris; but in the reformed cult of Hellenistic times he was replaced to a considerable extent by a new divinity, Serapis, and popular interest was transferred to the more appealing personality of Isis. She dominated the Hellenistic cult quite as Demeter held the supreme place in the Eleusinian mysteries, or the *Magna Mater* in those that emanated from Phrygia. In the ancient Osirian religion, the public ritual with its strong appeal to the masses was important. In the Hellenized worship of Isis, the significant ceremonials were those secret rites that had such deep meaning for the individual. These were only some of the ways in which the new cult showed adaptation to the very personal needs of individual religionists in the Hellenized world.[9]

So in the first and second centuries A.D. the Mysteries of Egypt became the Mysteries of Isis, just as in the Dark Ages they were to become the Mysteries of Hermes, centering on alchemy and the transmutation of lead into gold as a means of symbolizing the tenets of basically the same esoteric ritual and philosophy. The Mysteries always involved a hieratic initiation

---

[9] Harold R. Willoughby, *Pagan Regeneration: A Study of Mystery Initiations in the Graeco-Roman World* (Chicago: Univ. of Chicago Press, 1929), pp. 176-177.

SERAPIDIS
MACROBIANA DESCRIPTIO.

TypusSerapi-
dis hic phyſi-
cè expoſitus,
ad alios fen-
ſus anagogi-
cos, ethicos,
myſticos, pa-
ri analogia ap-
plicari poteſt.

Explicatio ſymbolorum Serapidis.

A Galathus, fœcunditas Nili.

B Nuditas iuuenilis, reflo-refcentiam poſt exun-dantionem Nili notat.

C Menſura incremento-rum Nili.

D Temporis Author Sera-pis.

E Tempus præteritum.

F Præſens per canem ad-blandientem.

G Futurum per lupum obliuioſum.

H Temporum ſucceſſio.

M Solis motus per humi-dum.

Serapis. From *Oedipus Aegyptiacus* (Rome, 1652), V. I., by Athanasius Kircher, p. 198. Courtesy Brown University Library.

into an arcane knowledge of immortality, knowledge achieved by a purification of the soul and a rite of passage through various prescribed trials and tests. It is a tribute to the truly sacred and secret character of this ritual that we know of its details only in fragments salvaged from ancient classical historians and a few Doctors of the Church. Even Herodotus, speaking of the performance of the Egyptian Mysteries at Saïs, felt constrained to tell his readers that "I could speak more exactly of these matters, for I know the truth, but I will hold my peace." What we do know, then, comes mainly from a handful of authors who are themselves the fathers of the occult tradition known generally as Hermeticism, which includes later alchemical and mystical commentaries as well as the few original texts which survived the wreck of the ancient world and the apparent extinction of learning during the early Middle Ages.

Poe's works, for example, contain learned references not only to Herodotus, Diodorus, and Plutarch, but also to Lucius Apuleius, who included in his *Metamorphoses* (better known in English as *The Golden Ass*) the most famous description of Isiac ritual which we possess. Apuleius, a Neo-Platonic philosopher of the second century A.D., followed Plutarch's model in holding back the most sacred details of the initiation rite as "things too holy for utterance," for "both tongue and ear would be infected with like guilt did I gratify such rash curiosity." Poe also mentions such authors as Tertullian and Iamblichus, both of whom discussed the Mysteries in one form or another, and he makes further reference to Demeter and Isis, who were considered by Diodorus to be interchangeable forms of the same goddess (the reform of the Osiris cult merged many aspects of the native Greek Eleusinian Mysteries with the Mysteries of Egypt). In "A Descent into the Maelström" there is even a reference by Poe to the seventeenth-century Jesuit occultist, Athanasius Kircher. Kircher's most famous work was the massive *Oedipus Aegyptiacus* (1652), a compendium of Egyptian, alchemical, and kabbalistic lore which contained in its final volume a description of the Mensa Isiaca, a hieroglyphic stone tablet once thought to describe in detail the full process of initiation, which Kircher relates to the *De Mysteriis Aegyptiorum* of Iamblichus, among others. There were, too, already in existence literary transmutations of these sources, such as Jean Terrasson's eighteenth-century romance, *Sethos,* and Novalis' *The Novices of Saïs* (1798). Coming closer to the time of Poe, we could say, as H. Bruce Franklin says of Melville's knowledge of Egyptian myth, "For contemporaneous versions and explanations [he] could have opened the pages of innumerable magazines, travel books, encyclopedias, and polemical tracts."[10]

But, for Poe, there is firm evidence of a more specific contemporary source for his acquaintance with a highly romanticized narrative of initiation into the Mysteries of Isis. In 1840, a year after "Usher" was published, Poe reviewed *Alciphron: A Poem* (1839) by the Irish poet, Thomas Moore, who had already caught the public fancy for things exotic with his long Oriental fantasy *Lalla Rookh. Alciphron,* however, was only a redoing in verse of what Moore had already done in his short prose romance, *The Epicurean* (first published in 1827) with which Poe was undoubtedly familiar, for in

---

[10] H. Bruce Franklin, *The Wake of the Gods: Melville's Mythology* (Stanford: Stanford Univ. Press, 1963), p. 73.

his review of *Alciphron* he mentions that the narrator is head of the Epicurean sect at Athens, a fact that is mentioned only in the romance and not in the poem. Burton R. Pollin has already traced the influence of *Alciphron* and *The Epicurean* on Poe's prose fantasy, "Shadow—A Parable,"[11] but no one has yet considered its influence on "The Fall of the House of Usher." For Moore's work provided not only that Romantic-Gothic eclecticism which gives the tale a novel and even sensational character, but also the underlying monomyth of initiation ritual which secretly unifies and deepens its metaphysical dimension.

Poe begins his review by praising Moore in no uncertain terms for his imaginative re-creation of a lost and exotic world, writing that "Amid the vague mythology of Egypt, the voluptuous scenery of the Nile, and the gigantic mysteries of her pyramids, Anacreon Moore has found all of that striking *materiel* which he so much delights in working up, and which he has embodied in the poem before us" (*Works*, X, 60). Like Byron, Poe refers to Moore as "Anacreon," for in 1804 Moore had first made his name with a translation of the *Odes of Anacreon*, by the Classic poet famous for his short lyrics on the subjects of love and wine. Both *The Epicurean* and *Alciphron*, which Moore admits were directly influenced by Terrasson's *Sethos*, attempted to accomplish something much more ambitious, however. Poe's summary of the poem (which can stand for the romance as well) gives some indication of the scope of Moore's philosophical and antiquarian interest:

The design of the story (for plot it has none) has been less a consideration than its facilities, and is made subservient to its execution. The subject is comprised in five epistles. In the first, Alciphron, head of the Epicurean sect at Athens, writes, from Alexandria, to his friend Cleon, in the former city. He tells him (assigning a reason for quitting Athens and her pleasures) that, having fallen asleep one night after protracted festivity, he beholds, in a dream, a spectre, who tells him that, beside the sacred Nile, he, the Epicurean, shall find that Eternal Life for which he had so long been sighing. In the second, from the same to the same, the traveller speaks, at large and in rapturous terms, of the scenery of Egypt; of the beauty of her maidens; of an approaching Festival of the Moon; and of a wild hope that amid the subterranean chambers of some huge pyramid lies the secret which he covets, the secret of Life Eternal. In the third letter, he relates a love adventure at the Festival. Fascinated by the charms of one of the nymphs of a procession, he is first in despair at losing sight of her, then overjoyed in seeing her in Necropolis, and finally traces her steps until they are lost near one of the smaller pyramids. In epistle the fourth (still from the same to the same) he enters and explores the pyramid, and, passing through a complete series of Eleusinian mysteries, is at length successfully initiated into the secrets of Memphian priestcraft; we learning this latter point from letter the fifth, which concludes the poem, and is addressed by Orcus, high priest of Memphis, to Decius, a praetorian prefect. (*Works*, X, 60-61)

For our purposes, the most interesting segment of *The Epicurean* is chapters six to eleven, which, as Poe indicates, contain a full and highly dramatic rendering of an initiation into the Egyptian Mysteries.[12] It is in-

---

[11] Burton R. Pollin, "Light on 'Shadow' and Other Pieces by Poe; Or, More of Thomas Moore," *ESQ: A Journal of the American Renaissance*, 18 (No. 3, 3rd Quarter, 1972), 166-172.

[12] In his Preliminary Notice to the joint edition of *The Epicurean* and *Alciphron*, Moore writes:

My original plan, in commencing the story of the Epicurean, was to write it all in verse, and in the form, as will be seen, of letters from different personages. But the great difficulty of managing, in rhyme, the minor details of a story, so as to be clear without becoming prosaic,

teresting, too, that Poe refers to these Mysteries as "Eleusinian," thus reflecting, like the anonymous author of *The Modern Eleusinia*, the eclecticism which merged all these forms of secret cult worship under the general heading of "Egyptian secrets." The Eleusinian Mysteries centered on the myth of Persephone, daughter of the earth goddess Demeter, and her rape and abduction to the Underworld by the dark daemon god Pluto. Eleusinian ritual involved the symbolic interment of Persephone and a search for her by Demeter in a passion drama which was so similar to the death of the sun god Osiris and his enchainment by the evil force, Typhon, that Lucius Apuleius (in discussing the Mysteries of Isis) says of his initiation that "I drew near the confines of death, I trod the threshold of Proserpine, I was borne through all the elements and returned to earth again."

This examination returns us to the beginning of "The Fall of the House of Usher" and the effect of that structure and its surrounding landscape on the spirits of the narrator. For, the sight of the House of Usher does not inspire awe and feelings of the sublime, but rather a shrinking dread and those dim apprehensions about impenetrable secrets, solemn catacombs, and morbid depths which Egyptian architecture was supposed to awaken in the Romantic mind. Indeed, the narrator confesses to experiencing only "an iciness, a sinking of the heart—an unredeemed dreariness of thought which no goading of the imagination could torture into aught of the sublime" (*Works*, III, 273). The Gothic mode of architecture was an objective correlative, one might almost say, for a sublime response on the part of the onlooker. But in the Gothic mode of literature, the literature of horror, as it is sometimes called, the transcendent feeling of the sublime is replaced by a numinous, nameless dread. Poe's narrator cannot even torture his imagination into producing a minimally sublime transport, for in gazing upon the House of Usher, he has the same forebodings as those nineteenth-century Romantics who meditated upon the ruins of the Temple of Karnak or the Great Pyramid at Giza.

---

and, still more, the diffuse length to which, I saw, narration in verse would be likely to run, deterred me from pursuing this plan any further; and I then commenced the tale anew, in its present shape. Whether I was wrong or right, in this change my readers have now an opportunity of judging for themselves.

He adds, then, that "In the letters of Alciphron will be found,—heightened only by a freer use of poetic colouring,—nearly the same details of events, feelings, and scenery which occupy the earlier prose narrative." I have in general used, in relation to Poe, the prose narration of *The Epicurean*, as found in the 1839 edition with illustrations by Turner: *The Epicurean, A Tale, and Alciphron, A Poem* (London: John Macrone, 1839).

Let us turn, then, to a detailed consideration of this most famous of Gothic short stories. The opening of Poe's tale, I suggest, is in the general Romantic tradition of a meditation on ruins, made popular by such eighteenth-century works as Volney's *The Ruins, or a Survey of the Revolutions of Empires* (1791), and popularized by countless nineteenth-century poets and graphic artists. In Poe's contemporary America, we need only look to a series of paintings like Thomas Cole's *The Past* and *The Present* (1838), Asher B. Durand's *The Morning of Life* and *The Evening of Life* (1840), or John Vanderlyn's *Marius Brooding on the Ruins of Carthage* (1807) to find an appropriate aesthetic parallel. But Poe's meditation, I would again emphasize, is on a very particular kind of ruin, a ruin in which the Mysteries of Egypt and Isis have been, or are about to be, performed. This is the famous Gothic Waste Land which confronts the narrator of "Usher":

> During the whole of a dull, dark, and soundless day in the autumn of the year, when the clouds hung oppressively low in the heavens, I had been passing alone, on horseback, through a singularly dreary tract of country, and at length found myself, as the shades of the evening drew on, within view of the melancholy House of Usher. I know not how it was—but, with the first glimpse of the building, a sense of insufferable gloom pervaded my spirit. I say insufferable; for the feeling was unrelieved by any of that half-pleasurable, because poetic, sentiment, with which the mind usually receives even the sternest natural images of the desolate or terrible. (*Works*, III, 273)

The narrator continues his attempt to define the effect of these stern images on his spiritual faculties by concluding with an elusive but significant reference:

> I looked upon the scene before me—upon the mere house, and the simple landscape features of the domain—upon the bleak walls—upon the vacant eye-like windows— upon a few rank sedges—and upon a few white trunks of decayed trees—with an utter depression of soul which I can compare to no earthly sensation more properly than to the after-dream of the reveller upon opium—the bitter lapse into every-day life—the hideous dropping off of the veil. (*Works*, III, 273)

Like a skull half-sunk in the desert sands, or a sphinx partially uncovered by desert winds, the House of Usher confronts the narrator with the shock of a sepulchral *memento mori*, and, in describing its effect, he thinks automatically of a fragment of the Mysteries associated with Egypt, the land of death, sphinxes, and pyramids, and their reigning goddess, Isis. His phrase, "the hideous dropping off of the veil," refers to a motif better known to the early nineteenth century than to us, though it was revived, appropriately enough, in the 1870's by that grand mistress of the occult and esoteric, Madame H. P. Blavatsky, founder of the Theosophical Society. In her *Isis Unveiled, A Master-key to the Mysteries of Ancient and Modern Science and Theology,* which attempted to merge Eastern mysticism with the Western occult tradition founded on Hermeticism and Neo-Platonism, Madame Blavatsky announced that:

> In our studies, mysteries were shown to be no mysteries. Names and places that to the Western mind have only a significance derived from Eastern fable, were shown to be realities. Reverently we stepped in spirit within the temple of Isis; to lift aside the veil of "the one that is and was and shall be" at Saïs; to look through the rent curtain of the Sanctum Sanctorum at Jerusalem; and even to interrogate within the crypts which once existed beneath the sacred edifice, the mysterious Bath-Kol.[13]

Madame Blavatsky finished her typically obscure rhetorical flourish with a mention of the "Bath-Kol," the mysterious oracle of God which certain rabbis maintained had spoken spontaneously within the precincts of the Tabernacle at Jerusalem, but her reference to the veil of Isis has the same source as Poe's reference to "the hideous dropping off of the veil" in his description of the melancholy effect of the House of Usher. For, in his treatise on the Egyptian Mysteries *De Iside et Osiride,* Plutarch, the first-century Roman historian, had written of the Egyptian priesthood that:

> . . . their philosophy is involved in fable and allegory, exhibiting only dark hints and obscure resemblances of the truth. This is insinuated, for example, in the sphinx, a type of their enigmatical theology, and in such inscriptions as that engraved on the base of Minerva's statue at Saïs, whom they regard as identical with Isis: "I am every thing that has been, that is, and that shall be; nor has any mortal ever yet been able to discover what is under my veil."[14]

Only those fully initiated into the cult of Isis, which conferred upon her initiates the like status of godhood or immortality, were permitted to lift the veil of Isis. Hence the equation by Poe's narrator of a sickness unto death and ultimate despair with an unwarranted and blasphemous "hideous dropping off of the veil." The reference, as mentioned in connection with Radcliffe, was a common one in Romantic literature. Novalis writes in his *The Novices of Saïs,* for example, that "I, too, then will inscribe my figure, and if according to the inscription, no mortal can lift the veil, we must seek to become immortal; he who does not seek to lift it, is no true novice of Saïs."[15] Thomas Moore, in *The Epicurean,* has his hero Alciphron say of Isis (after he has arrived in Egypt to study "the mysteries and the lore") that "At Saïs I was present during her Festival of Lamps, and read, by the blaze of innumerable lights, those sublime words on the temple of Neitha;—'I am all that has been, that is, and that will be, and no man hath ever lifted my veil.'" And, as in Hawthorne's *Blithedale Romance,* where Zenobia suggests

---

[13] H. P. Blavatsky, *Isis Unveiled* (New York: J. W. Bouton, 1884), I, vi.

[14] Lewis Spence, *The Mysteries of Egypt, or The Secret Rites and Traditions of the Nile* (London: Rider and Co., 1929), pp. 52-53.

[15] Novalis [Friedrich von Hardenberg], *Die Lehrlinge zu Saïs* (1798), trans. by Ralph Manheim, preface by Stephen Spender (New York: Curt Valentine, 1949), p. 17.

Isis. From *Oedipus Aegyptiacus* (Rome, 1652), V. I., by Athanasius Kircher, p. 189. Courtesy Brown University Library.

by her legend of "The Silvery Veil" that the Veiled Lady's mysterious drapery might even conceal "the face of a corpse" or "the head of a skeleton," *The Epicurean* contains an episode in which Alciphron raises the veil of a strangely silent figure at a feast and finds it to be a hideous mummy.[16]

Like the silver skeleton present at the banquet of Trimalchio in Petronius' *Satyricon*, the mummy is a reminder to remember death in the presence of life; and its effect on Alciphron is once again much like the effect of the House of Usher on Poe's narrator, for the Epicurean confesses, "This silent and ghostly witness of mirth seemed to embody, as it were, the shadow in my own heart." It is a witness, too, in much the same way in which the pyramids, as watchtowers of time, generate shadowy fancies in the mind of Alciphron when he contemplates the ruins of the monuments of Memphis. Usher's House, we might note, is also as mummified as the corpse of any embalmed pharoh of the Dynasties, for Poe writes of its "extraordinary dilapidation" that

there appeared to be a wild inconsistency between its still perfect adaptation of parts, and the crumbling condition of the individual stones. In this there was much that reminded me of the specious totality of old woodwork which has rotted for long years in some neglected vault, with no disturbance from the breath of the external air. (*Works*, III, 276-277)

The total effect of the House of Usher on Poe's narrator, then, is paralleled by the effect of the Pyramids of Memphis upon Moore's Epicurean:

There was a solemnity in the sunshine resting upon those monuments—a stillness, as of reverence, in the air that breathed around them, which stole, like the music of past times, into my heart. I thought what myriads of the wise, the beautiful, and the brave, had sunk into the dust since earth first saw those wonders; and, in the sadness of my soul, I exclaimed,—"Must man, alone, then, perish? must minds and hearts be annihilated, while pyramids endure? O Death! even upon these everlasting tablets—the only approach to immortality that kings themselves could purchase—thou hast written of our doom, awfully and intelligibly, saying,—'There is for man no eternal mansion but the grave.'" (*The Epicurean*, p. 26)

Alciphron perhaps voices those thoughts too deep for tears which oppress Poe's narrator, who, gazing at the mansion of the Ushers, also thinks unconsciously of the "long lapse of centuries" and "the consequent undeviating transmission from sire to son, of the patrimony with the name, which had, at length, so identified the two as to merge the original title of the estate in the quaint and equivocal appellation of the 'House of Usher'" (*Works*, III, 275). The narrator, unable to articulate the feeling of insufferable gloom which causes such "an iciness, a sinking, a sickening of [his] heart," here matches Alciphron, who exclaims, "My heart sunk at the thought; and, for the moment, I yielded to that desolate feeling, which overspreads the soul that hath no light from the future." It is precisely to exorcise this feeling that

---

[16] For a Gothic tale which, like *The Epicurean*, forms a curious link between the eclectic imagery of "The Fall of the House of Usher" and the "Legend of the Silvery Veil" in *The Blithdale Romance* (through the common use of the ritual of Egyptian Mystery initiation and the process of various trials and inquisitions), see the anon. "The Sphinx: An Extravaganza, Etched in the Manner of Callot," *Blackwood's Magazine*, 24 (October, 1828), 441-452. This story has been reprinted in Ronald Curran, ed., *Witches, Wraiths and Warlocks: Supernatural Tales of the American Renaissance* (New York: Fawcett World Library, 1971), pp. 123-144.

Alciphron undertakes his mission to undergo the trials of mystery initiation, in the hopes of gaining an immortality which will forever banish his fears about the vanity of human wishes and the transience of human accomplishment. The meditation on ruins thus merges naturally and imperceptibly with the immemorial *ubi sunt* tradition, but, whereas Alciphron manages to shake off his feeling of ultimate desolation, the same emotion continues to pervade and to permeate the atmosphere of the House of Usher, as well as to afflict its master, the unhappy Roderick.

If the House of Usher can be considered, in its effect at least, to be a structure of Egyptian dread and magnitude, combining the uses to which such an image was put by the Romantic mind—temple, crypt, and prison— then Roderick Usher is indeed the master of this temple, as well as its entombed Pharoh and its holy prisoner. He is the priest-king, chief celebrant, and hierophant of its Hall of Labyrinths, the Osiris who must descend into the depths of night in order to be reborn again in mystic marriage with his sister-wife, Isis. As Harold Willoughby writes,

According to ancient cosmology, the sun each night visited the subterranean regions. In the rite of initiation, therefore, the votary as a new Osiris made both the infernal and the celestial journey like the sun. At midnight he saw the sun brightly shine in the realm of the dead, and likewise he mounted up into the heavens and saw the gods celestial as well as the gods infernal. In doing all this he was but playing the part of the dying and rising god Osiris in the salvation drama of the Isis cult. (*Pagan Regeneration,* p. 190)

In visiting the House of Usher, the narrator is also visiting the House of the Dead, being guided (like the neophyte of the Isis rituals) through the subterranean regions, the vaults and crypts within the pyramid or underneath the Temple of Isis itself: "A valet, of stealthy step, thence conducted me, in silence, through many dark and intricate passages in my progress to the *studio* of his master" (*Works,* III, 277). This master, the true conductor of the mysteries, is, again, Usher himself, for his very name echoes the meaning of the term "hierophant" which, as Carl Kerényi tells us in his study of the Eleusinian rites, means the priestly demonstrator of the holy mysteries.[17]

The narrator of "The Fall of the House of Usher" is an unwilling initiate who has failed to comprehend the significance of the Mysteries he has witnessed and the passion-drama in which he has participated. Thus, he reports his experience in Gothic terms which frame the narrative according to the conventions of the *Schauerroman,* the tale which is more of Germany than of the soul. He can be considered as a partially unreliable reporter, like those early Church Fathers, who talk of the initiation rites as only so much nonsense and pagan mumbo-jumbo, more mystification than mystery. This latter supposition accounts for Usher's characterization of the narrator as a madman precisely before the climax of the ritual Usher has been enacting, with his sister Madeline playing the part of the Isis-Persephone figure. The narrator is "mad" precisely because he does not recognize, or realize, the import of the chance for divine wisdom and revelation, with the concomitant gift of immortality, which has been offered to him by the gods themselves.

---

[17] C. Kerényi and C. G. Jung, *Introduction to a Science of Mythology: The Myth of the Divine Child and the Mysteries of Eleusis* (London: Routledge and Kegan Paul, Ltd., 1951), p. 194. The hierophant was the only one permitted to exhibit the *hiera,* the sacred objects, to the initiates.

The first part of "The Fall of the House of Usher" can thus be read as an esoteric or even subterranean performance of an Egyptian Mystery rite, with Usher assuming the part of the hierophant and the narrator as an uncomprehending witness. The story follows, indeed, the five stages of Mystery initiation outlined by Lewis Spence in his study, *The Mysteries of Egypt*. The first part can be seen as the necessary steps of contemplation, purgation, and a journey through the higher and lower regions, while the climax can be considered as embodying the culminating aspects of union and rebirth (*Mysteries of Egypt,* p. 205).

Long discipline and contemplation were a requisite part of the initiation process itself. As Edouard Schuré writes of the questing neophyte:

Before rising to Isis Uranus, he had to know terrestrial Isis, had to learn the physical sciences. His time was divided between meditations in his cell, the study of hieroglyphics in the halls and courts of the temple, as large as a city, and in lessons from his teachers. He learned the science of minerals and plants, the history of man and peoples, medicine, architecture, and sacred music. In this long apprenticeship he had not only to know, but to become.[18]

In this respect, the narrator is the apprentice and Roderick is the master of the peculiar Pythagorean discipline taking place within the Halls of the Temple which is the House of Usher. While in Egypt studying the Mysteries, Pythagoras was said to have learned the fundamentals of geometry and the theory of the celestial orbs as well as all that pertained to computation and numbers. These he used to construct his abstract philosophy of numerical and harmonic progression. Thus Poe's narrator says of his intimacy with the recesses of Usher's spirit, "We painted and read together, or I listened, as if in a dream, to the wild improvisations of his speaking guitar" (*Works*, III, 282). We do get a more direct hint, however, as to exactly what texts are studied in the discipline. "Our books," he remarks

—the books which, for years, had formed no small portion of the mental existence of the invalid—were, as might be supposed, in strict keeping with this character of phantasm. We pored together over such works as the Ververt et Chartreuse of Gresser;

18 Edouard Schuré, *The Great Initiates: A Study of the Secret History of Religions* (1889; rpt. ed., West Nyack, New York: St. George Books, 1961), p. 151.

the Belphegor of Machiavelli; the Heaven and Hell of Swedenborg; the Subterranean Voyage of Nicholas Klimm by Holberg; the Chiromancy of Robert Flud, of Jean D'Indaginé, and of De la Chambre; the Journey into the Blue Distance of Tieck; and the City of the Sun of Campanella. (*Works,* III, 287)

As T. O. Mabbott and others have noted, "All of Usher's library . . . consists of real books, and, although Poe may have seen few of them, they all concern in one way or another the idea that spirit is present even in inanimate things and that the world, or macrocosm, has relations to the microcosm, man."[19] The books have usually been seen as only an extension of Roderick's belief in the sentience of all things. Yet it is not the books themselves and their content (for some, like Klimm's *Subterranean Voyage,* are merely satirical studies in the vein of Swift's *Gulliver's Travels*) but rather their titles which take on an occult significance. Most of them deal with a journey to the underworld, and we have seen that the journey of the sun god Osiris to the infernal regions was a central part of Egyptian ritual. "I drew near the confines of death," said Apuleius, "I trod the threshold of Proserpine, I was borne through all the elements and returned to earth again." And, he adds to this mystic revelation, "I saw the sun gleaming with bright splendour at dead of night, I approached the gods above, and the gods below, and worshipped them face to face" (*Mysteries of Egypt,* p. 70).

Swedenborg's *Heaven and Hell,* for example, deals not only with an occult theory of correspondences but also with "the gods above" and "the gods below" as seen face to face by this Swedish mystic. Most of the other titles in Usher's library concern subterranean journeys and what one should expect to find in these infernal regions, thus paralleling the most famous *vade mecum* to the underworld, the sacred Egyptian *Book of the Dead.* For the Mysteries performed in life were considered only as a prelude to the same ritual to be enacted after death. The descent into an artificial darkness in the Temple of Isis was thought to be a symbolic re-creation and anticipation of the descent of the soul into Hades through the Door of Death. As Plutarch wrote, "When a man dies, he is like those who are being initiated into the mysteries. . . . Our whole life is but a succession of wanderings, of painful courses, of long journeys by tortuous ways without outlet" (*Pagan Regeneration,* p. 61). And Thomas Taylor, the eighteenth-century translator of so many mystic and Neo-Platonic texts, added in his *Dissertation on the Eleusinian and Bacchic Mysteries* that "as the rape of Proserpine was exhibited in the shews of the mysteries, as is clear from Apuleius, it indisputably follows, that this represented the descent of the soul, and its union with the dark tenement of body."[20]

What Lewis Spence has to say about the antiquity of the sacred Egyptian texts, however, may explain why Poe includes among the library titles in the dark tenement of the House of Usher such an item as Campanella's *City of the Sun.* "The Book of the Dead," he writes, "was preceded by the Pyramid Texts, which recount the manner in which Egyptian royalty succeeded to union

---

[19] T. O. Mabbott, notes to "The Fall of the House of Usher," in *The Selected Poetry and Prose of Edgar Allan Poe* (New York: Modern Library, 1951), p. 418. Mabbott's views are summarized in a posthumous essay entitled "The Books in the House of Usher," *Books at Iowa,* 19 (1973).

[20] Thomas Taylor, "A Dissertation on the Eleusinian and Bacchic Mysteries" (1790), in *Thomas Taylor the Platonist,* ed. by Kathleen Raine and George Mills Harper (Princeton, New Jersey: Princeton Univ. Press, 1969), p. 383.

with the god [Osiris]. His soul bathed in the sacred lake, he underwent lustration with Nile water, and he then crossed the Lake of Lilies in the ferry-boat. He ascended the staircase of the sun and reached the city of the sun, after magically opening its gates by a spell, being announced by heavenly heralds" (*Mysteries of Egypt,* p. 87).

The titles in Usher's library, then, comprise an esoteric guide to the underworld of Usher, itself a journey into the blue distance of Mystery initiation. This journey ends with a transcendent vision—the City of the Sun, the golden state of Isis unveiled, in holy union with her brother-husband Osiris, who himself has been resurrected after death and dismemberment by the ecliptic powers of darkness. These latter powers the Egyptians personified by the god Set, whom Greeks designated as the wind monster Typhon. In the Eleusinian Mysteries, which Poe obviously thought were identical with the original Egyptian rites, the liturgy charted the course of Persephone through the precincts of Hades, to which she had been abducted by the god of the underworld Pluto. In the passion drama performed in the labyrinths of the House of Usher, this shadowy part is taken by the physician who has in his keeping Roderick's sister. Madeline is temporarily interred in one of the numerous vaults within the main walls of the building, for, like Persephone, she will be resurrected in the return to life and union which is the hierogamic marriage of Isis and her hierophant, Roderick, acting the part of the reborn sun god.

The proper guide for the descent into these infernal regions is thus *The Book of the Dead.* As Spence tells us, this book "is a magical book, inasmuch as the sorcery of everyday life is placed at the disposal of the dead in order that they may escape destruction in the journey toward the Otherworld by means of spells and magical invocations" (*Mysteries of Egypt,* p. 77). The chapters of this most antique of volumes describe the monsters and enemies that the dead soul will encounter in its wanderings, revealing their secret names which, when uttered, allow the soul to control a host of destructive demons. Thus "Belphegor," in Poe's eclectic catalogue of demonology, is the name of the Ammonitic devil who lurked in the shadows of rocks and crevices, seducing the daughters of Israel until he was openly denounced by the angry prophet Hosea.

Another important section of *The Book of the Dead* is devoted to the judgment of Osiris, in which the soul is interrogated by forty-two judges to determine whether it is fit to take equal station with the sun god or be devoured by the howling monster who waits without. The last three books mentioned as part of Usher's library function precisely as this kind of symbolic scripture, familiarizing the soul with the demons to be met in the coming infernal journey; and following, as *The Book of the Dead* should follow, the Pyramid Texts. The list even culminates in a work that can be translated quite literally as the book of "The Watches of the Dead." Poe's narrator continues:

One favourite volume was a small octavo edition of the *Directorium Inquisitorium,* by the Dominican Eymeric de Gironne; and there were passages in Pomponius Mela, about the old African Satyrs and AEgipans, over which Usher would sit dreaming for hours. His chief delight, however, was found in the perusal of an exceedingly rare and curious book in quarto Gothic—the manual of a forgotten church—the *Vigilae Mortuorum secundum Chorum Ecclesiae Maguntinae* (*Works,* III, 287)

We have thus come to the trials, inquisitions, and tortures that the questing soul, the aspirant of the Mysteries, must face if he is to obtain the right to confront Isis unveiled, for the *Directorium Inquisitorium* cherished by Roderick is actually a work by Nicholas Eymeric de Gerone, inquisitor-general for Castile in 1356, which gives an account of the tortures of the Inquisition. It is for this that the instruction, purgation, and discipline have been instituted and the reason that the arcana, the *Hiera* (the sacred objects), have been revealed to the narrator, who is to accompany Usher on the infernal journey in the same way in which the neophyte is conducted, or ushered, by the hierophant.

One of the most important of these arcana, prophetic of the entombment of the sun god, is the series of strange paintings which Roderick executes as part of the discipline which occupies his waking hours before the descent into the Underworld. As the narrator writes of the uncanny effect of these paintings:

From the paintings over which his elaborate fancy brooded, and which grew, touch by touch, into vagueness at which I shuddered the more thrillingly, because I shuddered knowing not why;—from these paintings (vivid as their images now are before me) I would in vain endeavor to educe more than a small portion which should lie within the compass of merely written words. By the utter simplicity, by the nakedness of his designs, he arrested and over-awed attention. If ever mortal painted an idea that mortal was Roderick Usher. For me at least—in the circumstances then surrounding me—there arose out of the pure abstractions which the hypochondriac contrived to throw upon his canvas, an intensity of intolerable awe, no shadow of which I felt ever yet in the contemplation of the certainly glowing yet too concrete reveries of Fuseli. (*Works*, III, 283)

The narrator refers here to the Swiss artist of the weird and the grotesque, friend of Blake and a fellow-illustrator of visions and nightmares. But Usher's paintings are abstract in the same way that his musical studies are intense, formal, and intricate, for they form part of the larger pattern of exact instruction in the larger monomyth of the Mysteries. They are also like the "scenic representations," the "chambers of imagery," which Thomas Moore's Alciphron has to pass through in order to gain admittance to the sanctuary of Isis. Edouard Schuré, in his imaginative re-creation of an initiation ceremony, based on the same Romantic sources with which Poe was familiar, writes of one segment of the ritual that:

A Magus called a *pastophor,* a guardian of sacred symbols, opened the grating for the novice and welcomed him with a kind smile. He congratulated him upon having successfully passed the first test. Then, leading him across the hall, he explained the sacred paintings. Under each of these paintings was a letter and a number. The twenty-two symbols represented the twenty-two first Mysteries and constituted the alphabet of secret science, that is, the absolute principles, the universal keys which, employed by the will, become the source of all wisdom and power. (*The Great Initiates,* p. 146)

Schuré relates these arcana to the Tarot deck and suggests that the Tarot cards themselves represent symbolic fragments of initiation into the Mysteries of Egypt and Isis. Although only one of Roderick Usher's awe-inspiring paintings is described (and it seems to have no relation to Tarot symbolism), Usher does act as a *pastophor* in exhibiting it to the narrator. The work fits into the chain of occult symbolism that is developed through the titles of the books in Usher's library. As the narrator relates:

One of the phantasmagoric conceptions of my friend, partaking not so rigidly of the spirit of abstraction, may be shadowed forth, although feebly, in words. A small picture presented the interior of an immensely long and rectangular vault or tunnel, with low walls, smooth, white, and without interruption or device. Certain accessory points of the design served well to convey the idea that this excavation lay at an exceeding depth below the surface of the earth. No outlet was observed in any portion of its vast extent, and no torch or other artificial source of light was discernible; yet a flood of intense rays rolled throughout, and bathed the whole in a ghastly and inappropriate splendour. (*Works,* III, 283)

Usher's painting might be entitled "The Burial of the Sun," for (as Willoughby has already noted, referring to the statement of Apuleius that "I saw the sun gleaming with bright splendour at the dead of night") the novice made the same journey as the sun god Osiris. *The Book of the Dead* tells us that this journey involved a descent into the nether regions of night and darkness and then an ascent up the golden staircase of the sky to final enthronement in Heliopolis, the holy City of the Sun. Thus at the end of his initiation into the Mysteries of Isis, Apuleius writes, "I was adorned like the sun and made in the fashion of an image." Willoughby comments of Lucius' symbolic resurrection that "This was essentially a rite of deification, and Lucius with his Olympian stole, his lighted torch, and his rayed crown was viewed as a personification of the sun-god" (*Pagan Regeneration,* p. 191). The ancient Egyptians called part of the original ritual which centered around the resurrection of Pharoh as a representative Osiris figure "the Rite of the Golden Chamber," and it is just such a golden chamber which Usher limns—the inner vault, the *sanctum sanctorum,* the burial chamber of a pyramid and the tomb of a god.

The ghastly and inappropriate splendor of Usher's vault is paralleled, too, by the unearthly phosphorescence of a cavern that Moore's Alciphron stumbles upon as part of his Mystery initiation in the depths of a pyramid at the necropolis north of Memphis. Moore writes:

While occupied in these ineffectual struggles, I perceived, to the left of the archway, a dark, cavernous opening, which seemed to lead in a direction parallel to the lighted arcades. Notwithstanding, however, my impatience, the aspect of this passage, as I looked shudderingly into it, chilled my very blood. It was not so much darkness, as a sort of livid and ghastly twilight, from which a damp, like that of death-vaults, exhaled, and through which, if my eyes did not deceive me, pale, phantom-like shapes were, at that very moment, hovering. (*The Epicurean,* p. 53)

Usher's painting, I think, does not so much look forward to the development of modern abstract art and non-objective expressionism as it looks backward to Pythagorean geometry and the mysterious labyrinths of the pyramids. It is not Usher, however, but his sister Madeline who is interred in such a vault, for, being the exact twin of her brother ("sympathies of a scarcely intelligible nature had always existed between them"), she undergoes the passion of Persephone, prematurely buried in the sinks of Hades, while he undergoes the passion of Osiris, slowly being torn apart and dismembered while she struggles for resurrection in the tomb. Her malady, as Poe specifically tells us, is cataleptic in nature; and the first trial of the Mystery initiation was a literal simulacrum of the death of the neophyte and his wandering, as a lost and questing soul, through the infernal regions. Schuré even speaks of "the seeming cataleptic death of the adept and his resurrection," but that resurrection is accomplished only by the trials and tortures foreshadowed in a book like the *Directorium Inquisitorium*—trials which are ultimately "elemental" in nature.

Lucius Apuleius had said of his initiation into the cult of Isis that "I was borne through all the elements." The elemental trials which are common both to *The Epicurean* and "The Fall of the House of Usher," then, are the ordeals of earth, fire, water, and air. In Usher's case, the trial by earth is obviously the entombment of his sister Madeline in the crypt, as well as his own entrapment in the labyrinthine dungeon of the house of his fathers. Similarly, the trials by air, fire, and water all culminate in the whirlwind which gathers in the vicinity of the mansion at the end of the tale, and in the vaporish activity of the tarn, which is supercharged with a weird phosphorescence. The tarn thus becomes the molten barrier which must be passed or endured if the initiation is to be successful. The narrator describes the scene in the following terms:

The impetuous fury of the entering gust nearly lifted us from our feet. It was, indeed, a tempestuous yet sternly beautiful night, and one wildly singular in its terror and its beauty. A whirlwind had apparently collected its force in our vicinity; for there were frequent and violent alterations in the direction of the wind; and the exceeding density of the clouds (which hung so low as to press upon the turrets of the house) did not prevent our perceiving the life-like velocity with which they flew careening from all points against each other, without passing away into the distance. I say that even their exceeding density did not prevent our perceiving this—yet we had no glimpse of the moon or stars—nor was there any flashing forth of the lightning. But the under surfaces of the huge masses of agitated vapor, as well as all terrestrial objects immediately around us, were glowing in the unnatural light of a faintly luminous and distinctly gaseous exhalation which hung about and enshrouded the mansion. (*Works,* III, 291)

In this context, it is interesting to note that Set or Typhon, the legendary force of darkness that temporarily overcame Osiris, was often conceived of as a storm or whirlwind. In fact, in Jacob Bryant's *A New System, or An Analysis of Ancient Mythology* (first published in 1774) the author says of the Greek Typhon (from which the modern term "typhoon" is partially derived): "By this was signified a mighty whirlwind, and inundation: and it oftentimes denoted the ocean; and particularly the ocean in ferment."[21] Certainly the tarn of Usher is in ferment, an unholy ferment which combines all the elements of earth, water, fire, and air, though the narrator attempts to explain away such unnatural appearances by reassuring Roderick with the Radcliffean explanation that they "are merely electrical phenomena not uncommon—or it may be that they have their ghastly origin in the rank miasma of the tarn." In *The Epicurean* Alciphron's trial by the elements of air and wind can be profitably compared with the sound and fury of Poe's tempest and its effect on the beholders of this midnight cyclone. The glare of an unnatural light during the hours which should be consecrated to darkness may also again remind us of Apuleius and his testimony that "I saw the sun gleaming with bright splendour at dead of night." Moore writes of the trials of air and fire:

Just then, a momentary flash, as if of lightning, broke around me, and I perceived,

---

21 Jacob Bryant, *A New System, or An Analysis of Ancient Mythology: Wherein an Attempt is made to divest Tradition of Fable; and to reduce the Truth to its Original Purity,* 3 vols. (London, 1774-1776), II, 323. The influence of Bryant and his fellow mythagogues on early Romantic literature has been traced by E. B. Hungerford in *Shores of Darkness* (New York: Columbia Univ. Press, 1941).

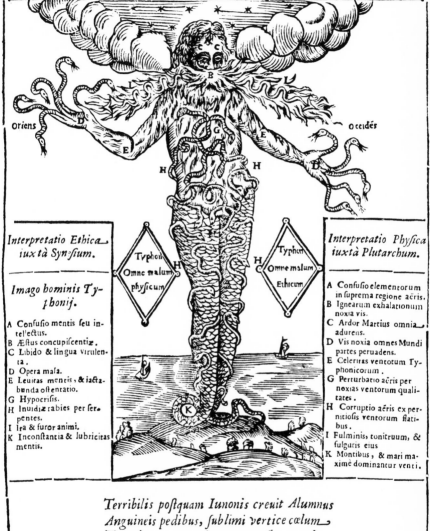

Typhon. From *Oedipus Aegyptiacus* (Rome, 1652), V. I., by Athanasius Kircher, p. 221.
Courtesy Brown University Library.

hanging out of the clouds, and barely within my reach, a huge brazen ring. Instinctively I stretched forth my arm to seize it, and, at the same instant, both balustrade and steps gave way beneath me, and I was left swinging by my hands in the dark void. As if, too, this massy ring, which I grasped, was by some magic power linked with all the winds in heaven, no sooner had I seized it than, like the touching of a spring, it seemed to give loose to every variety of gusts and tempests, that ever strewed the sea-shore with wrecks or dead; and, as I swung about, the sport of this elemental strife, every new burst of its fury threatened to shiver me, like a storm-sail, to atoms! (*The Epicurean*, pp. 58-59)

Thus is Typhon, the Lord of Winds, unleashed with the same power that, with its "impetuous fury," almost lifts the narrator and Usher off their feet in Poe's tale. The "brazen ring" is missing from Poe's version of the trials, but there is a "shield of brass" and a whole pattern of hierarchical symbolism (which centers on the progression of the planetary metals) embodied in the fanciful history which Poe calls the "Mad Trist" of Sir Launcelot Canning. This is the work which the narrator reads to Roderick at precisely the same time that Madeline frees herself from the tomb.[22] Yet, beneath the Gothic exterior of this pseudo-Grail romance once again lurks another Egyptian Mystery—the art and science of transmuting these metals, known popularly as alchemy, which also helps to structure the monomyth of "The Fall of the House of Usher." I have already explored this connection elsewhere,[23] but what is important about the "Mad Trist" in the context of the original Egyptian Mysteries is the fact that it functions as a pageant or dumb show of the trials and torments that the questing aspirant has to endure. The ordeals of entering the City of the Sun, the "palace of gold, with a floor of silver," include the struggle with the monster of doubt and will, the Dragon "of pesty breath," Typhon, and the successful confrontation with the obstinate hermit, the Master of the Mysteries, who holds the key to the gates of full initiation. At the same time, Madeline is enduring the trial of earth, the ordeals of the labyrinth, and the premature burial which shadows forth the death of the old self and

---

[22] The entire device of juxtaposing a dramatic reading from a strange old book with noisy interruptions that coincide with events related in the text Poe once again took from Mrs. Radcliffe. In the sixth chapter of Volume IV of *The Mysteries of Udolpho*, Ludovico, servant of the Count De Villefort, agrees to spend a night in a haunted suite of rooms where the sentimental heroine Emily has heard groans, while, "immediately after, a dead weight fell against the door, with a violence, that threatened to burst it open" (p. 542). Ludovico arms himself for the ordeal of the watch with a bottle of wine and a book by which (like the "Mad Trist" as used by the narrator of "Usher") he "endeavoured to abstract his mind from melancholy." Mrs. Radcliffe's description of this chivalric work—containing the legend which Ludovico reads to the accompaniment of mysterious sound effects, "The Provençal Tale"—provides a parallel ancestry for Poe's "Mad Trist." Mrs. Radcliffe writes of the book:

> It had been lent to him by Dorothée, who had formerly picked it up in an obscure corner of the Marquis's library, and who, having opened it and perceived some of the marvels it related, had carefully preserved it for her own entertainment, its condition giving her some excuse for detaining it from its proper station. The damp corner into which it had fallen, had caused the cover to be disfigured and mouldy, and the leaves to be so discoloured with spots, that it was not without difficulty the letters could be traced. The fictions of the provençal writers, whether drawn from the Arabic legends, brought by the Saracens into Spain, or recounting the chivalric exploits performed by the crusaders, whom the Troubadors accompanied to the east, were generally splendid and always marvellous, both in scenery and incident; and it is not wonderful, that Dorothée and Ludovico should be fascinated by inventions, which had captivated the careless imagination in every rank of society, in a former age. (*Mysteries of Udolpho*, pp. 551-552)

It is in this mouldy volume that a work like Canning's "Mad Trist" might be found.

[23] Cf. my essay, "Usher Unveiled: Poe and the Metaphysic of Gnosticism," *Poe Studies*, 5 (1972), 1-8.

the rebirth of a new, untrammeled soul. This struggle issues in the final Mystery which the narrator is permitted to witness, the full *hieros gamos* of priest and priestess, Osiris and Isis, Roderick and Madeline, which fulfills the paradox that absolute purity of soul can only be attained by a physical ravishment. Since both Madeline and Roderick have attained the status of gods, however, their union is a sublime, awe-inspiring one which the narrator chooses to report under the guise of a typical Gothic catastrophe, echoing that "utter astonishment and dread" which he first evinced upon his entry into the catacombs of Usher:

> As if in the superhuman energy of his utterance there had been found the potency of a spell—the huge antique panels to which the speaker pointed threw slowly back, upon the instant, their ponderous and ebony jaws. It was the work of the rushing gust —but then without those doors there *did* stand the lofty and enshrouded figure of the lady Madeline of Usher. There was blood upon her white robes, and the evidence of some bitter struggle upon every portion of her emaciated frame. For a moment she remained trembling and reeling to and fro upon the threshold, then, with a low moaning cry, fell heavily inward upon the person of her brother, and in her violent and now final death-agonies, bore him to the floor a corpse, and a victim to the terrors he had anticipated. (*Works,* III, 296-297)

The veil of Isis has been lifted, then, with sublime consequences for Madeline and Roderick, whose earthly tenement is superseded by the radiant glories of Heliopolis. But this revelation has only "hideous" repercussions for the narrator, who has failed to comprehend the full significance of the Mysteries he has witnessed. The closing scene of "The Fall of the House of Usher" is described in the terms of an apocalypse, a catastrophe like the archetypal Gothic climax of Horace Walpole's *The Castle of Otranto*, where a clap of thunder shakes the castle to its foundations, the walls are thrown down with a mighty force, and the poor witnesses think the last day is at hand. "There came a fierce breath of the whirlwind," the narrator of "Usher" exclaims, "—the entire orb of the satellite burst at once upon my sight—my brain reeled as I saw the mighty walls rushing asunder—there was a long tumultuous shouting sound like the voice of a thousand waters—and the deep and dark tarn at my feet closed sullenly and silently over the fragments of the 'House of Usher'" (*Works,* III, 297). This is not a description of an apocalypse, however, but of a new genesis, and it constitutes a conjunction rather than a catastrophe. Earth, water, air, and fire are now transcendently united, as Sun and Moon are sublimely conjoined. The initiation is complete, and, as the anonymous author of *The Modern Eleusinia* puts it, after the "deep bitterness, and tormenting darkness of Vice and Error," and "by the way of tears, and sacrifice, and toil," we have reached and actually witnessed "the soul's exaltation."

Beneath the Gothic tracery of the walls of "Usher" one can glimpse the massive Egyptian pylons which structure and support the House itself. But at the same time, we have traveled far from the hothouse Romanticism of Thomas Moore's *The Epicurean,* which points to the later Romantic decadence of works like *Salammbô, The Temptation of St. Anthony,* and *Salome.* Beginning in the nostalgia and yearning for the past which was perhaps the strongest of the early Romantic senses, the Egyptian style soon degenerated into the felicities of historical romance, as the search for a unifying monomyth was similarly transferred from the realm of literature to the realm of science. Moore's *The Epicurean* is what we would have to term, without any pejorative meaning intended, mere romance; it illustrates the early fascination with the exotic and the eclectic which was to return in an even more overwhelming degree toward the last days of the Romantic Age.

What was lost in this shift was the traumatic connection between landscape and consciousness, the widening of the sphere of sensibility which conjoined the sense of place with the sense of self and which made the Romantic imagination into a new medium and a new universe, a metaphysical temple full of enchanting clerestoreys as well as demonic tunnels and howling labyrinths. Mrs. Radcliffe, in associating the landscape of the Alps and the Appenines with the high consciousness and snowy sensibility of her heroine, Emily, had begun all unwittingly a process which was to culminate in the daring use of metaphor which made the landscape of the House of Usher into a simulacrum of the desert places of the human soul. The "hideous dropping off of the veil" witnessed by the narrator was at one and the same time a privilege and a curse; a privilege for those, like Usher, prepared to go beyond the "trembling of the veil" (as Yeats titled his own autobiography) and a curse for those, like the narrator himself, who delved into the Mysteries of the soul without putting aside their rationalism, failing to realize that the precinct which they had entered was, in fact, holy ground. Thus is the narrator of "Usher" afflicted by shadowy fancies and an unfathomable melancholia at the beginning of Poe's tale and thus is he cursed with an unmediated Faustian knowledge at its end.

The quest for a monomyth involving the trials and progress of the soul was to become, as we have mentioned, more and more of a secular rather than a literary endeavor, as the eclecticism in which Romanticism began at last exhausted and subverted the Romantic consciousness itself. Beginning with the attempt of Athanasius Kircher to produce a compendium of occult knowledge in his *Oedipus Aegyptiacus* (1652-1655), the scholarly synthesis of ancient religious history and the Mysteries of myth continued in a work we have already quoted, the enormously influential *A New System, or An Analysis of Ancient Mythology* (published by Jacob Bryant in three volumes from 1774 to 1776). Poe was undoubtedly familiar with this work, for he refers to Bryant's "very learned 'Mythology'" in "The Purloined Letter," and in *Eureka* he quotes with approval Bryant's declaration that "Although the Pagan fables are not believed, yet we forget ourselves continually and make inferences from them as from existing realities" (*Works*, XVI, 217). Bryant proceeded to reduce all antique mythologies to one grand monomyth, which could be traced to the primal event of the Flood, so that "All the mysteries of the Gentile world seem to have been memorials of the Deluge." Bryant's syncretism was continued by disciples such as George Stanley Faber, whose *Dissertation on the Mysteries of the Cabiri* (1803) bore the typically fulsome and self-explanatory subtitle: *Being an Attempt to Deduce the Several Orgies of Isis, Ceres, Mithras, Bacchus, Rhea, Adonis, and Hecate, from an Union of the Rites Commemorative of the Deluge with the Adoration of the Host of Heaven.* The historical quest, then, subsumed particular concerns with the nature and destiny of the individual soul in a general interest in mythology. The goal became the elusive monomyth that tied all myths together as a fossilized "epic of humanity" which portrayed the evolution from sympathetic magic to sophisticated religion. Sir James George Frazer climaxed this search in 1890 with the publication of the first two volumes of *The Golden Bough*, which was the virtuoso attempt of a trained classicist to solve the seemingly insoluble Mysteries of the Grove of Nemi.

Frazer, however, only resurrected and codified the occult and esoteric lore which had already provided such a treasure trove of eclectic symbolism for Romantics such as Moore and Poe. Moreover, Frazer also pointed to the connection between consciousness and landscape, between the individual and the magical environment which he inhabits, by emphasizing the legend of the Fisher King, whose psychic health and well-being ensured the fertility of his kingdom. The wounding of the King, who is also chief priest and hierophant —what Edouard Schuré calls "The Great Initiate"—causes his kingdom to lapse into decay and decline, producing the Gothic Waste Land which, as Stephen Mooney has pointed out, is common both to Eliot's famous poem and to Poe's "The Fall of the House of Usher."[24] In the notes to *The Waste Land*, Eliot listed among the sources for his poem the "Adonis, Attis, Osiris" chapter of Frazer's *The Golden Bough*, which dealt in massive detail with the folklore of the Mystery religions, and especially with the role of the sacred marriage, which we have already discussed in relation to Poe. He also cited Jessie Weston's book on the Grail legend, *From Ritual to Romance*, as a direct inspiration for "the title, . . . the plan, and a good deal of the incidental symbolism of the poem."[25]

---

[24] Stephen L. Mooney, "Poe's Gothic Waste Land" (1962), rpt. in *The Recognition of Edgar Allan Poe*, ed. by Eric W. Carlson (Ann Arbor: Univ. of Michigan Press, 1966), pp. 278-297.

[25] T. S. Eliot, notes to *The Waste Land*, in *The Complete Poems and Plays* (New York: Harcourt, Brace, and World, 1962), p. 50.

From Ritual to Romance is a scholarly classic which attempts to prove that the Grail romances are derived from the vegetation rites of those same Mystery religions and that the main features of the Grail story—the Waste Land, the Fisher King, the Hidden Castle with its solemn Feast, and the Mysterious Feeding Vessel, the Bleeding Lance and Cup—are elements transmuted from the original monomyth of initiation ceremonies. Under this rubric, Usher, with his obscure illness and impotence, is also of course another kind of Fisher King, while the House itself becomes the Hidden Castle or sinister Chapel Perilous and its surrounding landscape of decayed and noxious vegetation is the Perilous Cemetery or Waste Land noted by Mooney. The "Mad Trist" of Sir Launcelot Canning (the title of which is reminiscent of *The Geste of Syr Gawaine*, another Grail romance mentioned by Miss Weston) continues the chivalric imagery, for the trencher or ringing brass shield that Poe's hero Ethelred must win is very like the sacred vessel of the Attis rite, which, as she points out, was both tympanum and cymbal. Weston concludes that the Grail romances are veiled accounts of Mystery initiations and she deduces that:

> The earliest version of the Grail story, represented by our Blerheris form, relates the visit of a wandering knight to one of these hidden temples; his successful passing of the test into the lower grade of Life initiation, his failure to attain to the highest degree. It matters little whether it were the record of an actual, or of a possible, experience; the casting into romantic form of an event which the story-teller knew to have happened, had, perchance, actually witnessed; or the objective recital of what he knew *might* have occurred; the essential fact is that the *mise-en-scène* of the story, the nomenclature, the march of incident, the character of the tests, correspond to what we know from independent sources of the details of this Nature Ritual. The Grail Quest was actually possible then, it is actually possible to-day, for the indication of two of our romances as to the final location of the Grail is not imagination, but the record of actual fact.[26]

Poe's narrator, too, passes, or at least beholds, the first trials of initiation like the wandering knight at the threshold of the hidden temple, but his failure to recognize the full significance of the esoteric symbolism and ritual displayed by the hierophant loses him his chance for the highest degree. Indeed, the whole ambiguous narrative technique of "The Fall of the House of Usher" is implicit in Weston's description of this earliest of the Grail romances. When we turn to Eliot's *Waste Land* (which is an attempt to write another variety of *Modern Eleusinia* by imposing an occult monomyth on the chaos of contemporary life), we find the same kind of allusions to the presence of profounder Mysteries. The Egyptian mode surfaces in the name and practice of Eliot's sleazy fortune-teller, Madame Sosostris, and in her wicked pack of cards, the Tarot deck; to Weston, as to Schuré, there was no doubt that "parallel designs and combinations" of Tarot symbolism "were to be found in the surviving decorations of Egyptian temples" (*From Ritual to Romance,* p. 78).[27] Adding to the Egyptian symbolism, Eliot also utilized Far Eastern and Oriental sources, constructing a modernist eclecticism which actually dramatized the search for meaningful archetypes in much the same

---

[26] Jessie L. Weston, *From Ritual to Romance* (1920; rpt. ed., Garden City, New York: Doubleday and Company, 1957), pp. 204-205.

[27] The name of Madame Sosostris (who may be a satirical portrait of Madame Blavatsky herself) is no doubt Eliot's reworking of "Sesostris," the legendary Egyptian king and world conqueror mentioned in Leigh Hunt's poem, "The Nile" (1818).

way that Weston and Frazer used comparative techniques in their anthropological studies, or, though Eliot would have been horrified at the suggestion, much as Madame Blavatsky had sought for the monomyth amid all the esoterica of her *Isis Unveiled*.

What remains important is the fact that, while the unifying legend of the Grail romance and its occult meaning, uncovered by Frazer and Weston, made the quest for a monomyth possible again for Eliot in 1922, it was also possible for Poe in 1839. Ultimately, Poe and Eliot have the same sources and the same concerns, for, like all modern seekers for that myth (whether literary or anthropological), they try to reverse the direction of the quest away from romance and back toward ritual, that task which Jacob Bryant defined in his subtitle of *A New System, or An Analysis of Ancient Mythology* as the attempt "to divest Tradition of Fable; and to reduce the Truth to its Original Purity." An awareness of this tradition, in turn, may force us to realize that, given its antecedents, *The Waste Land* is more truly "Gothic" in character than its first readers ever imagined. But the tradition also demonstrates that Poe, in successfully using the monomyth of initiation ritual to structure and to deepen the vital eclecticism of "The Fall of the House of Usher," was not only an adept of Gothic prestidigitation, but that he had mastered as well the most complex thaumaturgies of Romantic art.

Byron and the Metaphysic of Self-Destruction

JOHN W. EHRSTINE

The dark, rebellious Byronic hero has rarely been understood, partly because the type, as Byron developed it, is a composite and evolutionary figure, and partly because this hero has rarely been approached with the care that the demonic deserves. In Byron, wrestling with darkness is not a pose, but a poetic quest. In criticism, following that quest leads one into multiple problems, into a "Gothic labyrinthe of unknown windings," to borrow the phrasing of one of Byron's later characters. These various problems, however they may get twisted by the poet's life, usually admit of reduction to two central issues, and by extension these are the major critical issues in our understanding of Byron's poetry. The first is: Does Byron's poetry have any philosophical centrality, or does his poetic thought circle persistently in a kind of intellectual play which he himself came to call "*mobilité*"? The other abiding concern does not admit of such easy formulation, but may perhaps be stated in this way: Beyond the dark lamentation or the sharp wit of his poems, and beyond the intricacies of his biography, does Byron have any hope for man? When dealing with the darker aspect of Byron's poetry, this second concern is often phrased in alternative ways. Is Byron's Gothicism a genuine psychological and religious struggle? If so, then does his poetry arrive at a metaphysical view of hope or despair? Is his final vision positive or negative?

Though the questions are always raised, Byron's total canon is rarely taken into account in arriving at answers. What is needed is a new way to approach Byron's poetry, a way which will not exclude one or another aspect of his work. Such an approach must of course draw upon the poet's entire corpus, seeing each item as the product of the same poetic, and developing, mind.

Woven through the substantial fabric of Byron's poetic world are to be found the elements of what I wish to call his metaphysic. Byron himself uses the word "metaphysical" in such a context. When he refers, rather flippantly, to his "gay, metaphysical style," Byron seems to point to particu-

JOHN W. EHRSTINE, Professor of English at Washington State University, has written on Medieval and nineteenth- and twentieth-century literature, including *William Blake's Poetical Sketches*.

larly symbolic poems: *Lara*, Canto Third of *Childe Harold's Pilgrimage, Manfred*, and *Cain*, for example.[1] These are works in which he is able to embody more comprehensively his particular view of the human condition. Although he did not apparently think of all of his work in this way, surely all of his poems and plays were part of what he more frequently called "the march of [his] mind," and hence they may be assumed to contribute to, and participate in, certain governing poetic concerns. These in their turn form a central metaphysic, which is the substance or structure of that "metaphysical style," and which will serve as a comprehensive approach to his poetry, if we can formulate it. For the present purposes, what will emerge in particular clarity is Byron's use of Gothicism as a literary mode for the expression of poetic thought. In Byron's case, the intellectual burden of the poetry is often the relentless pursuit by an individual mind, in all its isolation, of the demonic root of evil. The point of this quest is the hope that the individual might work through, even past, the principle of evil, or the principle of The Fall.

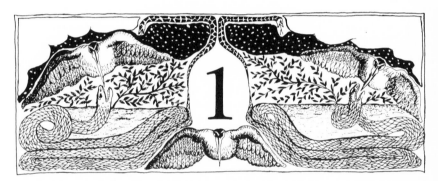

It is fair to say that Byron, as the darkest of the British Romantic poets, begins with failure. From the outset, his gaze falls on a collapsed world. It is not surprising then that some recollection of innocence is an important poetic theme. In Paradise—either the Garden of Genesis, or the innocent state into which we were born—the universe had appeared to be good. There had been unity to it, and between it and the individual. Even the early lyrics are everywhere filled with this theme, and the usual emphasis is on the loss of unity man experiences by his fall.

Consider, for example, one of the many early poems to Mary Chaworth:

Hills of Annesley, bleak and barren,
   Where my thoughtless childhood stray'd,
How the northern tempests, warring,
   Howl above thy tufted shade!

---

[1] Truman Guy Steffan, *Lord Byron's Cain* (Austin: Univ. of Texas Press, 1968), pp. 6-7, cites the relevant passages in Byron's commentary, and discusses his probable meaning. Hereafter, references to Byron will be cited in *The Works, Poetry,* ed. E. H. Coleridge (London: John Murray, 1904-1905), *Letters and Journals,* ed. Rowland Prothero (London: John Murray, 1898-1901); both are hereafter indicated in notes and text as *P* and *LJ*.

Now no more, the hours beguiling,
  Former favourite haunts I see;
Now no more my Mary smiling
  Makes ye seem a heaven to me.

(P, I, 210-211)

Ironically, the former scene of innocence is "bleak and barren," and the "northern tempests, warring" are scarcely Edenic. Even though this hyperborean landscape was warmed and unified by "my Mary smiling," the disparities admitted of synthesis partly because of the "thoughtless" child perceiving them. In any case, that world only "seem[ed] a heaven," and in retrospect that seeming Paradise was as evil as it was good. One important detail in Byron's metaphysic is embodied here: for him, the fall from unity is accompanied by the knowledge that what man thought was paradisal was actually not; the unity he felt was a hoax.

Accompanying the destruction of unity and innocence is another constant detail: the inevitable arrival of guilt, even if such guilt is only one's chagrin at having been fooled by life. More deeply, guilt is the residue of what one has lost, and the acts one has committed, however innocently, which brought about his collapse. Man then incurs guilt before he knows that it will cancel his innocence. Thus he is left, like Adam, with only the recollection of his fall.[2] More deeply still, in Byron the guilt will likely turn to self-hatred, a state in which what one is is split apart from what he would wish to be. Individual integrity is consequently shattered. These observations lead us to a cluster of motifs in Byron's poems. An insistent implication throughout is that to live in a state of disunity is to live in tyranny. Enslavement under some cosmic tyranny is man's existential fate after he falls from innocence. In this manner, both tyranny and fate are generically defined. In addition, tyranny of an analogous sort seems to be man's political inheritance. Even though man can imagine political freedom, in his fallen state he has achieved it only for moments in history.[3] Hence, individually or collectively, man's fallen existence is bifurcated into desire and reality. What is worse, neither existential nor political tyranny in human life is static. For Byron, tyranny is active, consistently producing some kind of perversion of what the human state ought to be. Tyranny is, then, a state in which *perverse* and *perverted* coalesce in meaning. Facing such a dilemma, the individual either sinks into the perversion in some way, or he acts.

The action which Byron sees tyranny producing may take many forms, but in each case the attempt is to escape entrapment by rebuilding unity, or integrity, in the individual life. The much-maligned theme of sexual love in Byron takes on new meaning when seen in this context. For example, without benefit of priest or society, Don Juan and Haidee are wed, and the reuniting of the sexes accomplishes a short-lived paradise.[4] They return to an almost prehuman, godly state of sexuality, a condition which is also glimpsed forlornly toward the end of *Manfred*.[5] Byron often conceives of a

---

[2] See *Don Juan* I, cxxvii; *P,* VI, 49.

[3] One of Byron's best poetic statements of this idea is *Childe Harold* IV, xciii-xcviii; *P,* II, 399-402.

[4] *Don Juan* II, clxxii-cciii; *P,* VI, 130-138.

[5] III, 2, 3-8; *P,* IV, 127. See also George Ridenour, *The Style of Don Juan* (New Haven: Yale Univ. Press, 1960), pp. 45-48.

similar reunification achieved by establishing a geographical haven-paradise of one sort or another. What is significant about Conrad's island in *The Corsair* is that in that little world, there is unity, and it is gained through the total separation of Conrad's island-world from the literal, perverted world with which he deals as a pirate.[6] Precisely the same situation exists with Lambro in *Don Juan*,[7] and in fact his island supplies the place where Juan and Haidee may reach their momentary union. Both of these attempts to create some lost unity—sexual love and the island paradise—are deftly brought together again in *The Bride of Abydos*. In his empassioned proposal to Zuleika, Selim conceives of their love as a metaphorical island, or microcosm, wherein he believes they may transcend the fallen world so long as they do not "disunite." He tells her,

With thee all toils are sweet, each clime hath charms;
Earth—sea alike—our world within our arms!

(11. 452-3; *P,* III, 176)

Another mode of attaining unity in a fallen world is the pursuit of knowledge, a theme visible in both *Manfred* and *Cain*. Manfred's complaint is that "The Tree of Knowledge is not that of Life," and he is left with the guilt which his efforts to know, both by head and heart, have brought him.[8] More fundamentally, Cain wants to know why guilt or evil exist in the first place.[9] Cain, in fact, demonstrates yet another action which the tyranny of his world suscitates: violence. Out of despair and rage, he blindly kills Abel. And yet, blackly enough, his act is really no different from Selim's attempt to build his own world, or from Manfred's dogged quest for spiritual peace. The characterization in *Lara* shows a kindred act of rebellion, only it is rendered in more comprehensive terms. Lara leads a peasant revolt, but that potentially noble act is motivated by near lassitude, which in turn is generated by his own past failures, and by hatred of the tyranny of his life and his society.[10] Each of these heroes is driven into action by his longing for a reunified existence in which the fragments of his political and/or personal life may be put back together.

To move a step further, all of these familiar Byronic actions—besides being attempts to regain a unified world, or a oneness of identity—are acts of rebellion, and they may be aimed either at our existential or at our political slavery. The two are rarely separable. Writing a poem is a consummate act of rebellion in Byron's terms, for it is an attempt both to escape fallen reality, and to enter an island world of art where some unity is possible.[11] We may say, then, that in Byron's metaphysic, to act against tyranny is always to rebel; moreover, rebellious acts are acts of creativity. Finally action, rebellion, and creativity are demonic, and therefore something of the dark, or Gothic, or bizarre, will be part of the literary expression.

---

[6] The exuberant song, which forms section I of Canto the First, indicates this unity; *P,* III, 227-228.

[7] *Don Juan* III, xiii-lvii; *P,* VI, 147-158.

[8] I, 1, 12; *P,* IV, 85.

[9] For example, II, 2, 279-299; *P,* V, 249-250.

[10] II, ix; *P,* III, 356-357.

[11] For example, *Childe Harold* III, lxxxi-lxxxii; *P,* II, 266-267.

However, as several recent scholars have pointed out, the various curative actions which man attempts seem to be little better than the ailments.[12] Paradoxically, all man's endeavors to get beyond the tyranny of his condition also seem to fail. Indeed, they seem to force him to his "worst—his second fall."[13] There are any number of reasons for this renewed collapse, but certainly Byron implies that the guilt we sustain with each failure is a major one. We may gain some momentary synthesis, but it remains fragile, and the very seeds of evil and discord are necessarily part of the new, humanly created unity. Therefore, the transcendence must crumble, and man must feel guilty for it. In a fine stanza of *Childe Harold* IV, Byron draws together the failure inherent in sexual love, and the terms of this passage are not only characteristic, but particularly useful to the present argument:

Few—none—find what they love or could have loved,
Though accident, blind contact, and the strong
Necessity of loving, have removed
Antipathies—but to recur, ere long,
Envenom'd with irrevocable wrong;
And Circumstance, that unspiritual god
And miscreator, makes and helps along
Our coming evils with a crutch-like rod,
Whose touch turns Hope to dust, the dust we all have trod.

(cxxv; *P, II*, 421)

In addition to the overriding irony here of man's general lucklessness, the stanza stresses that "Antipathies" may be resolved, hence unity achieved, but only to bring on new paradoxes, greater guilt, and deeper bitterness.

In the world of Byron's poems, then, a composite, or underlying metaphysical pattern emerges out of the foregoing details. In the perversity of the fallen, Gothic world of man's experience, good and evil seem always embroiled. As man acts in rebellion to regain order, he can indeed synthesize these and other opposites, but the transcendence is only momentary. He then falls again, and is reawakened more deeply to the dark tyranny of his existence. The consequent, redoubled agony seems almost to be his punishment—the sign of his guilt—for having rebelled, for having resisted the perversity (which becomes perversion) all around him.[14] It is at this point that many suspect that Byron's view is ultimately only pessimistic, and that his poetic argument loses any other kind of centrality but its despair.

And yet, a second metaphysical pattern is also operative in the poems, and it stands over against the negative estimation of Byron. The poems suggest, repeatedly and tenaciously, that there is some honor and dignity in man's struggle to recreate unity. That is, man's struggle may be noble at the same time that it is almost invariably pitiful. Moreover, in the fallen world where good and evil are relative, we may be baffled morally by a particular hero's actions. The narrative voice in the *Turkish Tales*, for example,

---

[12] See Ridenour, *The Style of Don Juan*, p. 49; Robert F. Gleckner, *Byron and the Ruins of Paradise* (Baltimore, Md.: Johns Hopkins Press, 1967), p. 179.

[13] *Childe Harold* IV, xcvii; *P, II*, 402.

[14] Paul West, *Byron and the Spoiler's Art* (New York: St. Martin's Press, 1960), p. 103, rather overstates the case for such a point when he says that Byron thought that "to strive towards a full sense of one's separate identity was apostasy."

often seems to be unable to offer a moral judgment on the action he reports.[15] To the reader, such a figure will seem Gothic because he appears to be beyond orthodox good and evil.   The idea seems to be that any given hero cannot really be labeled wrong except when he loses his human dignity by struggling weakly.[16]   Sinking below man's rightful dignity is precisely what so angered Byron about Napoleon.[17]   Conversely, even so dark and compromised a figure as Lara retains some human nobility:

And Lara sleeps not where his fathers sleep,
But where he died his grave was dug as deep;
Nor is his mortal slumber less profound,
Though priest nor bless'd nor marble deck'd the mound. . . .

(II, 1165-8; *P*, III, 308)

These two consistent patterns or principles—the struggle to regain unity, together with repeated failure: counterpointed by the possibility of human dignity—are brought together with remarkable balance and skill in Byron's use of the myth of Prometheus.   While criticism has been somewhat confusing in its analysis of Byron's Prometheanism generally,[18] the poems make it perfectly clear, even without Byron's prose comments, that the Titan served him as a dominant image.   By focusing centrally on the lyric poem, "Prometheus" (*P*, IV, 48-51), and by gathering together some of the references elsewhere to the god, the growth of Byron's metaphysic will become clearer. Byron's poetic thought expands because he has elevated the Gothicism of the *Turkish Tales* to a mythological plane, and he gains a certain detachment, as well as comprehensiveness, by this means.

Byron seems to think that, at least on the surface of the Greek myth,

---

[15] Gleckner, p. 131, suggests something of this in discussing *The Giaour* and *The Bride of Abydos*.

[16] Robert Langbaum, *The Poetry of Experience* (rpt. ed., New York: W. W. Norton, 1963), p. 85, makes the central point that the dramatic monologue leaves us in tension between sympathy and judgment.   One may add that Byron is leaning in the direction of that form, its manipulation of point of view, and its aesthetic effect.

[17] For example, *P*, III, 308, and II, 241.

[18] Ridenour, *The Style of Don Juan*, p. 86, suggests that Knight "comes closer than most" to comprehending Byron's Prometheanism.

Prometheus plainly fails. Despite his gift, which is intended to "strengthen Man with his own mind," the god is "baffled . . . from [on] high." That is, Zeus as tyrant chains Prometheus to the mountain, and because of his rebellious and guilty act, Prometheus loses the very freedom he wished to secure for man. From his act, some evil likewise accrues to human beings. Despite the nobility of the god's theft, his is still a fallen gift to a fallen world. In *Childe Harold*, for example, man must "endure" the fire, and there is a price to be paid for possessing it.[19] Specifically in *Manfred*, the "Promethean spark" of intellect or spirit dehumanizes man, rendering him unfit for other human company.[20] In any number of poems, implicitly or explicitly, man's life would simply be easier if Prometheus had let him remain merely clay.[21] Hence Prometheus' creative and rebellious act leads to deepened failure, and fulfills the first metaphysical pattern outlined above.

And yet, the second of the two patterns also clearly operates. There is something unarguably positive in Prometheus' act. Fundamentally, he is the archetypal image of a hero, and he rebels against the archetype of a tyrant. The value of the Titan's rebellion lies in the differences between his act and man's analogous rebellious endeavors. For example, Prometheus has acted sacrificially. His rebellion against tyranny is not merely selfish, but engendered by his pity for man. The beginning of the ode reads:

Titan! to whose immortal eyes
   The sufferings of mortality,
   Seen in their sad reality,
Were not as things that gods despise. . . .

(11. 1-4)

Then, too, Prometheus refuses to submit entirely to Zeus's punishment, never losing his dignity, or his "patient energy." This condition may be accounted for by his assuming full responsibility for his act: he takes upon himself his guilt, rather than crumbling beneath the weight of it. In effect, he contains within himself the paradox of freedom and entrapment, or guilt and innocence, and is able to sustain that synthesis with no reassurance from without. The difference in the poetic effect is due to the intensity of Prometheus as symbol; he possesses a quality far more powerful than merely Gothic mysteriousness. And yet, Gothic he is: his is a dark act, a "theft," and it is morally perplexing.

Another important difference in the Titan's action is his overview of the situation. Prometheus has perceived the fate both of Zeus and of man. In creating man only to enslave him, Zeus initiates tyranny, and hence disunity. He must consequently fulfill the fate of tyrants, which is eventual ruin. Prometheus foresees this consequence, of course, but will not tell Zeus. The tyrant sows discord and perversion against which others must and will react. Tyranny, after all, forces the sensitive man into some kind of rebellious action. In a specifically political context, Barbarigo expresses this idea when, in *The Two Foscari,* he tells Loredano:

---

19 For example, IV, clxiii; *P*, II, 448.

20 I, 1, 154; *P*, IV, 90.

21 For example, see *The Deformed Transformed*, I, 1, 453-481; *P*, V, 494.

> . . . [the Giunta] have gone beyond
> Even their exorbitance of power: and when
> This happens in the most contemn'd and abject
> States, stung humanity will rise to check it.
>
> (V, 146-9; *P, V, 187*)

Unhappily, "stung humanity" may only destroy this particular tyrant, making way for another.[22] But such heavy irony is simply part of the self-renewing perversion Zeus (or his Judeo-Christian equivalent, Jehovah) has established in his selfish creation of man.

Regarding the Titan's awareness of man's destiny, we are told that Prometheus is a "symbol and a sign" indicating man's "force and fate." That fate is to be in part divine (11. 45-7), but also entrapped even as Prometheus now is. Given his dual nature of spirit and clay, man's force resides in his knowledge that, like Prometheus, his spirit may oppose itself to all its woes, as an act of "firm will" (11. 53-5). This resolve by no means eliminates the "woes" or the "Torture," but man's firm will is not simply pitiful or pointless either; it may lead him to some inner, self-contained reward. That is the only victory allowed even to the god. The poem is structured so as to assert this very idea. It opens with a question—"What was thy pity's recompense?"—and works its way through to an answer: Prometheus has "concentered recompense" (1, 5; 1. 57). The repeated word is scarcely accidental.

The poem then ends with seeming enigma, insisting that the interior reward makes death a "Victory." Byron's meaning here is both metaphorical and literal. To contain paradox—that is, to take into one's self the bifurcation of the fallen world, as Prometheus does—is to die unto the self. That is the essential state of being which the Titan gains by acting sacrificially. What is more, the human metaphorical possibilities for Promethean status form a theme upon which Byron places increasing weight after 1816, that especially pivotal period in his development.[23] Notably in *Manfred,* this theme is of major significance to Byron's poetical meditations about the unavoidable guilt and selfishness of fallen man. Moreover, to be able to die literally gives man a victory that even the god Prometheus is denied: fate had refused him "even the boon to die" (1. 23). From this point of view, death may be seen as the final self-containment, the ultimate balance, of paradox. As such, death becomes not so much a consummation devoutly to be wished as a transcendent state energetically to be lived and earned. The Gothic "labyrinth" of this life, even of this cosmos, produces death, to be defeated only by making that death into metaphor. In that case, the demonic pursuit of evil is not only restated at a cosmic thematic level, but psychologized by Byron into an imaginative interior quest.

"Prometheus" fulfills the two patterns of Byron's metaphysic already discussed: his perception of tyranny drives him to action; but in turn his attempt to reestablish unity collapses, enchaining him, and adding a burden to man's existence. Yet even in chains, Prometheus retains his heroic stature. Beyond that, he introduces a third principle: by willing himself to contain paradox, the Titan creates a unity which is entirely within himself. That is to say that

---

[22] For example, see *Sardanapalus,* V, 1, 323-326; *P, V, 105.*

[23] See Ridenour, "Byron in 1816," in *From Sensibility to Romanticism,* ed. Hilles and Bloom (New York: Oxford Univ. Press, 1965), pp. 453-465; and Ward Pafford, "Byron and the Mind of Man," *Studies in Romanticism,* 1 (1962), 105-127.

he reaches unity by containing the tyranny of dualism. Hence, whatever the philosophical negativism present in Byron's poems, the 1816 lyric establishes at least the possibility of a positive, though unorthodox, victory for the individual. A Promethean victory is not without its ironies, but nothing in Byron ever is. There is but stern comfort in Byron's conclusion that the only way to synthesize any of the opposites incessantly facing man after his fall is to contain them. That synthesis is the only unity, the only release from perversion, tyranny, or fragmentation that human beings can achieve. The Byronic hero, then, is not merely Gothic, tempestuous, and guilty; especially in the later heroes we are given portraits of men who, in attempting to contain these dark and inevitable consequences of the human sojourn on earth, become selfless and sacrificial in the process.

Yet Prometheus is only one of Byron's two central images. Cain is the other, and in dealing with the Genesis story, the poet expands his metaphysic through the richer parallels he is able to draw upon in the more detailed Biblical myth. To demonstrate this expansiveness, we may add another thematic dimension in Byron's poetry.

As mentioned earlier, in Byron's metaphysic the writing of poetry is viewed as a consummate act of rebellion, an act the potency of which other acts of creativity may achieve. But we can understand this act only by viewing Byron's statements about poetry in the poems. Critics have dwelt too long on his epistolary disclaimers concerning the value of poetry, and on his cavalier attitudes toward writing.[24] For instance, Byron offers for consideration a number of serious implications in the much celebrated sixth stanza of *Childe Harold* III:

'Tis to create, and in creating live
A being more intense, that we endow
With form our fancy, gaining as we give
The life we image, even as I do now.

Here the poet is said to gain "A being more intense" from his creativity. That is, by creating, "even as I do now," the poet acquires freedom, Prome-

---

[24] It has been too easy to misinterpret many of Byron's more flippant comments on his own poetry. As examples, consider *LJ*, II, 369, 402; and IV, 86, 196-197.

theus-like, through a transcendent identity. While this freedom differs from, say, *The Corsair's* island paradise, it does so only in being entirely metaphorical or imaginative. The impetus is the same. Byron implies, however, that the poet is punished for his creativity as either Conrad or Prometheus is: at the poem's completion, as at the completion of an act, the poet must return to reality and abide its separation from his poetic, or active, existence. In *The Lament of Tasso,* Byron gives us a finely lachrymose statement of the poet's particular fall back to reality.[25] Even here in this sixth stanza, the terms for the punishment of such rebellion are implied:

What am I? Nothing: but not so art thou,
Soul of my thought! with whom I traverse earth,
Invisible but gazing, as I glow
Mix'd with thy spirit, blended with thy birth,
And feeling still with thee in my crush'd feelings' dearth.
(my italics)

When the creative act is done, the poet, while "feeling still with thee," apparently becomes visible again; that is, corporeal and fallen. As Gleckner has pointed out, a poet would be driven to incessant creativity to avoid this increasingly painful, repeatable fall.[26] In addition to this alloy in the value of creative action, the poet ironically murders his characters when a poem is completed. Witness the dismissal of Harold in Canto IV:

Ye! who have traced the Pilgrim to the scene
Which is his last, if in your memories dwell
A thought which once was his, if on ye swell
A single recollection, not in vain
He wore his sandal-shoon and scallop-shell;
    Farewell! with *him* alone may rest the pain,
If such there were—with *you,* the moral of his strain.

(clxxxvi; *P,* II, 462-3)

"Farewell! with *him* alone may rest the pain"; the line is a bit uneasy and ominous. The poet at this point appears more like Zeus or the Jehovah of *Cain,* arbitrarily creating and destroying.

Some often overlooked lines of "Prometheus" are useful at this juncture, and they are lines to which Byron clearly wanted to draw attention because they form the only spot in the ode where he constructs four consecutive rhymes. He speaks of

. . . the deaf tyranny of Fate,
The ruling principle of Hate,
Which for its pleasure doth create
The things it may annihilate. . . .

(11. 19-22)

Although the description is of Zeus, these lines easily apply to the poet who likewise creates out of "the ruling principle of Hate" (hatred of self, of fallen existence, and so forth). The hate in turn has grown out of "the deaf tyranny" of his own human fate, the entrapment he is trying to surmount.

---

25 II, 33-43.
26 *Byron and the Ruins of Paradise,* pp. 251-252.

Moreover, the poet creates—albeit inadvertently—things he does indeed annihilate. Presumably, if Harold could speak, we would find him as enraged at his creator as Cain is at Jehovah in the later play!

Byron explores this analogy further. Near the outset of the fourth canto, he offers another statement about creativity in terms which we will recognize:

> The beings of the mind are not of clay;
> Essentially immortal, they create
> And multiply in us a brighter ray
> And more beloved existence: that which Fate
> Prohibits to dull life, in this our state
> Of mortal bondage, by these spirits supplied,
> First exiles, then replaces what we hate;
> Watering the heart whose early flowers have died,
> And with fresher growth replenishing the void.
>
> (v; *P*, II, 332)

If the poet can maintain his own dignity, and thereby go on creating long enough and deeply enough, some permanent improvement accumulates. As in Canto III, his creations still possess "A being more intense," since here they "are not of clay"; they possess the invisibility of which the narrative voice had spoken. And yet, Byron goes further here because now a poet's creations conquer "our mortal bondage," the tyranny of the Gothic, fallen world. The result of this advance is stated in the crucial seventh line: the transcendent aspect of creativity "First exiles, then replaces what we hate. . . ." If that circumstance is so, the poet does not fall back into reality entirely at a poem's finish; some of the transcendent value remains, and "replaces" what he hated in reality. In that case, we may assume the poet does not simply destroy; he annihilates some of the evil of his world. In fact, he annihilates some of himself because the hatred resides within him, and emanates outward onto the already-fallen universe. Consummate self-hatred is the attribute of Satan in *The Vision of Judgment*: "And *where* he gazed, a gloom pervaded space."[27] Presumably, if the poet did not create, and hence destroy, his self-hatred, he would advance negatively toward Satan's condition, projecting his gloom onto an indeed gloomy universe. *Lara* is very nearly an example of this process, and in some ways *The Prisoner of Chillon* another.

Because the speaking voice of *Childe Harold* is actively creating, however, Byron can carry his metaphysical-aesthetic speculation one step further in Canto IV. Following the famous stanzas on his curse of forgiveness (cxxxii-cxxxv), a remarkable transformation occurs at cxxxviii:

> The seal is set.—Now welcome, thou dread power!
> Nameless, yet thus omnipotent, which here
> Walk'st in the shadow of the midnight hour
> With a deep awe, yet all distinct from fear;
> Thy haunts are ever where the dead walls rear
> Their ivy mantles, and the solemn scene
> Derives from thee a sense so deep and clear
> That we become a part of what has been,
> And grow unto the spot, all-seeing but unseen.
>
> (*P*, II, 432)

---

[27] Stanza xxiv; *P*, IV, 495.

Not only does he welcome the "dread power," associated with the monuments of the dead and the past which surround him, but he describes this new state of being as "all-seeing but unseen." The narrative voice of the poem has become permanently invisible as the poet of Canto III had been only during the act of creation. The symbolism and logic here are dazzling. If out of hatred we create only to annihilate, and if the creativity of the mind "First exiles, then replaces" what we hate, then those who become truly poets destroy themselves through total imaginative replacement. This desire is to become invisible, "all-seeing but unseen," and also to gain "concentered recompense," the unity and selflessness of "Prometheus." If we take Coleridge's view for a moment, and assume that art contains opposites in synthesis, then by dying unto the self, both Prometheus and the speaker of *Childe Harold* become art itself in that they each become the action they take.[28] They contain paradox, and die metaphorically. The enigmatic victory of death in "Prometheus" now becomes more clearly an imaginative process. Byron gives us a later, more lengthy account of this state of being in *The Prophecy of Dante*, the point of which is that one may be a poet without writing a line; such a one becomes "the new Prometheus of the men,/ Bestowing fire from heaven. . . ."[29] These are poets of action, who entirely replace themselves by becoming one with the action they take. The active pursuit of the evil of our fallen state is at this point no longer merely demonic, even though it may, by an inversion of irony, bear that appearance, as it does in *Cain*. In the case of "Prometheus," dying unto self, reaching "concentered recompense," is more than Zeus can achieve, since he is always the tyrant and hence the architect of his inevitable ruin. As one turns to *Cain*, it appears that it may be more than Jehovah can do, too.

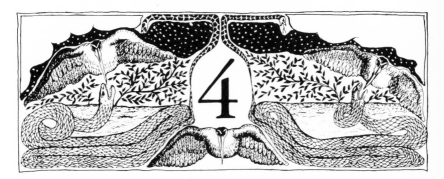

Attention may now be more cogently turned to Byron's other central mythic figure, Cain. To my mind, the most striking aspect of Byron's metaphysic in *Cain* is that Jehovah looks astonishingly like the poet of *Childe Harold* III and IV. Byron is not merely forcing the geological theories of Cuvier, and

---

[28] My point is slightly different from Wilson Knight's insistence that Byron's life and poetry coalesce into "poetry incarnate"; see especially *Lord Byron: Christian Virtues* (London: Routledge, 1952), Chapters III and IV *passim*.

[29] IV, 14-15; *P*, IV, 265.

his fondness for the figure of Cain, to serve obtuse and heretical purpose; but he is putting his material to poetic use, and he again expands his metaphysic —and its Gothic demonic elements—to more sustained mythic and cosmological dimensions. Yet the interior, psychological expansion is likewise brilliantly maintained since Lucifer clearly materializes from Cain's imagination, and the flight in space (Act II) is a journey within Cain's own mind. In this present context, two of Lucifer's speeches to Cain are particularly germane:

> But let [God]
> Sit on his vast and solitary throne,
> Creating worlds, to make eternity
> Less burthensome to his immense existence
> And unparticipated solitude; . . .
>   At least we sympathise—
> And, suffering in concert, make our pangs
> Innumerable more endurable,
> By the unbounded sympathy of all
> With all! But *He*! so wretched in his height,
> So restless in his wretchedness, must still
> Create, and re-create——

(I, 1, 147-63; P, V, 218-9)

And again, as Cain wonders why a previous world has fallen:

> By a most crushing and inexorable
> Destruction and disorder of the elements,
> Which struck a world to chaos, as a chaos
> Subsiding has struck out a world: such things
> Though rare in time, are frequent in eternity.

(II, 2, 80-4; P, V, 243)

From both speeches, it would appear that God creates worlds only to annihilate them when He is done, and His purpose (His "ruling principle of Hate") is to ameliorate His loneliness. He is also called "the Invisible" within the play. Since the poet was "Invisible but gazing" in the act of creation in *Childe Harold*, it may be deduced that God, at least from man's point of view, is as selfish as the poet in creating. He, too, is trying to gain the state of invisibility. It is to Lucifer's advantage, of course, to push this Jehovah-conception of deity as hard as he can, for he must encourage Cain's propensity to see Jehovah (whom Cain tellingly distinguishes [III, 1, 248] as "God in Heaven, Jehovah on Earth") operating this way.

If Jehovah functions as the poet does, then eventually one could assume that He would also die into existence, as one critic has recently hinted at,[30] and become fully God. He must create His poems to restore unity and entirety that has been lost. Then Jehovah also poetically "replaces" what He hates, and there would seem to be some progress toward an ultimate reunion; He would eventually become what He crafts, or would become the action He takes. However, until some abiding and transcendent unity is achieved, until Jehovah becomes God, He is driven to "Create, and re-create" endlessly. With the blackest of irony, Byron suggests that Jehovah uses man, even as the poet uses Childe Harold, or Selim uses Zuleika in *The Bride of Abydos*.

---

[30] Jerome McGann, *Fiery Dust* (Chicago: Univ. of Chicago Press, 1968), p. 269.

Byron leaves some ambivalence as to Jehovah's progress, however. Apocalypse could implicitly arrive when Jehovah dies unto Himself, contains all paradox (comprehended by Himself and Lucifer, or spirit and flesh), and becomes God. On the other hand, Jehovah might be like Zeus, an unregenerate tyrant whose arbitrary whimsy man must endure till He falls. Whether some searing Romantic Irony operates here or not,[31] the world Cain must deal with is filled with existential and political tyranny. Facing the injustice of life, he is driven to act. Lucifer serves to make him fully aware of the extent of the fall of man and the universe, and in rage Cain rebels. Byron borders on savagery here as Cain's act is Gothicism carried far toward stark realism. And yet the grimly absurd murder of Abel is a creative, poetic act in which Cain takes another step toward invisibility, toward the annihilation of self, and toward the containing of paradox. What he will have to realize is that killing Abel in no way annihilates what he hates. In fact, he says he does not hate Abel. Byron seems to imply that if Cain can take on himself his own guilt, he, too, may become a "new Prometheus," possessing "concentered recompense." But we are left not knowing if he can bear so staggering a fate.

After tracing these implications in Byron's metaphysic, it is impossible, I think, to say that his poetic view is either positive or negative. It is both. His Gothic pursuit of the demonic finally passes through a straightened place, and metaphorizes death. The same moral vertigo exists in one's reaction to *Cain* as in Dante's *Inferno*, when, suddenly, climbing down Satan's thigh becomes an ascent toward a positive pole. Byron's terms are different, being less orthodox: our condition is negative because it is tyrannous, which is to say fallen and labyrinthine; yet our struggle against those things engendered by tyranny—perversion, disunity, fragmentation—may move us toward human dignity, and toward a reunified self. That struggle Byron saw as potentially positive, if only for the individual. More importantly, to contain this paradox in synthesis constitutes—and defines—freedom in Byron's poems. The Romantic concept of self, oriented, as it generally is, toward the psychology of the individual imagination, receives particularly modern stress in Byron.

---

[31] For an enlightening discussion of this elusive term, see Chapter 2 of G. R. Thompson's *Poe's Fiction: Romantic Irony in the Gothic Tales* (Madison: Univ. of Wisconsin Press, 1973).

The idea is not that the Byronic mind becomes the center of the universe, as Hazlitt rather peevishly quipped,[32] but that the only integrity, the only unity, Byron thinks one may attain in the universe is within his own mind. If he gains it, the individual gains the status of art; his humanness becomes as invisible (as to its mode of being) and as durable as poetry itself. In fact, he dies into his poems, and though this act, this metaphysical self-destruction, will appear to be demonic, it is finally no more Satanic than Paul's saying, "It is no longer I that lives, but Christ in me."

It is clear that Byron took some time arriving at the metaphysical awareness he presents in "Prometheus." This particular lyric poem and *Manfred* and *Childe Harold* III and IV were, in my view, extremely important poems for him to write, all being axial in related ways. And indeed he had come very close to a resolution in *Parisina*, the last of the *Turkish Tales*. The hero of that poem, Hugo, is the first Byronic hero to contain paradox successfully. He is as much sinned against as sinning, and yet Hugo accepts, without bitterness or recrimination, his own guilt. He dies with "unshackled" eyes (*P*, III, 523). The crucial difference between Hugo and Manfred is that the latter, while also taking on his own guilt, does so symbolically; he is aware of the dimension of what he is doing, and that his act is emblematic of what all men must do if they have the strength. His quest is subsequently not merely for himself. Once having arrived at the metaphysic of self-destruction, Byron developed the idea in a number of ways. Morse Peckham has pointed out that the great difference between Manfred and Don Juan is that the latter knows that guilt lies with the "condition of things," not with himself.[33] Without denying the point, one may say that Manfred achieves a paradoxically similar innocence by taking guilt and responsibility upon himself. Juan is comic, Manfred tragic. For all its greatness, *Don Juan* is not a work in which Byron fully realized his metaphysic. Rather, it is especially in the plays, following Manfred's tragedy of perception, that the idea of "concentered recompense" receives its fullest and clearest statement.

---

[32] *The Spirit of the Age,* in *The Complete Works,* ed. P. B. Howe (rpt. ed., New York: AMS Press, 1967), XI, 71. Hazlitt also admitted his peevishness (XI, 77).

[33] *Beyond the Tragic Vision* (New York: George Braziller, 1962), p. 106.

Exuberant Gloom, Existential Agony, and Heroic Despair: Three Varieties of Negative Romanticism

ROBERT D. HUME

This is a speculative essay. Critics can agree hardly at all on what "Romanticism" means, and consequently a good many relevant works which fail to fit that .vague rubric satisfactorily are dubbed Gothic, or anti-Romantic, or simply consigned to limbo. My aim here is to suggest some distinctions among the various sorts of "Dark Romantic" writing. I am far from wanting to categorize, or to construct rigid pigeonholes. Rather, I want to offer an experimental construct designed to clarify the great differences in character and impact among the works of a number of writers—particularly Beckford, Byron, Lewis, Mary Shelley, and Maturin.

Necessarily, we begin with terminology, for there are as many definitions of Romanticism as critics willing to propound them. One can only beg indulgence, explain one's choice, and disavow any claim to exclusive truth. Post-Lovejoy, a critic either suits himself, or like Wellek, goes in search of a crucial element common to many otherwise-disparate writers. And, in fact, Wellek's notion of a missing link turns out to be quite serviceable. After a broad survey, he concluded that belief in "organicism" was the key: for the moment, never mind what that means. Negative Romanticism (*not* meaning disbelief in organicism) is a term I take, of course, from Morse Peckham's well-known development of Wellek's view. In essence Peckham argues that Romanticism can be defined as the revolt of the European mind against a static-mechanical concept of the world, and the rebel's subsequent acceptance of belief in a world of dynamic organicism. Negative Romanticism is the term Peckham proposes to describe the outlook of those who have rebelled against static mechanism but not yet arrived at faith in organicism.[1]

ROBERT D. HUME, Associate Professor of English at Cornell University, has published widely on Restoration, eighteenth-, and nineteenth-century literature. His most recent book is *The Development of English Drama in the Seventeenth Century.*

[1] René Wellek, "The Concept of 'Romanticism' in Literary History," *CL*, 1 (1949), 1-23, 147-172; Morse Peckham, "Toward a Theory of Romanticism," *PMLA*, 66 (1951), 5-23. Throughout this essay, I shall use the term "Negative Romanticism" to apply specifically to writers in the 1780-1830 period, "Dark Romanticism" more broadly.

But why is this approach significant or helpful? The aim is to find common ground among many writers, and since their products are so varied and contradictory, the critic is forced to look to genesis, to the attitudes, outlooks, and aims of the writers themselves. A considerable measure of truth resides in an embarrassingly hoary cliché: with the Great Chain of Being in disrepair and revealed religion no longer offering a satisfactory explanation for man's puzzles and the state of society, writers are left to make sense of a barren and alien world. And in truth an astonishing number of the writers in the "Romantic" period seem to be engaged in a quest for sense of place and identity—a point well made by Northrop Frye.[2] This quest, the central pattern of Romantic writing, takes a form described by Peckham as secular conversion. *The Rime of the Ancient Mariner, The Prelude*, and *Sartor Resartus* in particular he analyzes as showing a movement from a Negative Romantic state of doubt, despair, personal and religious isolation, to a "center of indifference," to a triumphant acceptance of organicism, and hence to a satisfactory understanding of man's place in the scheme of things. So viewed, a great deal of writing can be tidily organized: the scheme is indubitably handy. *Childe Harold* and *Manfred* give us the misery of the man who has not yet seen into the life of things; *Don Juan* presents the passive hero at the center of indifference; the "Intimations" Ode and the *Rime* are triumphant assertions of the text, "For every thing that lives is Holy," as Blake puts it. (I am embroidering freely on Peckham here, so not all blame should attach to him.) Romantic writing, so viewed, is an expression of acute need for emotional, religious, and sometimes metaphysical certitude, and in its heights celebrates attainment of such assurance.

Of course, whether the conversion works in any lasting way may be questioned. D. G. James, employing an entirely different but not incompatible construct, argues that the Romantics achieve their heights by placing impossible demands for certitude on creative imagination—and finding the results unsatisfactory or ultimately insubstantial, they collapse back in despair, turning to the church (Wordsworth and Coleridge) or "science" (Arnold) for their security.[3] Keats' *Hyperion* poems are a quintessential example of a desperate struggle to overcome the sensed limitations of imagination in the face of an overwhelming desire to find certitude with it. For my purposes, this success or failure is neither here nor there. The Romantic quest may well, as James says, lead to failure and despair. But the literary expressions of the quest are generally posited on a fundamental optimism about the result. Whatever the pains of the present (and they may be considerable), the Romantic poet hopes to find clarity and solutions to the problems and discontents which oppress him. Paradise Lost themes are extremely common, as in Wordsworth's childhood state, Blake's struggles to regain Eden, Shelley's platonism, Byron's laments amidst the ruins of paradise. But as a rule, the stronger the belief in the paradise, the stronger the hope that it can be regained. *The Triumph of Life, The Prelude, Sartor*, and *Jerusalem* all present a fulfillment of the quest which seems satisfactory, at least temporarily. Even *Dejection: An Ode* is able to bring the poet to the heights. When a Roman-

---

[2] *A Study of English Romanticism* (New York: Random House, 1968), Chapter 1.

[3] *Scepticism and Poetry* (London: Allen and Unwin, 1937); *Matthew Arnold and the Decline of English Romanticism* (Oxford: Clarendon Press, 1961).

tic Quest poem presses too hard, and examines its own grounds too curiously, it breaks off in dismay, as the *Hyperion* poems do.

I take it that the central impulse behind most of what we call Romantic writing stems from a profound discontent with inherited religion and world views, and the social and philosophical condition of man. A revolt against the limitations and uncertainties of the human condition combines with political-social consciousness to produce a drive to regain paradise—whether through Shelley's socialism, Blake's imagination, Coleridge's philosophy, or Keats' mythology. Common to all these men is a drive for special understanding, a determination to achieve more than the ordinary human view of the world. Wordsworth's craving to see into the life of things, Blake's indifference to corporeal vision, and Coleridge's inability to accept Kant's arguments for the radical limits of the powers of reason and imagination are all instances of profound dissatisfaction with the ordinary, limited, mechanical views of man's place in the world. The resulting quest can be thrilling and noble; it can also be completely disastrous. In James' view, the Romantics one and all are overreachers, striving for the unreachable and necessarily falling back into personal crisis. Nonetheless the great Romantic poems mostly express the hope of achievement, and to travel hopefully can seem quite fine to both author and reader.

Many works springing from the Romantic genesis, however, express not hope but bafflement, confusion, and despair. In *Vathek, Frankenstein, Moby-Dick,* and *Manfred,* for example, we find even more explicit presentation of the Romantic themes: the drive to attain special knowledge and understanding, determination to "break through the mask," striving for more than ordinary human power. Like Romantic writing, these works seem to spring from profound discontent with man's condition. By this formulation, the Romantic group strives hopefully for solutions, seeking an understanding of man's place in the scheme of things. The other group, unable to travel hopefully, thrashes out its discontents in other fashions, posing paradoxes, dwelling on the writer's pain. Many of the resulting works are termed Gothic. I am avoiding that term here for two reasons: I have used it elsewhere in a more restricted sense,[4] and I wish to avoid its connotations—hence my borrowing of Negative Romanticism. The writers who display this outlook are possessed by the Romantic discontents, but entirely lack the Romantic faith in man's ability to transcend his condition or transform it, practically or imaginatively. The result is an obvious tendency to despair and misery, and often to a perverse fascination with the power of blackness.

The reactions to Romantic discontent vary greatly, running from triumphant affirmation of organicism in the great poems to the bitter despair of *Melmoth the Wanderer.* To break up this spectrum of responses into Romantic/Negative Romantic (or to apply my own Gothic/Romantic formulation) can be convenient analytically, but is undoubtedly an oversimplification. Even so, the distinction between hope and struggle for a "breakthrough," versus an expression of bafflement at its inaccessibility, is real enough. The vision of the man trapped in such bafflement will be profoundly pessimistic, the reverse of Romantic optimism. And the literary results—Dark Romantic

---

4 "Gothic versus Romantic: A Revaluation of the Gothic Novel," *PMLA,* 84 (1969), 282-290; cf. subsequent controversy with Robert Platzner, *PMLA,* 86 (1971), 266-274.

writing—will consist largely of the exploration of dilemma, ugliness, and evil, and often the expression of despair and exploration of perversion. But just as Wordsworth is not Blake, and Coleridge not Keats, so we find vast differences among the Dark Romantic writers. My aim here is to identify three basic varieties of the Dark Romantic position. Other sets of distinctions could be formulated, but I think this one useful. Basically, it is an elaboration suggested by the Wellek-Peckham hypotheses. The Romantic is defined by profound discontent leading to secular conversion and faith in organicism. But where the incipient Romantic fails to achieve the conversion and is left trapped in his predicament, we have the Faustian crisis.

Northrop Frye remarks that Prometheus can conveniently stand as the central Romantic figure. Indeed the unbinding of Prometheus, the expanding of his knowledge and consciousness to encompass the greater gnosis, stands perfectly for the archetypal Romantic endeavor. Blake, Wordsworth, Coleridge, and Keats all struggle to arrive at such gnosis. But to the Dark Romantic, the non-believer to whom gnosis seems a complete impossibility, Prometheus is nothing better than a bitter mockery. Indeed *Frankenstein* (subtitled *The Modern Prometheus*) is an explicit rebuttal of the Prometheus myth: Mary Shelley takes the Promethean ambition, lets it overvault itself, and brings out of it only desolation, death, and despair.

For the Dark Romantic, Faust makes a more plausible archetypal figure. Dissatisfied with all human knowledge and learning, painfully isolated, and feeling himself cut off from Nature (Goethe, 11. 454-59), Faust's discontents drive him to seek a breakthrough to knowledge at any price and involve him deeply in evil. His restless, tormenting dissatisfaction makes him demand what he believes cannot be fulfilled. The terms of the pact Goethe concocts are explicit in this respect: Faust says that if ever once his lofty aspirations are satisfied, however briefly, Mephistopheles wins (11. 1671-1706). In essence, he bets that the Promethean gnosis does not exist, or is too paltry to satisfy him. The essence of the Faust figure is titanic, tormenting aspirations for knowledge and power, agonizing frustration, and finally adoption of unholy means. Attitudes toward the protagonist can vary drastically. Marlowe's form of the story moves to Faust's damnation; Goethe's to his ultimate salvation. Faust can be punished for his presumption or rewarded for his temerity. One can glory in his enterprise or castigate its folly. Almost any form of the story will seem ambivalent to a degree. This variety proves useful if one wants to take Faust as an archetype for some rather diverse Dark Romantic works.

The pattern of the traditional Faust story is strikingly recurrent in Dark Romantic writing. The discontent theme is a key initial element: the protagonist is driven to evil, cannot or will not repent, and is destroyed. This basic form of the myth we will find essentially full blown in *Vathek, The Monk, Frankenstein, Melmoth the Wanderer, Moby-Dick*, and Thomas Mann's *Doktor Faustus*. Of course, the author may choose to concentrate on only one part of the whole. *Werther* is an emotional bath in the cheap and melodramatic forms of Romantic discontent; de Sade finds that evil is the rule of nature, and proceeds to wallow in it; in *Manfred* Byron gives us plenty of discontent and fair hints of evil, but concentrates on the state of the protagonist just prior to his destruction. A work can spring from the Faustian genesis without reproducing the whole of the story.

Presentations of the Faust pattern can vary drastically also in seriousness. Here we move toward my main point. The works I have been referring to range from heroic tragedy (*Melmoth* and Mann's *Faustus*) down to the near-burlesque (*Vathek*). Starting—or so I am asserting—from the same sort of genesis, and employing the same archetypal pattern, these authors are coming out with radically different results: plainly the impact of these works will be widely divergent in kind, and it is up to us to sort out the various types of Negative Romanticism represented here.

Vathek is a distinctly puzzling work. Its influence has been observed in Keats, Benjamin Disraeli, Hawthorne, and Meredith; Byron, Poe, Mallarmé, and Swinburne expressed enthusiasm for it; the work is popular with undergraduates today. And yet withal the critic has a devil of a time explaining just what the thing is, or what should be made of it.[5] Certainly the work is an Oriental tale replete with quasi-scholarship and elaborate footnotes. Its place in that tradition is both undeniable and rather unhelpful, since the basic character of the work is not to be explained with reference to other examples of the form. *Vathek* is often treated as a Gothic novel on the grounds that it exploits horror and magic machinery in *Schauer-Romantik* fashion. The connection is genuine, yet I must agree with the work's recent editor that *Vathek* is not centrally of the Gothic type. Its horrors reach the point of burlesque, and its continual return to a detached and even comic tone set it apart. But if the type remains a problem, the meaning of the work—if any—is a real teaser. Professor Parreaux, the leading Beckford scholar, proposes a grandiose reading in terms of social history at the time of the Industrial Revolution, making *Vathek* into an aristocratic manifesto against bourgeois morality. This interpretation is exceedingly ingenious, but like Mr. Lonsdale, I cannot accept it. More simply, one is tempted to indulge in biographical psychologizing. Few pre-twentieth-century novels display their author's psychology so nakedly. Anyone

---

[5] *Vathek* was written in French in 1782 (when Beckford was 21); it was first published in Samuel Henley's English translation in 1786 (reissued in 1809); differing French versions appeared in 1786, 1787, and 1815. References here are to the text of the third English edition (1816), which represents Beckford's correction of Henley's translation. This text is reprinted in Roger Lonsdale's excellent Oxford English Novels edition (Oxford, 1970), from which page numbers are given.

knowing some basic facts—about Beckford's famous coming of age party at Fonthill in 1781, his relations with his mother, his sexual involvement with his cousin's wife, and the homosexual scandal over the thirteen-year-old William Courtenay—will have trouble not finding these matters spread all over *Vathek*. Indeed, they clearly are. But if we are to consider the work anything more than an overblown, adolescent, psycho-sexual fantasy, we will have to get away from the purely biographical reading. Lonsdale throws down the gauntlet, remarking that the "difficulty of attaching any clear meaning or satiric purpose to *Vathek*" tends "to force its readers back on the author himself for enlightenment." I accept the challenge: in my opinion *Vathek* represents an important permutation of the Negative Romantic position, and I think it makes a perfectly comprehensible statement without extrinsic biographical reference to the author.

Taken in its bare structural terms, *Vathek* is simply a variation of the Faust legend. Vathek, "ninth Caliph of the race of the Abassides," possesses insatiable sensual appetites and a burning desire "to know every thing; even sciences that did not exist" (p. 3). He proceeds to construct a gigantic tower, driven by "the insolent curiosity of penetrating the secrets of heaven." Here on page four we have the overreacher theme full blown. Ascending the tower, Vathek is first enraptured by the grandeur and height he has attained—and then utterly cast down by an "unwelcome perception of his littleness" when he sees the stars as high above him as before (p. 4). Like Faust, Vathek is at first proud of his attainments; then made utterly contemptuous of them. For a while he suffers a Faustian dejection, but insatiable curiosity drives him on, despite warnings: "Woe to the rash mortal who seeks to know that of which he should remain ignorant; and to undertake that which surpasseth his power!" (p. 11). Naturally Vathek gets an offer of a Faustian pact, made by the Giaour: "Wouldest thou devote thyself to me? adore the terrestrial influences, and abjure Mahomet? On these conditions I will bring thee to the Palace of Subterranean Fire . . . [where] Soliman Ben Daoud reposes, surrounded by the talismans that control the world" (p. 22). The remaining five sixths of the story is set up as a kind of pilgrimage to the Dark Mountain. Along the way Beckford includes a fine parody of the Gretchen episode. Violating the laws of hospitality, Vathek seduces and carries off the daughter of a virtuous old Emir—the joke being that Nouronihar is entirely willing and every bit as eager to sell out to the powers of darkness as Vathek is himself. Just before the final scene of damnation, Beckford includes a powerful episode in which Vathek is offered the possibility of grace. This scene seldom attracts comment, but it has a good deal of serious impact. Paralleling Marlowe's form of the story, good Genii intercede with Mahomet and make one last effort to save Vathek. One, in the form of a shepherd, succeeds in shocking Vathek and Nouronihar into temporary fear and contrition. He warns them that they must abandon all impious ambitions, for "this moment is the last of grace allowed thee." But as with Faust, Vathek's pride is his damnation. "Vathek . . . was at the point of prostrating himself . . . but, his pride prevailing, he audaciously lifted his head, and glancing at him one of his terrible looks, said: 'Whoever thou art, withhold thy useless admonitions: thou wouldst either delude me, or art thyself deceived. If what I have done be so criminal, as thou pretendest, there remains not for me a moment of grace. I have traversed a sea of blood, to acquire a power, which will make thy equals tremble: deem not that I shall retire, when in view of the port. . . . It matters not where it may end'" (pp. 103-105).

Damnation through despairing pride is central to Marlowe's *Dr. Faustus*, *Manfred*, *Melmoth*, *Moby-Dick*, and other major Dark Romantic works. The final section of *Vathek*, the vision of damnation, attains a stark sublimity of genuine tragic impact and power. Eblis, a revamped Satan from *Paradise Lost*, presides in "pride and despair" over a world in which "insatiable as your curiosity may be, shall you find sufficient objects to gratify it" (p. 111). The damned are there, we learn, because their "curiosity . . . could not be restrained by sublunary things" (p. 113) and they sought "impious knowledge" (p. 117). The final page provides a highly explicit summation and moral. "Such was, and such should be, the punishment of unrestrained passions and atrocious deeds! Such shall be, the chastisement of that blind curiosity, which would transgress those bounds the wisdom of the Creator has prescribed to human knowledge; and such the dreadful disappointment of that restless ambition, which, aiming at discoveries reserved for beings of a supernatural order, perceives not, through its infatuated pride, that the condition of man upon earth is to be—humble and ignorant" (p. 120). Thus Beckford quite bluntly preaches the doctrine of man's necessary limitation and ignorance. If there were not another side to the work, *Vathek* would simply be a reworking of the Faust story with an odd setting.[6]

Two major features of *Vathek*, however, change its whole character. One is its riotous energy, obvious fascination with the protagonist's crimes, and burlesque exaggerations. The other is Beckford's steady stream of flippancies and snide remarks. Consider the latter first. On page one, we are told that when the mighty Vathek was angry, "one of his eyes became so terrible, that no person could bear to behold it; and the wretch upon whom it was fixed, instantly fell backward, and sometimes expired." Beckford promptly adds a suave, detached comment: "For fear, however, of depopulating his dominions and making his palace desolate, he but rarely gave way to his anger." This sort of deflation is one of the principal features of Beckford's descriptions. Some examples. A prisoner escapes during the night, killing his guards. Vathek, "in the paroxism of his passion . . . fell furiously on the poor carcases"—now Beckford drops the trap—"and kicked them till evening without intermission" (p. 7). Vathek has sacrificed fifty beautiful young boys; seeing his master threatened with violence by the parents—who are annoyed—Vathek's Vizier begs the court eunuchs to rescue their master, whereupon we are told, "Bababalouk and his fraternity, felicitating each other in a low voice on their having been spared the cares as well as the honor of paternity, obeyed the mandate" (p. 28). Eating some very welcome fruit provided by pious dwarfs, Vathek repents his disrespect to Mahomet: "as he continued to eat, his piety increased; and in the same breath, he recited his prayers and called for the Koran and sugar" (p. 52)—shades of Bibles and Billets-doux. When Vathek discovers that Nouronihar is still alive (her father has pulled the *Romeo and Juliet* drug trick), they have a rapturous reunion. However, "at the mention of the subterranean palace, the Caliph suspended

---

[6] Lonsdale (xix-xxi) makes the interesting point that the original reviewers took the final "moral" at face value. The only one who complained did so on the grounds that indolence and childish innocence should not be preferred to the pursuit of knowledge.

his caresses"—one sees Beckford's crack coming—"(which had indeed proceeded pretty far)" (p. 84). A bit later the happy couple pause to frolic in a flowery meadow, are discommoded by "the bees, who were staunch Musselmans," and considering it "their duty to revenge the insult to their dear masters," "assembled so zealously to do it with good effect, that the Caliph and Nouronihar were glad to find their tents prepared to receive them" (p. 101). The cumulative effect of these deadpan comments is devastating. Had Beckford been Shakespeare, he would have had Lear stop on the heath to deliver a complaint about the quality of London Fog raincoats.

This exuberance of style is merely one part of an overall case of tearing high spirits. The whole tale goes by in a flash, proceeding in a headlong rush without textual divisions from beginning to end. The very fast pace and almost kaleidoscopic rapidity with which horrors and calamities flash by greatly lighten the impact of the story. The very verve and energy of the narration belie the content. Some of the episodes are plain wild farce— for example, that involving the mysterious stranger who rolls himself into a ball, passes out of the city, and vanishes into a chasm (pp. 18-20). The scene in which fifty boys are thrown into an abyss as a sacrifice is presented so coolly that the monstrousness of the deed scarcely strikes us—and we later learn that Beckford has had them rescued in midair by a good Genius anyway (p. 97). Or at the end of the scene in which Vathek desecrates the besom, Beckford's bland exaggeration removes all seriousness: "Bababalouk did all in his power to console the ambassadors; but the two most infirm expired on the spot: the rest were carried to their beds, from whence, being heart-broken with sorrow and shame, they never arose" (p. 41).

Many of the most elaborately overblown horrors are provided by Vathek's mother, Carathis. Her ambition is to "enjoy some intercourse with the infernal powers" (p. 31), and in a mysterious tower she keeps "materials for the advancement of science" (p. 37)—mummies, "the oil of the most venomous serpents; rhinoceros' horns . . . together with a thousand other horrible rarities." Helped by her assistants—fifty female negro mutes blind in the right eye—she strangles a good number of Vathek's most faithful subjects in order to add them to a sacrifice they had interrupted: "the fumes of the mummies, at once overpowered their senses. It was a pity! for they beheld not the agreeable smile, with which the mutes and negresses adjusted the cord to their necks: these amiable personages rejoiced, however, no less at the scene. Never before had the ceremony of strangling been performed with so much facility" (pp. 34-35). Right at the end, Carathis explains that she arranged her affairs before descending to the dark city. "Availing myself . . . of the few moments allowed me, I set fire to the tower, and consumed in it the mutes, negresses, and serpents, which have rendered me so much good service: nor should I have been less kind to Marakanabad, had he not prevented me, by deserting at last to thy brother. As for Bababalouk . . . I undoubtedly would have put him to the torture; but being in a hurry, I only hung him, after having decoyed him in a snare, with thy wives: whom I buried alive by the help of my negresses; who thus spent their last moments greatly to their satisfaction" (p. 117).

One is left to ask what we can make of all this. A potentially grandiose and tragic story of existential discontent and the pursuit of forbidden knowledge is told in very disconcerting fashion. Beckford's obvious glee in recounting horrors and crimes rings oddly against the imaginative power with which he presents Vathek's boredom, impious quest, and pride. Sadistic sexual fantasies (for example, the sacrifice of the boys) are mingled with ironic ones: "These vigilant guards [eunuchs], having remarked certain cages of the ladies swagging somewhat awry, and discovered that a few adventurous gallants had contrived to get in, soon dislodged the enraptured culprits and consigned them, with good commendations, to the surgeons of the serail" (p. 43). Homosexual passion appears prominently, especially in the extended descriptions of the beautiful young Gulchenrouz. Homosexuality, recurrent sacrifice fantasy, and sadism all help lend the work a malaise that its tearing high spirits and comic asides cannot wholly remove. Lonsdale finds the tone distractingly unstable and the "point" frustratingly ambiguous. He is right in one sense at least: as a literary result, an independent entity and work of art, *Vathek* seems awkwardly contradictory. Probably there is a good deal of truth in Lonsdale's conservative summation: "Perhaps no more definite meaning should be sought for in *Vathek* than is suggested by its role as a vehicle for the imaginative projection of private fantasy and emotional turmoil, which the obtrusive comic tone and polished style essay to keep under some kind of control" (p. xxviii).

Personally, granting the artistic shortcomings, I am prepared to value *Vathek* rather higher. What we find in it, I think, is an existential crisis defused by comic exaggeration. Perhaps one will say that the work is insufficiently "serious" to support such a reading. But that is my point: the potentially serious is here made light. The author obviously has a powerful imaginative empathy with Vathek's Faustian discontent, and this feeling encourages indulgence in palliatives, especially sexual fantasy. But here neither the discontent nor the fantasy is fully indulged. In the world of de Sade, or *Frankenstein*, or at times in *The Monk*, we are directly and morbidly fascinated with evil. In *Vathek* a comic perspective is maintained: a significant residue of pessimism and unhappiness remains, but the author's exuberant energy and humor vastly temper the impact of the story. *Vathek* starts from the Negative Romantic crisis and encompasses a Faustian quest which ends in a fairly impressive tragedy and moral, but the author's view of his subject deflates the tale with burlesque exaggeration. The result is a dark-tinged but high-spirited comedy.

Chameleon Byron has proved the bane and despair of Romantic categorizers. Peckham develops his notion of Negative Romanticism largely as a strategy for locking Byron into some kind of comprehensible position vis-à-vis the rest of the Big Five. Byron's refusal to play Wordsworth, or even Shelley, forces the critics to look for ways to reconcile him to his criticism-ordained group. All this is quite unnecessary. Definitions of Romanticism, whether language, myth, philosophy, biography, or imagination oriented, will apply poorly to Byron. The problem lies in attention to literary results: what Byron produces is markedly distinct. Genesis is another matter. In the past thirty years critics have been so shy of biography and the intentional fallacy, so determined to deal with texts-in-themselves, that author-oriented criticism has become downright disreputable in some quarters. In light of the crude kinds of biographical criticism once popular, one cannot regret this reaction, but given the extent to which Romantic writers delve into the Self, some attention to the circumstances and feelings which make them write seems justified. Peckham's bold hypothesis makes many scholars uncomfortable because it relies, essentially, on inference about authors from their works. Basically, this approach demands that one ask what kind of outlook would give rise to the results we possess. This is neither biographical importation nor intentional fallacizing; indubitably it is speculative, but it can be stimulating and instructive. Byron offers especially fruitful ground for such reading: his sense of poetry as personal performance rather than independent imaginative prophecy brings the man—or his self-projections—out all over his poetry.

Byron writes from After the Fall. This, I take it, is the point of Gleckner's Ruins-of-Paradise thesis.[7] I find his study overschematic, too insistent on making every poem conform to a pattern. A given work may be related only tangentially or not at all to what we later see as the central thrust of a writer's concerns. Nonetheless, in an astonishing number of Byron's productions, one can see the Paradise Lost theme. Blake and Byron are seldom brought together, but they share a lasting preoccupation with the Fall. Blake's central preoccupation is explaining how the Fall—usually conceived as psychic disintegration—came about and can be reversed. Byron, similarly suffering

---

[7] Robert F. Gleckner, *Byron and the Ruins of Paradise* (Baltimore: Johns Hopkins Press, 1967).

the pangs of the outcast, sees no possible answer to either problem, and so can only grapple with the pains of the fallen state. The two men come into epiphanic contrast with *Cain* and *The Ghost of Abel,* the one a bitter protest against existential paradox, the other a serene affirmation of the transcendental power of imagination. Byron lives with the pain of corporeal vision; Blake is untroubled: "Nature has no Outline: but Imagination has. Nature has no Tune: but Imagination has! Nature has no Supernatural & dissolves: Imagination is Eternity." The two poets stand at polar extremes of the "Romantic" response. Wordsworth, Coleridge, Keats, and Shelley seek the gnosis Blake attains and retains; Byron cannot believe in the gnosis enough to join the quest, and so looks for other ways to ameliorate his condition. Shelley in *The Triumph of Life* or Keats in the *Hyperion* poems makes a painful, even heroic struggle toward knowledge, while Byron tries to come to terms with its unavailability.

The bulk of Byron's work may conveniently be visualized as falling into three categories: statements of predicament, High-Faust solutions, and Low-Faust solutions. The best exemplars are *Childe Harold, Manfred,* and *Don Juan,* respectively. The "Tales," mostly early expressions of *Sturm und Drang* discontent, can be read as imaginative manifestations of the Childe Harold mood: call them escapist fantasy or adolescent daydream if you like, but beneath the excesses and self-indulgence is a serious substratum.[8] Undoubtedly though the clearest statement of the Byronic predicament is *Childe Harold.* As the title says, the work is a pilgrimage—or, as we learn, a quest for belonging. The epigraph from *Le Cosmopolite* might suggest a need for merely social adjustment, but we quickly learn in Canto I that the problem is psychological and even metaphysical. Harold, once "given to revel and ungodly glee," succumbs to "the fulness of satiety," and "sore sick at heart" goes into exile in search of the Everlasting Yea. Harold's predicament is Byron's, as the emergence of Byron himself in Canto III suggests. There explicitly the theme is isolation, the individual cut off from man and nature, alone and joyless and wandering: "I stood and stand alone" (III, cxii). Canto IV brings us to Rome, where Art paradoxically brings some shred of comfort, even in the face of continuing negations. The basic theme of the whole, however, is irremediable alienation.

If the Romantic poet is to believe in the solutions he seeks, he must have faith that his imagination can create or put him in touch with truth. Blake's faith in imagination and Shelley's notion of the projected *epipsyche* find no parallel in Byron's view of his creations. "What am I? Nothing," he says; Harold is "not so," his creator hopes (III, vi), but by now persona has been swallowed and digested by creator, and its shadowy remains are no grounds for faith in the infinite. Canto III is the crucial one. In it Byron considers his state and isolation, examines and rejects ways out. Harold—here representing the imaginative product of the poet—fades into insubstantiality just as significance is demanded of him. So Byron cannot create his own meaning. Can he perhaps find it in nature à la Shelley? The question is raised, the urge is obvious, but no great comfort can be found there either. So the

---

[8] I have discussed these works in detail in "*The Island* and the Evolution of Byron's Tales," *Romantic and Victorian: Studies in Memory of William H. Marshall,* ed. W. Paul Elledge and Richard L. Hoffman (Rutherford, N.J.: Fairleigh Dickinson Univ. Press, 1971), pp. 158-180.

problem remains: how are alienation and pain to be ameliorated? Byron's solutions in life range from frenetic dissipation to the determined heroism of his Greek expedition. In art he tries two tacks: the exaltation of the miserable rebel to heroic dimensions, and the comic reduction of the predicament to tedium and insignificance.

Manfred, as a number of critics have realized, is essentially a highly personal recension of the Faust myth. It takes the criminal-outcast hero of the *Sturm und Drang* tales, and inflates him to vast proportions. A new degree of identification with the protagonist is reached: in the early tales there is never really any doubt that the heroes are egregiously flawed, and Byron's imaginative empathy (and ours) with them is Wertherian self-indulgence. Manfred we are to take seriously. The time of the poem is compressed: we see only the very end of Manfred's life. Nonetheless, the basic elements of the Faust story are all present: alienation from man and nature, violent existential discontent; raising of spirits; inclination to suicide; mortal sin; destruction of a virtuous female (here with incest as an added fillip); raising of the dead; despairing pride; and final damnation. Says Manfred, "Philosophy and Science, and the springs/ Of wonder, and the wisdom of the world,/ I have essay'd . . . But they avail not." His crimes (incest and trafficking with devils aside) are vague, but, we gather, dreadful. Internal compulsion has driven him beyond proper human knowledge and experience. After the phantom of Astarte disappears, Manfred is "convulsed" and a Spirit comments, "This is to be a mortal/ And seek things beyond mortality." In Act III the Abbot argues that "there still is time/ For Penitence and pity"; Manfred answers with Marlovian pride and despair: "It is too late." But here our response changes its character. Marlowe's Faust's despair, like Vathek's pride, is wrong: the audience is to disapprove their obdurateness. Manfred's persistence is made heroic: we agree with him that the Abbot cannot comprehend the extent of his agony and crime and do not condemn his refusal to repent. This response is validated in the final lines of the poem, when Manfred tells the demons "yet I do defy ye." He insists:

> *Thou* didst not tempt me, and thou couldst not tempt me
> [shades of Goethe's Faust]
> I have not been thy dupe, nor am thy prey—
> But was my own destroyer, and will be
> My own hereafter.—Back, ye baffled fiends!—
> The hand of death is on me—but not yours!

The essence of *Manfred* lies in its glorification of stupendous crimes and heroic despair: Manfred is so titanic a Faust that he rises superior to mere devils and damns himself.

The ending of the poem is quite fine, and yet grossly unsatisfactory for an author who obviously put a good deal of himself into Manfred. Byron can imagine himself at the top of Manfred's tower, shaking his fist at the heavens and defying all the powers of Hell. But Manfred expires with suitable grandeur and mysteriousness; Byron must descend to breakfast the next morning. *Manfred* represents one pole of Byron's response to *Weltschmerz*—puff it up to significance and tragic grandeur. The other pole is devaluation: reduce the pain to fatuity and insignificance. Manfred is grand, mysterious, arch-criminal, and hyperactive, a man driven by superhuman discontents to terrible crime. Don Juan goes to the opposite extreme. He is a dummy, an extravagantly passive figure who is tossed from pillar to post by circumstances, and goes through it all with bland amiability and ease. Cannibalism, love, hair-breadth escapes make no impression at all on him. Nothing can satisfy Manfred's cravings; Juan, anti-Faust, has no cravings.

Don Juan is delightfully satiric. But is it a satire? On what? The poem has been read as a comic "resolution" of Byron's Romantic agonies. But wherein is the resolution? The poem gives us a drastic contrast between the supremely *un*conscious Juan and the hyperconscious narrator. Juan is a football to be kicked from one situation to the next. What does the narrator find which is so satisfactory? Essentially, he is occupying himself with a self-concocted game. Beckett's Krapp and the tramps in *Godot* play games to keep feeling alive amidst nothingness: Byron's narrator here plays games to minimize feeling. The *modus operandi* of the whole poem is neatly epitomized in the ridiculous "Fragment" found "On the back of the Poet's MS. of Canto I."

I would to heaven that I were so much clay,
As I am blood, bone, marrow, passion, feeling—
Because at least the past were pass'd away—
And for the future—

So far we have a straightforward if facile statement of *Weltschmerz*, a routine outcropping of the oblivion theme common in Negative Romantic writing and so strong in *Manfred* ("What wouldst thou . . . ? . . . 'Oblivion, self-oblivion!'"). However, Byron continues:

(but I write this reeling,
Having got drunk exceedingly to-day,
So that I seem to stand upon the ceiling)
I say—the future is a serious matter—
And so—for God's sake—hock and soda-water!

Concluded thus, oblivion theme and serious *Weltschmerz* are reduced to complete fatuity, the feeling obliterated, the whole rendered innocuous.

A comparison with Beckford here is instructive. Beckford burlesques the Faust myth, directly undercutting a passionately felt *Weltschmerz*. Byron, working toward the same ends, does nothing so simple. One could imagine the Manfred story replete with snide remarks, not reduced to bathos but sardonically narrated. Why does Byron not produce such a subversion? Like Beckford, he seeks to devalue serious feeling. Perhaps one answer—a hypothesis at least—is (a) his near-solipsistic imprisonment in a consciousness for which nature remains external and remote; combined with (b) his sense of the utter remoteness of innocence. To expand: "nature" is not for Byron organic and vital, something in which he can participate; rather, nature is physical, inanimate, and external, a set of objects to be perceived, and available only in a form distorted by the perceiving consciousness. This perception gives rise to a painful sense of satiety and aimlessness, but unlike Beckford, Byron cannot be so naive as to think longingly of a state of innocence to which this realization has not yet penetrated. Even in *Manfred* Byron gives us a Faust myth which emphasizes pain rather than quest: plainly he does not believe in the quest even to the limited degree Beckford does. So when

Byron comes to produce a devaluation, he has no use for simple travesty. To one with Byron's view of material reality, a serious Faust-quest is self-travesty. In short, he will aim not to subvert the quest but to negate or deny it. Byron is always performer rather than prophet: in *Don Juan* he finally admits this. But what then does the performance do?

Consider the figure of the hero—specifically the "Byronic" hero. Satiety and painful consciousness combine paradoxically with insatiable cravings to produce a tormented overreacher. Byron's object in his epic farce is devaluation. Notice his method though. Instead of exaggerating and ridiculing his hero's ambitions, Byron removes them. Perhaps this accounts for the substitution of the Don Juan figure for Faust. A Faust without titanic aspirations does not exist; nothing can happen to him. But a Don Juan, traditionally as insatiable as Faust, can be used, can be subjected to experience, even if he must be made radically passive. The necessity and point of Juan's wanderings is precisely that he must be at the mercy of experience, observed aloofly by a sardonic narrator now freed from the complications of empathy. Juan's passivity, a marvellous joke and a drastic reversal of his mythic role, is the perfect negation of quest. Juan bounces from crisis to crisis: each one ought to be grounds for serious feeling, his and ours, and never is. From glorification of feeling in *Manfred* Byron turns to obliteration of it. The narrator dissociates himself from this curious nonquest, a progression which can end only in death or midair. Accidental or not, the Sternean dangle at the conclusion of Canto XVI makes an excellent stopping point. The mock-Gothic rousing of expectations, comically punctured and abandoned, epitomizes well the method of the whole poem. I shall argue later that *Vathek* and *Don Juan* stand in essentially the same relation to Romantic affirmation—but with this difference: Beckford deflates the Romantic quest, Byron negates it.

A strong case can thus be made for saying that *Don Juan* represents not a comic solution to Byron's existential agonies, but rather a refusal to take them seriously, a retreat into self-reductive gamesplaying. Byron seems to deny even the existentialist "election of death," and by deprecating and mocking himself as poet and narrator he refuses to take seriously even the pain of a nihilist's view of the world. Byron ironically repudiates the validity of irony, and denies the significance of denial, maneuvering himself into the role of hyperconscious spokesman for the insignificance of consciousness. A brilliant overview of Byron along these lines has recently been put forward by Frank D. McConnell.[9] I am indebted to his reading, though overall I find it one-sided. To see how right McConnell is in emphasizing Byron's pervasive reductionism and self-devaluation, one has first to see how strong the opposite tendencies are—the searing dissatisfactions, the urge to ride them into the ultra-Faust solution of *Manfred* rather than the anti-Faust denial of the problem in *Don Juan*.

---

[9] "Byron's Reductions: 'Much too Poetical,'" *ELH*, 37 (1970), 415-432.

Byron makes a particularly good instance of the Dark Romantic because he gives us almost the whole possible spread of response. In *Childe Harold* we see the statement of predicament, especially in the pervasive sense of isolation and alienation, the protagonist cut off from man and nature. *Cain* is an extended and explicit analysis of the problem, bringing protagonist and author face to face with insoluble questions. "Why art thou wretched? Why do I exist?/ Why are all things so? . . . Why is evil?" Self-knowledge is no help. Lucifer asks, "have I not . . . Taught thee to know thyself?" Cain can only answer sadly, "Alas, I seem nothing." The pain of recognizing human and personal insignificance is a major Romantic starting point. Among Dark Romantic writers, the response is often Faustian overreaching, an attempt to reach *Übermensch* status. This is the pattern of *Manfred*, as we have seen. But in Byron especially the drive toward the heroic seems to collapse back on itself, necessitating a compensatory reductionism: Byron is too acutely self-conscious and self-critical long to hold a Nietzschean pose. The plays—manipulative puppet shows—are prelude to *Don Juan*, in which Byron dresses himself as chief puppet in the narrator's guise, and proceeds to put the show through its endless and unchanging changes—literally, as McConnell remarks, "boring himself to death with the playing of his narrative role."

The central form of Dark Romanticism is essentially an acute perception of evil with little move toward either solution or escape. I am calling this Existential Agony. Poe is perhaps the most perfect exemplar of this condition in its elemental form. But plainly a variety of results in practice can be identified even within the No Exit school of Dark Romantics. I very much want to avoid restrictive classification, but the common types should be mentioned. A basic differentiation can be made between works which present, explore, and often analyze the condition of existential torment (*Childe Harold, Cain, Frankenstein*) and those which seem to be a reaction to such feeling. Since the genesis is wretchedness, acute discontent without prospect of alleviation, such works are usually morbid, gloomy, bitter. Often they are "perverse." An author caught in the No Exit syndrome will grow fascinated with pain, evil, and paradox. The Power of Blackness (as Harry Levin titles a study of Poe, Hawthorne, and Melville) is very strong for such authors, even without the possibility of heroic elevation so well achieved by Melville in *Moby-Dick*.

Poe's fascination with evil can be called morbid, but it is not perverse. A large number of No Exit writers explicitly concern themselves with abnormal sexuality. De Sade's religion of pain is the famous instance: the celebrated, almost endless catalogue of the type in nineteenth-century literature is of course Mario Praz's *The Romantic Agony* (1933). The beauties of the horrid, the pleasures of pain, the attraction of the Fatal Woman are there charted at length. Speaking facilely, one can say that many of the authors Praz discusses take an emotional dive into pain, seeking satiety in that, if no other relief avails.

The Power of Blackness—fascination with evil and pain—is apparent in all Dark Romantic writers, but at times it is offset by ironic devaluation or travesty in an attempt to relieve the existential misery which gives rise to the writing in the first place. *Vathek*, we have seen, gives us serious imaginative empathy with both the Faustian predicament and the sadistic excesses of the protagonist; it also, by travesty, reduces both to innocuous insignificance. Byron's admiration for Beckford is well known, and parallels have been drawn (especially by M. K. Joseph) between *Vathek* and the "Oriental tales." The comparison is apt enough: both combine a glorying in crime with an overinflation which destroys seriousness. I would also argue, however, that both in method and results *Don Juan* shows some interesting connections to *Vathek*. Here I am seeing the work in a different light than Peckham, who views *Don Juan* as a transitional midpoint, a center of indifference between the Negative Romantic crisis and the Romantic affirmation. I would see *Don Juan* as an ameliorative devaluation of existential crisis, a palliative which leads not to the Everlasting Yea and Wordsworth, but toward vacuity and the antics of *Godot* and *Endgame*. Writing from the Romantic perspective, Peckham sees his pattern of secular conversion as natural, right, and proper. Writing from the Negative Romantic position, I see the conversion as unnatural, improbable, and self-delusory. Take the despairing visions of Poe and Maturin: the evil presented is real enough, so how is organicism to convince them that in erring reason's spite, whatever is, is right? Or even tolerable?

Living in a mental hell, one very natural response is to burlesque it. M. G. Lewis' *The Monk* is a perfect example of a work which shuttles uneasily between the serious *Schauer-Romantik* and the devaluative mode. The horrors are exaggerated, though not nearly as much so as in *Vathek;* more tellingly, the narration has such exuberance and energy—and such a lack of morbid malaise—that one may enjoy the impact of the horrors while not feeling that they have serious significance. Indeed Beckford, Byron, and Lewis display some astonishing biographical parallels, homosexuality not least among them. In all three there is a curious theme of regret for a lost purity, a sense of innocence spoiled. The theme of childhood innocence is dramatically clear in the last paragraph of *Vathek*. "Thus the Caliph Vathek, who, for the sake of empty pomp and forbidden power, had sullied himself with a thousand crimes, became a prey to grief without end, and remorse without mitigation: whilst the humble, the despised Gulchenrouz passed whole ages in undisturbed tranquillity, and in the pure happiness of childhood." Just so does the whore dream of the nun. But paradise is unrecapturable. So the writer mocks and deflates his wretchedness, or wallows in it, or exalts his fallen state. Satanworship is one of the phenomena of the third possibility; it is a common element in many of the Heroic Despair works.

Milton's Satan—as interpreted by the Romantics—is one of the great archetypal overreachers, a stupendous being, who, rebelling and trying to go beyond his proper place, is cast out of paradise into perpetual torment but remains heroically defiant. The angel-outlaw, the man of vast gifts and potentiality for good whose powers are perverted to evil ends, is a central figure in Dark Romanticism. Faust is of this mold, but in that myth we usually remain acutely conscious of the folly and misery of the attempt at "breakthrough": little of its grandeur survives. If a writer wishes to emphasize the heroic side of such a figure, Satan is often an important source for the resulting characterization.

Blake, Shelley, and Schiller express their admiration for Milton's Satan; his characteristics crop up extensively in Gothic and pseudo-Gothic writing. Schiller's Karl Moor (hero of *Die Räuber*) is a particularly blatant imitation. Elements of the character are present in Mrs. Radcliffe's Montoni and Lewis' Ambrosio; the whole is readily apparent in Mrs. Radcliffe's Schedoni (in *The Italian*). Several of the protagonists in Byron's early tales are precisely of this mode. Interestingly, Byron produced near the end of his life in *The Island* an overt rebuttal of the satanic rebel. The story is an idiosyncratic recension of the Mutiny on the Bounty story; instead of siding with Fletcher Christian, Byron is extremely severe, and has him killed after stripping Christian of such grandeur as his doomed rebellion might seem to possess. What seems especially revealing, however, is the way Byron splits his protagonist into two: the wretched Christian, and his native ally Torquil, who is allowed to escape and live happily ever after. Byron's presentation of Torquil shows an explicit yearning for prelapsarian innocence. The Christian-Torquil contrast, and the final bittersweet contemplation of an unutterably distant and unrecapturable innocence rewarded, should remind us of Beckford. Indeed, *The Island* is *Vathek* writ by an older and sadder man, now able to revel hardly at all in satanic rebellion. Byron could not sustain (and Beckford never tries to) the hero's Satan-image: he falls back on reductionism and laments paradise lost.

Only in rare instances is the satanic raised from the level of the Gothic-outlaw to the heights of high seriousness. *Moby-Dick* is one instance; Thomas Mann's *Doktor Faustus* is another. The latter retains the Marlovian structure, but Adrian Leverkühn is invested with genuinely tragic grandeur. He is determined to achieve what is explicitly called "breakthrough" as a composer at any price. He pays the price, achieves what he wants, and suffers the consequences. His determination to create helps differentiate him from mere whiners about existential *Angst;* the way his story is presented in tandem with an account of both modern German culture and the collapse of Nazi Germany helps invest it with a tragic grandeur and scale beyond the personal and individual. Cataclysm and utter despair are the core of the novel, yet withal there remains a sublimity in Leverkühn's endeavor and its context which lends a rending poignancy. *Doktor Faustus* is a work I have read many times, but it never fails to move me to tears.

Within the original "Romantic period," *Melmoth the Wanderer* (1820) stands as the supreme statement of heroic despair. The work springs from and dwells tormentedly on acute consciousness of social, political, religious, and economic tyranny. The length and vast narrative complexity of the book forbid more than summary analysis. The imaginative center of the novel is the misery of sadistic nihilism. The "Tale of the Indians" summarizes and makes explicit what is elaborated elsewhere. There we find again the drastic contrast of agonized, self-damned criminal-wanderer (Melmoth) with pre-lapsarian purity (Immalee). She proves unable to redeem him: he has sold his soul to attain the knowledge of the *Übermensch*—and this knowledge consists, ironically, of despairing disbelief in love and human compassion. Obviously the pattern is again that of Marlowe's Faust, but as in Mann's version of the story, the protagonist is given a degree of self-knowledge and misery which invest him with tragic sublimity. Why *Melmoth* has not long since taken its rightful place as one of the major documents of Romanticism (albeit the Negative sort) is one of the mysteries of literary history.

That such heights and intensity were seldom and briefly reached is to be expected. *Melmoth* is the exception, not the norm. A major work which falls far closer to the norms of Negative Romantic patterns and traits is *Franken-stein,* a No Exit tale of overreaching. Victor Frankenstein is determined to "pioneer a new way, explore unknown powers, and unfold to the world the deepest mysteries of creation. . . . Life and death appeared to me ideal bounds, which I should first break through, and pour a torrent of light into our dark world."[10] The successful attempt to create life produces, of course, the monster: the death and desolation which follow provide a warning about breakthroughs well supplied with the nastiness and impact so lacking in *Vathek,* which ostensibly presents the same moral. Almost schematically, Mary Shelley's novel reverses and denies the Romantic quest for gnosis.

In the formulation I have developed here from Wellek, Peckham, and Frye, the Promethean-Romantic myth, a striving for gnosis, is set against Negative Romantic frustrations, the imaginative center of which, I have argued, is the Faust myth. In a broader sense, the Faust myth, or more par-ticularly the Faustian predicament, can be conceived as the jumping-off point for the morbid preoccupations of Dark Romanticism generally. (1) The basic Negative Romantic myth is the Marlovian form of the story: pain, No Exit, and damnation if the narrative covers that much of the tale. Prime ex-amples are *Cain* and *Frankenstein.* (2) Moving in one direction from this center, we find the travesty (*Vathek,* which actually includes damnation) and the anti-Faust devaluation (*Don Juan*). (3) Moving in the opposite direc-tion from the center, one comes to the ultra-Faust glorification, in which the grandeur of pain and endeavor lend a tragic-heroic compensation lacking in recensions of the basic myth, as in *Melmoth* and very nearly in *Manfred.*

Throughout all three types of response, as in the Romantic response in the conversion pattern proposed by Peckham, one finds implicit or explicit a demand for solutions, for breakthrough, for absolutes. All the Romantics' paradoxical answers and joy in sensed solutions do not really disguise their craving for ontological certitude, for an absolute security in their faith in "or-ganicism." As D. G. James suggests, this insistence on the ends of the quest places a tremendous pressure on the Romantic writer. For those who cannot believe in the possible achievement of the ends, the pains of existential dis-content loom large. These Negative Romantics can glorify the pain, or im-merse themselves in presenting, analyzing, and sometimes living it, or can try to drug and devalue it. The only real exit, lacking a Blakean imagination,

---

[10] *Frankenstein,* ed. M. K. Joseph, Oxford English Novels (Oxford, 1969), pp. 48, 54.

is the eschewal of ends and the acceptance of process. In oversimplified terms, this seems to be the message of Keats' "To Autumn," and to be the solution toward which Shelley works in *The Triumph of Life*. Curiously enough— and conveniently for my central conceit in this essay—Goethe arrives at exactly the same conclusion at the end of Part II of his *Faust*, a work which as a kind of *Divine Comedy* in modern rather than Medieval metaphysic stands at the heart of Romanticism and Negative Romanticism alike. Against mythic precedent, Goethe saves Faust because however futile the quest, it has driven Faust to strive, and though the endeavor has led him astray, the process itself is redemptive, though the sufferer cannot realize this in the midst of his existential discontents. Adopting a perspective which transcends the merely human, Goethe offers from the heights of old age the answer which solves the Romantic and Negative Romantic dilemmas alike, but is almost equally inaccessible to both parties:

Wer immer strebend sich bemüht,
Den können wir erlösen.

From the "Last Judgment" to Kafka's World: A Study in Gothic Iconography

VIRGINIA M. HYDE

When Lord Byron places his Childe Harold in a setting with "a castle and a prison on each hand,"[1] he happens to capture a conjunction common to the experience of Western European Christendom—the same which Franz Kafka evokes in the very titles of his major novels, *The Castle* and *The Trial*. Analogous to these spheres, one towering heavenward toward grace and one probing labyrinthine depths of guilt and punishment, are the circumscribed niches of the Last Judgment, the definitive iconography of Medieval Gothic art,[2] appointing a Celestial City on the right hand of God and a subterranean pit on the left. One of the most noteworthy aspects of the *dies irae*, probably the most important single scenic configuration to enter Europe from Byzantine art,[3] is its comprehensive orderliness, preserving the symmetry imposed by the priorities of stone construction for cathedral portals: before God or Christ as Pantocrater, enthroned in glory, humanity stands at the point of meeting between heaven and earth, death and life, immortality and mortality. The pathway past open graves to the Judge is all that remains of the fallen earth; while the central spheres and the right side are bright with pure gold leaf, signifying sublimity, the left side is contrastingly dark as a confining repository for chaos.[4]

VIRGINIA M. HYDE, Assistant Professor of English at Washington State University, is author of articles on ninteenth- and twentieth-century poets and is past section chairman of the *Medieval Tradition in Modern Literature* for the annual Conference on Medieval Studies at Western Michigan University.

[1] *Childe Harold's Pilgrimage,* Canto IV, 1 (line 2).

[2] Henri Focillon, *The Art of the West in the Middle Ages,* trans. Donald King; ed., Jean Bony (London: Phaidon, 1963), II, 76.

[3] Otto Demus, *Byzantine Art and the West,* Wrightsman Lectures, No. 3 (New York: New York Univ. Press, 1970), pp. 53, 122-131 *et passim.*

[4] This simplified schema includes the features common to most of the Byzantine patterns without entering into the additional properties of the several influential workshops' exemplars. See Demus, pp. 122-131, for major colonial and outlying experiments and for major embodiments of the scene at Cefalú, Monreale, Palermo, Venice, and Torcello.

Kafka, surrounded by the monuments of the famous Prague workshops of Gothic and Gothic Baroque Apocalyptic art, would have been familiar with the mosaic Judgment tympanum at St. Vitus' Cathedral, Prague, and the gold-encrusted illustrations of the Book of Revelation at nearby Castle Karlšteyn.[5] His literary art reveals a talent powerfully possessed by the vitality of a graphic tradition, even one from which formal patterns may survive apart from their original significations. Kafka produced a body of literature entirely eschatological in orientation and chiefly explicable in terms of the dualism featured in the Judgment—though his characteristic fiction looses "left-hand" elements from accustomed confines into the schema at large, introducing the demonic, deformed, and grotesque into the diverse arenas of life itself. His world is continuously located at a metaphysical boundary such as one of his characters discusses: "this tomb represents the frontier between the Human and the Other, and it's on this frontier that I wish to post a guard."[6] Such grafting of the supermundane upon the earthly —and eruptions of the "other" into the province of the human—seems peculiarly fitting to a Prague source, for Kafka was one of a group of Apocalyptic writers and painters which flourished in that city's expressionist movement in the first quarter of the twentieth century.[7] Indeed, Kafka's name was first associated with the Judgment when some of his works appeared in *Der jüngste Tag* (*The Last Day* in English, *Du Jugement dernier* in French), edited by his friend Kurt Wolff, in 1916. Still, reflecting the panorama which had confronted "Everyman" from the western facade of the cathedral through centuries of Christendom, Kafka's appeal is far from local as it addresses the reader's cultural memory. Thus, K., the land surveyor (*Landvermesser*) in search of Count Westwest in *The Castle*, suggests the famous "measurer" of the New Jerusalem's outer walls as depicted at Karlšteyn—as in countless other representations of the eschatological pilgrimage. Similarly, Joseph K., often termed an Everyman figure,[8] stands at a recognizable seat of judgment

---

[5] Vlasta Dvořáková, Josef Krása, Anežka Merhautová, and Karl Stejskal, *Gothic Mural Painting in Bohemia and Moravia, 1300-1378* (London: Oxford Univ. Press, 1964), pp. 51-65, 69-70. See also Plates VI, VII, XIV, XV, XVII, and Figures 115, 138, 140-155.

[6] *The Warden of the Tomb*, in *Description of a Struggle and The Great Wall of China*, trans. Willa and Edwin Muir and Tania and James Stern (London: Secker and Warburg, 1960), p. 302. The play, based on the monarchical history of his culture, is one of several Kafka works making explicit references to persons and places that are identifiable in the background of Prague or surrounding areas.

[7] Heinz Politzer, *Franz Kafka: Parable and Paradox* (New York: Cornell Univ. Press, 1966), pp. 8-10, 23-27. See also Klaus Wagenbach, *Franz Kafka: Eine Biographie seiner Jugend, 1883-1912* (Bern: Francke Verlag, 1958), pp. 65-98 et passim; Wagenbach, *Kafka par lui-même*, trans. Alain Huriot (Paris: Ecrivains de Toujours, n. d.), p. 126 et passim; Johannes Urzidil, *There Goes Kafka*, trans. Harold A. Basilius (Detroit, Mich.: Wayne State Univ. Press, 1968), pp. 9-21; Erich Heller, *The Disinherited Mind: Essays in Modern German Literature and Thought* (Philadelphia: Dufour and Saifer, 1952), pp. 185-201; Pavel Eisner, "Franz Kafkas *Prozess* und Prag," *German Life & Letters*, 14 (1960-1961), 16-25; Heinz Ladendorf, "Kafka und die Kunstgeschichte," *Wallraf-Richartz-Jahrbuch*, XXIII and XXV (1961, 1963).

[8] Eisner, p. 23. This representative character of the Kafka protagonist is the basis for a number of studies assuming the Everyman moral pilgrimage. See Kafka's relationship to the Salzburg *Jedermann* of Hugo von Hofmannsthal, in Politzer, *Parable and Paradox*, pp. 212-213. See also Rebecca West, *The Court and the Castle* (New Haven: Yale Univ. Press, 1957), pp. 279-305; William R. Mueller, "The Theme

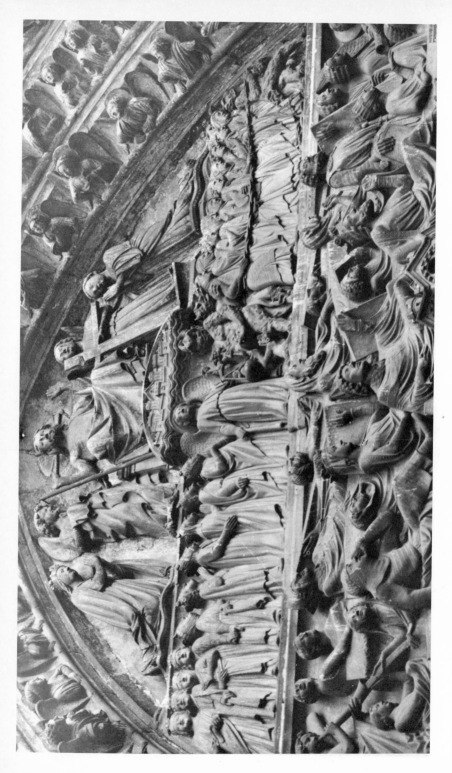

dramatically depicted in Karlšteyn's Great Keep with its *Apocalyptic Godhead and the Book of the Law,* on Prague Cathedral facade, and elsewhere.

Preeminently, then, Kafka stands as an exemplar not of an isolated but of a widely dispersed phenomenon, unfurling the Judgment scene down through the centuries. Undergoing a process of increasing abstraction in the arts, it passes from the massive modeling of the western tympanum, which Romanesque and Gothic architecture had pressed into rigid structural service, into other art media: monumental and miniature painting, epic and romance literature, the Doomsday play and the theater it influences.[9] A major metaphor not of the *roman noir* alone but of countless other literary works of the past two centuries, for example, is the cosmic court session, more and more fully internalized and fleeting, a flash of vision convicting a host of protagonists of sin: Hawthorne's Arthur Dimmesdale in a midnight vigil on a scaffold or Robert Browning in the revelation of the Judgment Seat ending his *Easter Day* shares this vision no less than does Franz Kafka's Joseph K., "seized in bed before [he] could get up"[10] and charged with a nameless and unanswerable offense.

The background of Kafka's native city, propitious for the development

---

The central importance of the Last Judgment in thirteenth-century Gothic iconography is attested by the principal portal of Notre-Dame de Paris (fashioned 1220-1230 and restored by Viollet-le-Duc in the mid-nineteenth century).

Following conventional arrangement, Christ the Pantocrator presiding over the division of resurrected humanity is at the visual center of the tympanum. At the sides of Christ two angels carry the instruments of the passion: nails, lance (right), and cross (left). Next to the angels are the Virgin Mary (right, crowned) and Saint John (left) interceding for sinful mankind. At the feet of Christ the Celestial City separates the upper from the medial tympanum panel. Here Saint Michael weighs supplicating souls in the fateful balance while a hideous devil and his dwarf imp clutch the scales, eagerly waiting to snatch a condemned wretch to add to the file of eternally damned being led in chains toward the infernal pit by two grotesquely grimacing demons. To the right of Saint Michael stand the serene elect, directing their eyes upwards to Christ and wearing crowns to signify the royal bliss of the orderly heavenly society.

In the bottom panel of the tympanum, the conventional representation of the resurrection is heralded by the Judgment trumpets sounded by angels from both sides of the panel. Various classes and conditions of humanity are represented in the agitated motion of the general awakening as the lids of tombs and coffins are abruptly cast aside. Surrounding the tympanum are the six concentric bands of the archivolt. At the bottom of the archivolt bands on the right hand of Christ an angel receives the souls of the elect into Heaven, while the damned are hurled headlong into the abyss from the left hand of the tympanum's medial panel. The abyss itself is portrayed in the lowest register of the left-hand base of the archivolt. Each of the bands of the archivolt contains a scene from Hell: the damned being boiled in a cauldron, the horses of the apocalypse throwing their riders, demons torturing the damned, and a demon breaking the heads of bishops and kings with a pointed hammer.

Below the archivolt to each side of the two massive portal doors are the Apostles, each carrying a characteristic object and looking toward the statue of the teaching Christ on the central pillar supporting the tympanum. This statue, carved by Geoffroy-Dechaume in 1855 to replace one destroyed in the eighteenth century, locates the symbolically important visual upward path to the Judgment seat and the apex of the archivolt. The path linking Christ the teacher with Christ the Pantocrator forms a terminator between the bright, celestial right hand of the Judgment scene and the benighted left hand of the tympanum's medial panel and the infernal region at the bottom of the left-hand side of the archivolt. To the right hand of Christ lies the golden path to glory, to the left the grim route to perdition. (Thomas C. Faulkner)

of his own art, goes far toward suggesting some of the conditions giving rise to Medieval forms, especially to Gothic fiction, in recent centuries. The writer grew up in the midst of Czech nationalism and on the eve of the world wars; but the turbulence of his time had complex origins deep in previous centuries, Prague having been a convergence point for the most heterogeneous cultural movements in the Middle Ages. Jewish by birth, Kafka lived, nevertheless, in an area which retained predominantly the stamp of Gothic church art, Prague being one of several locations where the Gothic style seems to have survived in its late (or "Gothic Baroque") phase centuries after the florescence of High Gothic.[11] The city's artistic apex had been at the High Gothic period in a lavish Italo-Byzantine style commissioned by Holy Roman Emperor Karl IV to heighten the majesty of his fourteenth-century reign; for Byzantine gold work had intrinsic symbolic value aside from its material worth. Later, occultists attempted to revitalize their aging community, confusing materialistic and spiritual goals by using alchemy and necromancy and thus making the city so famous for its late Medieval experimentalism that Faust himself paid a visit there.[12] Between East and West, influenced alike by two Catholicisms—Roman and Eastern Orthodox—and by major Reformation movements[13] and Hebraic tradition as well, this "Golden Capital . . . with its hundred towers" (Urzidil, p. 14) had maintained a condition of spiritual ferment, awaiting a new order, through centuries. In the city's youth lay a lost Medieval "golden age" of artistic splendor at odds with the more stultified ambience of its later centuries.

Thus Kafka's fiction inherits a civilization which has already experienced a decline to nearly total cultural atrophy, and his literature is typical of the Gothic novel in reflecting decay, often in literal descriptions of ruins. Though peculiarly well-realized by imagery from the graphic arts, Kafka's buildings and monuments tend to be as "wasted" as his infrequent landscapes. Still, such ruins gain their force by implied contrast to an earlier society of frequently Gothic lines. Thus, in *The Castle*, K.'s best view of the inaccessible castle suggests both decomposition of structure and degeneration of old Medieval authority:

. . . on approaching it [K.] was disappointed in the Castle; it was after all only a wretched-looking town, a huddle of village houses, whose sole merit, if any, lay in

---

of Judgment: Franz Kafka's *The Trial*," in *The Prophetic Voice in Modern Fiction* (New York: Association Press, 1959), pp. 83-109; Max Lerner, "The Human Voyage," in *The Kafka Problem*, ed. Angel Flores (1946; rpt. ed., New York: Octagon, 1963), pp. 38-46; W. H. Auden, "K's Quest," *Kafka Problem*, pp. 47-52; John Kelly, " 'The Trial' and the Theology of Crisis," *Kafka Problem*, pp. 151-171; Politzer, *Parable and Paradox*, p. 376.

9 Focillon, II, 116, 133, 144. See also David J. Leigh, S. J., "The Doomsday Mystery Play: An Eschatological Morality," *Modern Philology*, 67 (1970), 211-221, with "Appendix: The General Judgment in Medieval Theology," 221-223.

10 *The Trial*, trans. Willa and Edwin Muir (New York: Schocken, 1968), p. 43. Page references to this volume will appear in parentheses within the text, as will references designated to *The Castle*, trans. Willa and Edwin Muir (New York: Modern Library, 1969). German quotations from *The Trial* are from *Der Prozess* (New York: Schocken, 1946).

11 Focillon, II, 167, notes the continuing late Gothic style in several European locations, singling out Prague, "city of cabbalists," as a notable example. See Dvořáková *et al.*, p. 48, on the relatively late Gothic zenith in Prague, where the fourteenth century is roughly analogous to the thirteenth in more advanced European centers.

being built of stone; but the plaster had long since flaked off and the stone seemed to be crumbling away. . . . The tower above him . . . was . . . pierced by small windows that glittered in the sun—with a somewhat maniacal glitter—and topped by what looked like an attic, with battlements that were irregular, broken, fumbling, as if designed by the trembling or careless hand of a child, clearly outlined against the blue. It was as if a melancholy-mad tenant who ought to have been kept locked in the topmost chamber of his house had burst through the roof and lifted himself up to the gaze of the world.   (pp. 11-12)

The castle is all but displaced throughout the book by Kafka's famous labyrinth figure[14] separating the quester from his goal: the twisting street "did not lead away from the Castle" but "led no nearer to it either" (p. 14). Similarly, the streets dominate much of *The Trial*, in which the attics—mad inversions of "celestial" court rooms—are urban ruins "not properly boarded off" (p. 63).

The enigmatic nature of "the powers that be" in this apparently discontinuous cosmology (which rather unexpectedly makes *The Castle* an analogue rather than a sequel or contrast to the frustration-ridden *Trial*) has a long history of critical disagreement. One question is whether the castle hierarchy deals in "divine grace," according to Max Brod, or whether these minions are really a "company of Gnostic demons," as in Erich Heller's retort.[15]   Little doubt attaches to the immediate signification of the Gothic castle—and perhaps none to K.'s ideal castle; as Dorrit Cohn points out, "the ghost of tran-

---

[12] The Austrian Empire, into which Kafka was born, had a glittering past—especially 1344-1378, when Karl IV established Prague New Town, where Kafka had his parental home; Karl-Ferdinand University, which Kafka attended; St. Vitus' Cathedral; Castle Karlšteyn; and many other churches and public buildings as well as humanitarian reform measures. After this apex, social or religious unrest alternated with repressive hierarchical controls. Kafka saw the last days of the empire, under the house of Hapsburg, in 1918, to the accompaniment of social turmoil calling forth much of the Apocalyptic writing of his Prague "circle." See Dvořáková *et al.*, p. 49, and Urzidil, pp. 9-21.

[13] Dvořáková *et al.*, pp. 49-50, 143, details, among repercussions of the Hussite Revolution, the fact that St. Vitus' Cathedral remained unfinished until the nineteenth and twentieth centuries, though its major appointments were complete in the pre-Hussite period under Karl IV. See Urzidil, pp. 119-140, especially 122, telling of Kafka's witnessing in his own lifetime an event concurrent with the declaration of the Republic in 1918: "The Statue of Mary in the midst of the Altstädter Ring . . . was torn down . . ., thus opening up the view toward the bronzed gaze of . . . Jan Hus." See Kafka on the Statue of Mary in "Description of a Struggle." See also Thomas Mann, *The Magic Mountain,* trans. H. T. Lowe-Porter (New York: Knopf, 1926), p. 517, for the claim by one of Mann's characters that the Reformation was of "Eastern"—Central European—origins, a proposition to which the Hussite events would lend themselves.

[14] Politzer, *Parable and Paradox*, pp. 230-234; Hermann Pongs, *Franz Kafka, Dichter des Labyrinths* (Hamburg: Rowohlt, 1957); Bernard Groethuysen, "The Endless Labyrinth," in *The Kafka Problem,* pp. 376-390; Walter A. Strauss, "Franz Kafka: Between the Paradise and the Labyrinth," *Centennial Review,* 5 (1961), 206-222. In a recent article, Herman J. Weigand increases the likeness of the Kafka labyrinth to Hell by adding to "The Burrow"—a story set in an underground maze—the intrusion of "an enormous set of jaws," suggestive of the Mouth of Hell. See Weigand, "Franz Kafka's 'The Burrow' ('Der Bau'): An Analytical Essay," *PMLA,* 87 (1972), 165.

[15] Heller, p. 175, answers Brod's postscript to the German edition of *Das Schloss,* p. 484. The issue is relevant to *The Trial,* its hierarchy having the same characteristics.

scendence" does not dispel itself from these easily.[16] Even so, the equivocal metaphysics of K.'s modern situation suggest greater complexity in his use of the castle than a common Medieval image of security, power, and salvation would ordinarily evoke. The sense of ruined structure, lost connections, and closed routes is a major element pointing to a dark interpretation of Kafka's fiction, and a further look at his transcendentalism is an important step toward determining Kafka's place in the Medievalism of modern literature. Certainly, the forceful impact of his major situations—infinite quests and everlasting court sessions—and images—the castle, the judgment seat, the judge—depend upon implied contrast between certain original types and, with their decline, their reversal into apparent opposites of those types. It is, indeed, possible that a "golden age" background, of some sort, is altogether indigenous to "Gothic" writing of recent centuries. A look at the literature which includes the Gothic Revival in England suggests as much.

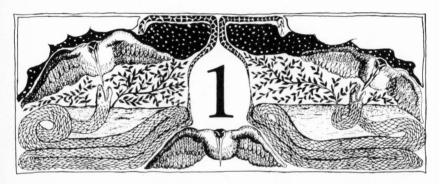

The Neo-Medieval mode of literature runs in dual channels throughout the nineteenth and twentieth centuries. One of these, idealizing the feudal past, occurs in the literature of historicism—represented in the historical novel— as well as in countless works of vaguely Utopian Romantic inspiration.[17] It forms the central vision of the German Nazarene and the Pre-Raphaelite Aesthetics of the last century and underlies pictures of domestic well-being in widely differing instances, such as Dickens' depiction of the Wemmicks' miniature Gothic castle, moated against encroachments from the world of business, in *Great Expectations* or Hans Castorp's memory of his ancestral christening bowl in Mann's *The Magic Mountain*. In this paradisaical tradition, the Pre-Raphaelite imagination yearns for a condition of societal unity and simplicity antedating the Renaissance and its twin phenomenon, the Reformation; the nostalgia seems based on an abiding reminiscence of divine

---

[16] Dorrit Cohn, "Castles and Anti-Castles, or Kafka and Robbe-Grillet," *Novel,* 5 (1971), 29.

[17] Avrom Fleishman, *The English Historical Novel from Walter Scott to Virginia Woolf* (Baltimore, Md.: Johns Hopkins Press, 1971), deals with this tradition in the first comprehensive history of the English historical novel. See also Devendra P. Varma, *The Gothic Flame* (1957; rpt. ed., New York: Russell and Russell, 1966), pp. 74-84; George Lukacs, *The Historical Novel,* trans. Stephen and Hannah Mitchell (London: Merlin, 1962); and notes 18, 20 below.

grace dwelling among men in their commonality—when, for all, the Church formed a home bridging nationalities and binding "classes" in a great stable chain throughout the Christian world. The very fact that Gothic was an eminently international style (Focillon, II, 46-76) seems to have witnessed to its freedom from an insular or divisive spirit. In short, whether or not such a virtual "golden age" had, in fact, existed in the youth of Western European civilization is less pertinent than the persisting intuition that it had.[18] As visualized, the condition of Medieval man was almost prelapsarian, his sins and his sorrows absorbed by the law administered by Church and State together and sanctioned or guided by doctrine implicit in humane letters and sciences alike.

This state of being had, supposedly, preceded the modern fragmentation of men's lives—"distinctions of class, of kind, of occupation, distinctions too numerous to review at a glance," as one of Kafka's narrators describes the loss of community.[19] Gothic humanism, to which the tradition of idealistic Neo-Medievalism looked back, had, in contrast to modern divisiveness, sought to embrace all contingencies of a man's life. Henri Focillon discusses it in these terms, describing the Medieval "mirror of nature" according to which Gothic art took its poised serenity at its height in the thirteenth century: "The world is in God, the world is an idea in the mind of God, art is the writing down of that idea. . . . When we say that the iconography of the thirteenth century is encyclopaedic, we mean, not only that it is universal and all-embracing, but also that, within its immense orb, of which God is the centre, a secret force binds together, and draws into its gravitational field, all the aspects of life"—and not life only but "even death, which was no more than a sleep in the Lord" (Focillon, II, 73, 71-72). The nineteenth-century "Medieval ideal," as distinct from the "Gothic fiction" motifs arising in eighteenth-century England,[20] thus finds its model in the equilibrious center of the Medieval Gothic culture rather than in its more tumultous Romanesque heritage (eleventh century) or its rather similarly agitated Flamboyant or

---

18 Alice Chandler, *A Dream of Order: The Medieval Ideal in Nineteenth-Century English Literature* (Lincoln: Univ. of Nebraska Press, 1970), the first full-length study of this aspect of late medievalism, finds it "partly historical but basically mythical" (p. 1). Besides relating it to enthusiasm for the older Church, she sees in it a search for fatherhood. See also David J. DeLaura, *Hebrew and Hellene in Victorian England: Newman, Arnold, and Pater* (Austin: Univ. of Texas Press, 1971), who traces some of the same "experience with history" in religious terms. Resurgent Neo-Catholicism in France, Peguy and Claudel perhaps standing out, has many features similar to those of the Medieval and historicist movements in England.

19 "Investigations of a Dog," in *Description of a Struggle and The Great Wall of China,* trans. Willa and Edwin Muir and Tania and James Stern (London: Secker & Warburg, 1960), p. 242. The volume title will be cited hereafter as *Description.*

20 Chandler, pp. 17-18, 20-23, attempts to account for differences between these traditions. Robert D. Hume, "Gothic Versus Romantic: A Revaluation of the Gothic Novel," *PMLA,* 84 (1969), 282-290, notes a religious attitude, a "concern with ultimate questions and lack of faith in the adequacy of reason or religious faith to make comprehensible the paradoxes of human existence" in the Gothic novel as well as in Romanticism generally—the Gothic being without hope of imaginative transcendence. See also Maurice Lévy, *Le Roman 'gothique' anglais, 1764-1824* (Toulouse: Association des Publications de la Faculté des Lettres et Sciences Humaines de Toulouse, 1968), pp. 53-66, who traces Gothic fiction sources to a Romantic mode—as opposed to the Classical—in the late Middle Ages and seventeenth century.

Baroque late phases (from the fifteenth century).[21] This ideal is reminiscent of the state of blessedness commonly depicted at God's "right hand" in the Judgment. A garden, the restored Eden, opens onto a city irradiating pure light. A hierarchy of angels receives the ongoing soul into the New Jerusalem, where, with the elders and saints, it takes its place in the bride of Christ.[22] Late heirs of this tradition tend to be writers of fantasy, often of modern Christian allegory, such as C. S. Lewis or Charles Williams.

The intimations of this bright side of Judgment, with its promise of redemption, while perhaps not entirely lacking in Kafka's fiction, are faint and often parodic, reduced very nearly to mere formal resemblances of the outward signs of beatitude. His protagonists, significantly including a number of animals, desire—without real expectation—a condition quite beyond their grasp and all but out of ken. Illustrating some of the complexities of this seeing "through a glass" with extraordinary darkness, the dog narrator of "Investigations of a Dog" laments, but exemplifies, the mortal incapacity to achieve other being despite a brief experience suggesting the light and harmony of celestial spheres. He recalls that "out of some place of darkness . . . seven dogs stepped into the light" and "from the empty air they conjured music." He adds:

I longed . . . to beg them to enlighten me . . . but . . . the music . . . cast me hither and thither, no matter how much I begged for mercy, and rescued me finally from its own violence by driving me into a labyrinth of wooden bars which rose round that place, though I had not noticed it before, but which now firmly caught me, kept my head pressed to the ground . . . though the music still resounded in the open space behind me.[23]

Heinz Politzer rightly refers to this music, as to music elsewhere in Kafka, as Apocalyptic, symbolizing "the perennially unattainable" and usually heralding "an ultimate vision of judgment, like the trumpets of Doom."[24] But whether the seven "musicians" are the visitants of a benign or a malign metaphysical order is not easy to determine. So are Kafka's transcendental projections, while often traced along lines of sacred Judeo-Christian myth, fraught with teasing ambiguities. For the beautiful, bright dogs from "out . . . of darkness" actually afflict their victim when they make him aware of prison bars, in effect binding him through a vision of transcendence serving only to accentuate the void of the labyrinth. In his morally equivocal positions, as in his customary focus upon the labyrinth regardless of his apparent subject, Kafka has deep affinities with the aesthetics of gloom associated with the Gothic Revival in literature, and he takes his place unmistakably in a tradition centering, like it, upon the dark and infernal nether regions and the fearful prodigies issuing from them.

---

[21] Focillon, II, 71-72, 176-177, 199.

[22] Meyer Abrams, *Natural Supernaturalism: Tradition and Revolution in Romantic Literature* (New York: Norton, 1971), pp. 37-46, shows that the Apocalyptic marriage, based on Biblical sources, has been a pervasive theme of literature, as in the Romantic vision of union between transcendent and mortal or spiritual and physical. Some of the unpromising love affairs in eschatological contexts in Kafka's works seem to be parodies of this marriage metaphor.

[23] "Investigations of a Dog," in *Description*, pp. 243-246.

[24] Heinz Politzer, "Franz Kafka's Language," *Modern Fiction Studies*, 8 (1962), 16-17. See also Politzer's *Parable and Paradox*, p. 244.

This dark tradition, like the "left hand" of a Judgment panel torn violently asunder from its original contexts, forms the complement—the murky mirror-image—to the strain of subliminal Romantic Gothicism of the "Medieval ideal." As in the masterpieces of such dark writers as E. T. A. Hoffmann, Brockden Brown, or Edgar Allan Poe, among others, supernatural power in the works of Kafka is usually highly suspect and quite possibly Satanic rather than Divine. While it is said that, for Kafka, in a culture experiencing spiritual paucity, "the shadow of God in his absence" continues to be the dominant presence in creation,[25] it becomes problematic in what way the "shadow" of God would not be identical with a black demiurge from the pit. Kafka's negativity, however, seems enforced upon his religious predisposition by a world view with which he is out of sympathy—a dilemma which he has in common with other writers on infernal themes. As the Devil tells Thomas Mann's musician-Faust, Adrian Leverkühn, the theology of the Divine has been absorbed into the man-made, enervated society:

Believe me, barbarism even has more grasp of theology than has a culture . . . which has known only culture, only the humane, never excess, paradox, the mystic passion, the utterly unbourgeois ordeal. But I hope you do not marvel that "the Great Adversary" speaks to you of religion. . . . Who else, I should like to know, is to speak of it today? . . . Since culture fell away from the cult and made a cult of itself, it has become nothing else than a falling away.[26]

For some readers, there often seems to be an unwritten wish in Kafka that his works might involve, like Goethe's *Faust*, some "Prologue in Heaven" with God's bargain over his Job figure: that the Devil might have power to "try" his characters only for a time.[27]

As Mann's Medieval sources suggest, highly "theological" invocation of the demonic is far from unique to the twentieth century. His "Great Adversary" sums up attitudes which underlie movements widely separated from each other in time and place, attitudes which would seem symptomatic of the cultural malaise occurring when a society has seemingly exhausted—or too rigidly codified—its original theocentric inspirations. Examples of similar motivation which come readily to mind from the history of the arts are those of the Anglo-French *Décadence* ending the nineteenth century, a movement linked with Satanism from that of De Sade during the French Revolution through that of Baudelaire and others in the following century. Such phenomena, along with the English Gothic novel, join hands, in some respects, with the occultisms rampant in the waning European Middle Ages, obsessed with the Dance of Death, Anti-Christ and Anti-Cosmos, and Tower of Babel motifs—as with sorcery, "the romance of the devil" (Focillon, II, 142). Here, then, not in Gothic proper but in Gothic Baroque art, appearing with

---

25 Hans Joachim Schoeps, "The Tragedy of Faithlessness," in *The Kafka Problem*, p. 287.

26 Thomas Mann, *Doctor Faustus*, trans. H. T. Lowe-Porter (New York: Knopf, 1948), p. 243.

27 Donald M. Kartiganer, "Job and Joseph K.: Myth in Kafka's *The Trial*," *Modern Fiction Studies*, 8 (1962), 31-34, suggests certain connections between the Book of Job and *The Trial*.

the decline of Scholasticism,[28] the elusive link existing between the Gothic graphic tradition and the *genre noir* seems to lie. Certainly, when Horace Walpole and his followers revived a "Gothic" style in eighteenth-century England, their most frequent themes—decidedly unlike those of the Scholastic world of the thirteenth century—evinced a preference for the dark pole to which Medieval Gothic itself had shifted in "the preoccupation with death, which weighed so heavily on the later Middle Ages" (Focillon, II, 166). Doubtless this is why Focillon remarks that the Gothic Revival in England takes the Middle Ages "in reverse" (Focillon, II, 205).

It cannot be forgotten that by far the majority of the painted representations of the ghastly, yawning Hell's Mouth—the mouth of Leviathan—and of the autonomous treatment of the torture of the damned, are products of the fifteenth century or later; that the majority of Anti-Christ drawings are products not of the Gothic period at all but of the "Northern Renaissance" or Reformation. Such themes as the Temptation of St. Anthony, swarming with demons, were revived from Romanesque carvings of the tenth and eleventh centuries to satisfy the late Medieval taste for the bizarre. In the Gothic cathedral at its height, this element "had always been present, but held in check by the discipline of the stone" high in the towers, in portal plinths, or beneath archivolts; these reserves offered ready sources to the Gothic Baroque (or Flamboyant) revival of the monstrous in the fifteenth century. Focillon writes:

The gargoyles, vestiges of the association of Romanesque biology in the architectural functions, had preserved its image, taut and rigid, at the summit of the buttresses. The grotesques which lent themselves to decoration bore witness . . . to the greatness of another age and its inexhaustible repertory of monsters. The Flamboyant style brought them back into the sculpture of the churches: in the convolutions of the ornament, Romanesque teratology lived anew, freed from its bondage and subjected to no law . . . as if the Middle Ages, near to their end, were yielding up all their dreams with precipitate haste and returning to the oldest among them. (II, 176-177)

Thus, along with literary Gothic's selective use of a set of motifs and an atmosphere from the decline of the great Medieval Gothic culture, this Gothic Revival inherits yet an earlier "revival" instinct with exaggerated and radically impellent life. Indeed, the multiple revival testifies strongly to the proposition that the terrifying aspects of otherworldliness have deep, perhaps perennial sanction within the popular consciousness. The Gothic novel's central situation of decline, which it assumes and emphasizes in its uses of ruins and death, and its usual atmosphere, subtly commingled of spiritual fear and sensationalism, seem inherent in its dark Medieval inspirations. It reproduces something of the hysteria of a dying age, racked by Apocalyptic expectations.

One uniquely ribald and frightful vision from the Gothic Baroque style

---

[28] Focillon, II, 140. See also Erwin Panofsky, *Gothic Architecture and Scholasticism* (Latrobe, Pa.: Archabbey, 1951), on the close association of High Gothic with the order of Scholasticism. Definitions of Gothic, cited by Lévy, pp. 7-76, bear out the idea that the interests of the Gothic Revival in literature lay outside Scholastic tradition, often centering on a late Gothic aspect of the Elizabethan age. See also John Harvey, *The Gothic World, 1100-1600: A Survey of Architecture and Art* (1950; rpt. ed., New York: Harper and Row, 1969), pp. 5-7, on Scholasticism; p. 9 on late Gothic style in England ("it must be admitted that much English work of the fifteenth century did . . . rely for effect upon a lavish display of repetitive carving and detail"); pp. 73-74 on Anglo-French interchanges of Gothic styles.

has particular relevance to Kafka—the Anti-Cosmos of Hieronymus Bosch, with whom, along with Pieter Brueghel, he has similar predilections for creating hybrid forms in his art—grotesques.[29]   Bosch was employed by Margaret of the Austrian Empire more than four centuries before Kafka was born in that empire.   The native places of both Bosch and Kafka— Netherlands and Prague [Bohemia]—are singled out by Focillon as centers not of "re-emergence but actual continuity" of Gothic art (Focillon, II, 204, 167).   Even a description of Bosch's "revelation of a new Apocalypse" is sufficient to suggest Kafka's works, enumerating their very subjects in several instances: the Netherlander's "school" belongs to "the last great reverie of the Middle Ages, with its monstrous piles of rock-work, its towers of Babel, its diabolic transformations of objects, its country-fair humour . . . combined with its sense of universal catastrophe" (Focillon, II, 205).   Something of the same audacity attaches to Kafka's use of a narrator who is a bridge with "bushy hair" and a tail coat,[30] and the same quality of unreality informs "The Metamorphosis," in which a young man has been transformed into a giant cockroach with a human brain.   Towers of Babel recur in Kafka, reflecting both his fascination with graphic arts and his acute sense of the unsubstantiality of human achievements.

Kafka's fiction contains a number of paintings and photographs, as well as monuments, to effect the stasis of an "eternal present."[31]   Less well known is his further use of graphic arts iconography as an allusive device in both descriptive and episodic passages.   The practice, in fact, accounts for much

[29] Karl-Heinz Fingerhut, *Die Function der Tierfiguren im Werke Franz Kafkas: Offene Erzählgerüste und Figurenspiele* (Bonn: H. Bouvier, 1969), p. 100. See also Wolfgang Kayser, *Das Groteske: Seine Gestaltung in Malerei und Dichtung* (Oldenburg and Hamburg: Gerhard Stalling, 1957), pp. 77, 157-161, 200-201, on Kafka; and Norbert Kassel, *Das Groteske bei Franz Kafka* (Munich: W. Fink, 1969).

[30] "The Bridge," in *Description,* p. 116.

[31] Cohn, "Castles and Anti-Castles," p. 42. See also Cohn's "Kafka's Eternal Present: Narrative Tense in 'Ein Landarzt' and Other First-Person Stories," *PMLA,* 83 (1968), 144-150; Martin Walser, *Beschreibung einer Form* (Munich: Carl Hanser, 1961), p. 150. See also Winfried Kudezus, "Erzählhaltung und Zeitverscheibung in Kafkas 'Prozess' und 'Schloss,'" *Deutsche Vierteljahrsschrift für Literaturwissenschaft und Geistesgeschichte,* 38 (1964), 192-207, noting exceptions to the pattern.

of the effect of densely stratified significance throughout his canon, chiefly evoking mythic and religious dimensions. The difficulty of considering Kafka in relation to Christian imagery would be great, indeed, if the frequent critical equation of him with his major protagonists were borne out by his fictional texts. But not only do his Joseph K. and K. distinguish themselves from their Jewish author by identifying themselves as Christians—the former in Catholic ritual and the latter in detailed memories of his home church—but his iconographic references are often demonstrably to Gothic Church art. Indeed, an early identification of iconography in Kafka—a study also demonstrating elements of inspiration from a Jewish service[32]—must suggest a curious displacement between some of his informing experiences and their appearance in "Christian" pictorial art forms. While "The Judgment," a story sharing the death sentence theme of *The Trial*, may dramatize part of the Day of Atonement service, a key description of a father as Judge and God draws upon one conventional stance of the Pantocrater of the Last Judgment: one hand aloft, the "giant" statuesque figure stands poised to pronounce a formulaic sentence of "death by drowning,"[33] which sends his son plunging from a bridge suggestive of the Bridge of Judgment.[34]

In *The Trial*, the merging of civil and Divine authority is adumbrated specifically in terms of artistic conventions. Titorelli, the "hereditary" painter of portraits for "the Judges," uses iconic patterns like those common in Medieval Byzantine workshops; in fact, "every Judge insists on being painted as the great old Judges were painted" (p. 152), each "on the point of rising menacingly from his high seat bracing himself firmly on the arms of it" (p. 147). Joseph K. learns that the painting's subject actually sits on a kitchen chair which the painter's art renders as the "high seat" or throne. K. watches Titorelli's use of conventions to give "celestial" identity to one likeness, a love token "for a lady": "a reddish shadow began to grow round the head of the Judge, a shadow which tapered off in long rays as it approached the edge of the picture. This play of shadow bit by bit surrounded the head like a halo" (p. 147). Kafka, by pointing out iconographic lines with which he "plays" throughout the novel, thus suggests a main reason for the vaguely supernatural aura pervading its court scenes.

The interrogation session in the second chapter of *The Trial* has surprising affinities with the configurations of the *dies irae*, though of a dingy slum variety taking ironic cognizance of the decline of its tradition. Joseph K., on a Sunday morning, climbs five flights of rickety stairs to encounter, in an attic, the congregated human family standing to left and to right of the enthroned Judge surrounded by gallery registers suggesting saints or elders. Drawn inwardly to this hearing, K. is admitted to it by a type of the female mediatrix—a "washer-woman" apparently cleansing people's "dirty linen" (pp. 37, 68)—who shuts the door ritualistically behind him. K. finds the cloudy air "too thick for him" and "the room . . . surely too full already," but a cherub-like, "red-cheeked" guide parts the multitude:

[32] Erwin R. Steinberg, "The Judgment in Kafka's 'The Judgment,' " *Modern Fiction Studies*, 8 (1962), 23-30.

[33] "The Judgment," in *The Penal Colony: Stories and Short Pieces*, trans. Willa and Edwin Muir (New York: Schocken, 1961), pp. 49-63.

[34] Robert Hughes, *Heaven and Hell in Western Art* (New York: Stein and Day, 1968), pp. 164-168.

A crowd of the most variegated people . . . filled a . . . two-windowed room, which just below the roof was surrounded by a gallery, also quite packed, where the people were able to stand only in a bent posture with their heads and backs knocking against the ceiling. . . .

K. let himself be led off, it seemed that in the confused, swarming crowd a slender path was kept free after all, possibly separating two different factions; . . . immediately to right and left of him K. saw scarcely one face looking his way, but only the backs of people. . . . Most of them were dressed in black, in old, long, and loosely hanging Sunday coats. These clothes were the only thing that baffled K., otherwise he would have taken the gathering for a local political meeting.

At the other end of the hall, toward which K. was being led, there stood on a low and somewhat crowded platform a little table, set at a slant, and behind it . . . sat a fat little wheezing man. . . . The fat little man now and then flung his arms into the air, as if he were caricaturing someone. . . . Only the people in the gallery still kept up their comments. As far as one could make out in the dimness, dust, and reek, they seemed to be worse dressed than the people below. Some had brought cushions with them, which they put between their heads and the ceiling, to keep their heads from getting bruised. . . .

The fuggy atmosphere in the room was unbearable, it actually prevented one from seeing the people at the other end. . . .

Here . . . the reek of the room and the dim light together made a whitish dazzle of fog. (pp. 37-46)

The scene's actions are as absurd as the parody of the place itself, the whole maintaining much of the tenor of popular "pearly gates" humor or of Lord Byron's version of the banal business transacted in the similar setting of his "Vision of Judgment."[35] Joseph K.'s Judge holds a watch, or time, in one hand and, producing a ledger "grown dog-eared from much thumbing," addresses K. in the Everyman tradition of Doomsday drama—by a representative occupation:

'Well, then . . . you are a house painter?' 'No,' said K., 'I'm the chief clerk of a large bank.' This answer evoked such a hearty outburst of laughter from the right party that K. had to laugh too. . . . There were even a few guffaws from the gallery. . . .

The left half of the hall, however, was still as quiet as ever, the people there stood in rows facing the platform and listened unmoved. (p. 40)

K.'s attempt to win sympathy from the "unmoved" underscores the ambiguity of his situation, as Kafka slyly presents it, for it is entirely uncertain whether "left hand" and "right hand" are from the viewpoint of the Examining Magistrate [Richter], the apparent Judge, or Joseph K., the possible Judge of himself.[36] Since the two "judges" face each other, the factions are, at least, of diametrically opposite designation to them. If the factions represent those of the usual judgment pattern—since the "strange assembly"

---

[35] Note the bureaucracy in the sky, according to Byron, "The Vision of Judgment" (lines 19-20, 32):

Terrestrial business filled naught in the sky
Save the recording angel's black bureau;

Six angels and twelve saints were named his clerks.

[36] Strother B. Purdy, "Religion and Death in Kafka's *Der Prozess*," *Papers on Language and Literature*, 5 (1968), 170-182; Frederick J. Hoffman, "Kafka's *The Trial*: The Assailant as Landscape," *Bucknell Review*, 9 (1960-1961), 89-105, suggest that Joseph K. judges himself.

(p. 41), meeting always on Sundays, seems ecclesiastical and is pointedly not political—they would signify good and evil, the blessed and the damned; it is, therefore, characteristic of the problems raised by Kafka's fiction that these poles can not be differentiated from each other. Indeed, the two are ultimately complicated further by "drifting together" (p. 44). When, at the conclusion of his hearing, K. turns to his fellows—supposedly "elderly men, some of them with white beards" (p. 42)—the comic situation becomes a terrifying one with the abrupt rapidity of a transformation in nightmare: "What faces these were around him! Their little black eyes darted furtively from side to side, their beards were stiff and brittle, and to take hold of them would be like clutching bunches of claws rather than beards" (p. 47).

The ghastly final impression is partly anticipated by incongruous circumstances throughout the sequence. In fact, the session ends when interrupted by the strange behavior—shrieking and "gazing at the ceiling" (p. 46)—of a "law student," or apprentice imp, who has the gracious washer-woman in an amorous grip in a corner of the room. He is later identified in repeated instances as a monster (*das Scheusal*) with a misshapen form (*die krumme Beine*) who carries this lady bodily away, presumably for the pleasure of the Judge. Moreover, animal imagery involving the student is surprisingly extensive, the crookedness of his bones suggesting actual coils (*die krumme Beine zum Kreis gedreht*), perhaps like those of a reptile; the inhuman picture of him is reinforced, as well, by his own actions, as when he assaults Joseph K.'s restraining hand: he "snapped at it with his teeth" (p. 58). Such details give ample warrant for wondering what his actual classification may be—one of the demon family, such as the Incubus; member of the animal kingdom; or fringe-dweller in the human race—and from what part of the infernal regions he may be a fugitive. In view of such typically Kafkaesque details, it is somewhat bewildering to find that Kafka's "realism" is a matter for debate and that one critic, for example, applauds him for using "no Gothic trickery, no monstrous or surreal properties."[37]

The events and characters of the interrogation scene represent those of the Judgment, erupting in a debased form into a modern, earthly setting but bringing with it the hordes of Hell. Thus monsters are unleashed from their traditional confines, and bestial, demonic, and commonplace elements mingle within a still-recognizably sacred *mise en scène*. This curious framework both draws upon and deflates Medieval Gothic form, as in the artful portrait-spoof of the spheres of stooping saints cushioning their heads from the constraining ceiling in the *dies irae* in the attic: drawing a bold arch across the upper registers of the scene, the description recalls the frequently convoluted or interrupted lines of haloes in the deterministic semi-circular contour of the Gothic tympanum. It is the atmosphere of hell, however, which prevails —and which is even contagious. In a later visit to the court milieu, Joseph K., taken for one of the guards or other officials by another accused man, suddenly assumes the character of a warden in Hell—to the point that "the man cried out as if K. had gripped him with glowing pincers instead of with two fingers" (p. 65). The domain of the law courts abounds generally with infernal imagery. At Titorelli's studio among court offices, for example,

---

[37] Hoffman, p. 90, goes so far as to say that "at no time are the officials or minions of the Law made to look like monsters or grotesques," p. 97.

there is nothing seraphic about the host of debauched little girls, at least one of them notably deformed,[38] who throng the stairways; and Joseph K. notices that, through "a gaping hole" in the painter's building, pours "a disgusting yellow fluid, steaming hot, from which some rats fled into the adjoining canal" (p. 141). Perhaps the most striking example of the radical displacement of Hell from any system of order is the chapter, "The Whipper"—termed by one critic "a bit of writing reeking of burning flesh"[39]—in which Joseph K. discovers that a back "lumber room" in his own place of employment harbors a flagellation which, tableau-like, is always in the same stages when he opens the door. The episode is not so much an action as an action-scene, a fact underlying the atemporal character of damnation.

Theological interpretation of *The Trial* stands largely on the chapter, "In the Cathedral," which introduces a new atmosphere just before the novel's end. No longer the decadent and at times gruesome world of most of the book, the Gothic cathedral setting presents an even more dreadful spectacle—the grand and the solemn abandoned to silence and obliterated by darkness. And it presents—in contrast to the previously crowded approximation of the General Judgment, however parodic—man's fearful solitude at the beck of a more personal call. Though without imagery of decomposition and impoverishment, the chapter's keynote is loss. First, a mysterious Italian—a stock figure of the Gothic novel—fails to keep an appointment to see the cathedral's art treasures with Joseph K. Subsequently, forms serve only to emphasize their own emptiness, and the very art in the cathedral's interior is multiply disquieting: a "recent" painting depicts the death of a deity, the Entombment of Christ (p. 205), and the great pulpit remains empty, even during a "sermon." The effect of the pulpit's decor in the growing shadows of a daylight eclipse seems a picture of cosmic conflict without a victor: "The outer balustrade and the stonework . . . were wrought all over with foliage in which little angels were entangled" and "the deep caverns of darkness among and behind the foliage looked as if caught and imprisoned there" (p. 205). Another omen of an eschatological kind is the deformed verger, seemingly a

---

[38] Kartiganer, p. 41, finds that "the picture of Hell is complete" at this point.

[39] Charles Neider, *The Frozen Sea: A Study of Franz Kafka* (1948; rpt. ed., New York: Russell and Russell, 1962), p. 109.

caricature of one of the Horsemen of the Apocalypse, who motions Joseph K. toward his appointed place for an irregular service: "With something of the same gait, a quick, limping motion, K. had often as a child imitated a man riding on horseback. . . . How he stops when I stop and peers to see if I am following him!" (p. 206).

Kafka's use of the monumental Gothic setting is not ironic, as in the iconographic play with the attics, but tragic—and powerfully so—as hallucinatory spatial effects, like great throes of expansion and contraction, rack the cathedral before the full force of the darkness negates visual form altogether. In striking contrast to the great pulpit and the expanses of the building, a fantastically constrictive side pulpit catches Joseph K.'s eye: "It was so small that from a distance it looked like an empty niche intended for a statue. . . . The whole structure was designed as if to torture the preacher" (pp. 206-207). Countering such diminutive architectonics is K.'s agorophobic experience of space approaching infinity and only exaggerated by the presence of surrounding structure: "K. felt . . . a solitary figure between the rows of empty seats . . . ; and the size of the Cathedral struck him as bordering on the limit of what human beings could bear" (pp. 208-209). In the absence of sound, light, and a coordinated sense of structure to give definition to space, the setting and time alike become uncertain; in effect, the scene is preempted utterly by the single arena of the protagonist's soul: "it was no congregation the priest was addressing, the words were unambiguous and inescapable, he was calling out: 'Joseph K.!'" (p. 209). As if from far reaches of memory, K., his life suspended in a futile wait, thinks of "an old woman before an image of the Madonna" who "ought to be there too" but is "somewhere or other" else; neither the expected guest nor even an unknown fellow worshipper relieves his loneliness before the "prison chaplain" (p. 210). An impression that the cathedral equates with the "prison" seems complete as the official and his ward wander circularly through the darkness, thus following the figure of the labyrinth while discussing a "doorkeeper" and a supplicant who are equally "deluded" or "deceived" (p. 217).

The expanding application of the spatial and mental maze to the world and human existence is implicit in the fact that the chapter parallels earlier episodes in which the labyrinth of meaningless chaos invades other structures —K.'s apartment, where he is arrested unaccountably; the painter's studio and other civic buildings, where absurd hearings proceed; and K.'s bank, where at least one cell houses eternal punishment. Kafka's choice of the Gothic cathedral for the culminating revelation of the world as "prison" without transcendence is particularly appropriate. The Gothic cathedral—which had traditionally mirrored all creation and corresponded even in measurements to the size and shape ascribed to the universe[40]—now reflects the radical disjunctures of Kafka's fictional world, a world going void in "black night" at noon.

---

[40] Otto von Simson, *The Gothic Cathedral* (New York: Pantheon, 1962), pp. 13-33; Erwin Panofsky, ed., *Abbot Suger on the Abbey Church of St.-Denis and Its Art Treasures*, trans. Panofsky (Princeton, Princeton Univ. Press, 1946), pp. 63-65 *et passim;* Panofsky, *Gothic Architecture and Scholasticism;* St. Augustine, *The Trinity*, trans. Stephen McKenna (Washington, D.C.: Catholic Univ. of America Press, 1963), IV, 4-6; Macrobius, *Commentary on the Dream of Scipio*, trans. and ed. William H. Stahl (New York: Columbia Univ. Press, 1952), pp. 23-39.

Yet it is precisely Kafka's allusive evocation of an old world order of faith and grandeur—a High Gothic "golden age"—which gives the darkness its particular density. Thus the splendor of the cathedral, the one grand structure in *The Trial*, only underscores the tragedy of its ultimate lack of reality or function for the protagonist. Darkness is presented in pointed contradistinction to the very forms which it conceals and to its antithesis, light: "All the stained glass in the great window could not illumine the darkness of the wall with one solitary gleam of light" (p. 211). Similarly, a lamp which Joseph K. holds has "long since gone out" (p. 221). Characteristically, Kafka inserts a religious artifact into the nadir point of this exposé of the labyrinth in the cathedral: "The silver image of some saint glimmered into sight immediately before [K.], by the sheen of its own silver, and was instantaneously lost in the darkness again" (p. 221). The gloom from which K. cannot extricate himself includes an air of spiritual decadence accented by his proximity to the relic which can shine with its "own silver" while he has neither inner nor outer illumination. A further contrast—the implied one from the New Testament parable of wedding guests who must have their lamps trimmed for the Apolcalyptic union of the blessed on the Last Day[41]—relates the scene to cosmic eschatology.

It is probable that particular meaning attaches to bright objects as well as lights in Kafka's imagery,[42] informed by the Byzantine code for sacred art. This art of the icon in which he knew the scenes of Apocalypse, including the Last Judgment, posits mystic virtue in the pure gold and silver with which it clads its immortal subject in light, leaving the profane untouched by these precious substances. Thus it is well-known for its "golden ground," the lambent play of light comprising a background not of earth but of heaven.[43] Kafka's pointed introduction of the comprehensive *dies irae* and the microcosmic cathedral into his text serves to establish the original contexts and the point of departure for his own variations upon the old Byzantine and Byzantine-Gothic formulae. Certainly, the ambiguous lights in Kafka's parodies of ecclesiastical art cannot be thoroughly appreciated without the knowledge that his models are chiefly distinguished by their brilliance of real gold and silver.[44] It is entirely propitious to his creation of Manichean de-

---

41 Von Simson, pp. 113-115, points to the admonitory significance of the wise and foolish guests in Gothic iconography: they are features of the Western (Judgment) Portal of some cathedrals.

42 Ladendorf, "Kafka und die Kunstgeschichte," *Wallraf-Richartz-Jahrbuch,* 23 (1961), 313-320, deals with Kafka's use of light from the painterly tradition, finding it ultimately a device of Impressionism well-schooled in ancient art.

43 Focillon, II, 116-117; Demus, pp. 233-236. See also Dvořáková *et al.,* p. 63, on the ideological design of the Byzantine art in Prague: "The linking of the heavenly and earthly spheres is entrusted to the transparent medium of precious stones and crystals which, according to Augustinian conceptions, were suffused with the light of the spirit and formed from above just as man can be formed only by the hand of God."

44 Eisner, p. 23, identifies some models for the cathedral art in *The Trial*. See Dvořáková *et al.,* pp. 68-69, on statuary at St. Vitus' Cathedral; pp. 101-107, on "golden ground" at Emmaus Monastery; p. 63 (cited), on Byzantine ornamentation at Castle Karlšteyn: "The central idea of the interior has its starting-point in the chancel where on the breast of the vaulting is a golden sun, a silver moon and the five other then known planets. They are in the surface firmament, thickly sown with golden stars, which is designed to create the illusion of the heavenly sphere itself, where

signs of light and dark, to his very development of the *roman noir*, that the height or "golden" period of his particular culture was coterminous with its extensive use of the Byzantine style.

As if a glimpse of the sphere of light gives the greatest pain to the denizens of Hell or of a hellish earth,[45] Kafka continues to work with variations upon the pattern of vision and imprisonment economically contained in "Investigations of a Dog." The human position is unredeemed, among the beasts, and it is significant that both Joseph K. in *The Trial* and K. in *The Castle* are associated with dog imagery (Fingerhut, pp. 215-223). Joseph K. dies, in his own words, "like a dog" (p. 229) at his execution. K., too, was destined by his author for a similarly unremitting "trial" ending in his dying "worn out" by his quest.[46] The condition of both, like that of the dog narrator, is defined by its lacks: their world is one ranging atmospherically from dingy to black, at all times outside the "golden ground" of paradisaical experience.

Perhaps the most striking of Kafka's Medieval tropes for the lost connection with transcendence is the castle—chiefly notable for its absence—in the novel of that name. The dim outlines of the castle merely vex the quester with their "illusory emptiness" (p. 3); and K., despite his active pursuit of the rituals of pilgrimage, meets only with the same sequence of ambiguously authorized bureaucrats that faces Joseph K. The chain of command governing the lives of both characters seems empty in its upper reaches so that the protagonists, seeking authority above themselves, range uneasily through the arena of a broken link pervaded by a vertiginous *horror vacui*. Thus, in *The Trial* there are mere "legends" of the High Court which can acquit an accused man (p. 154), and "the really great lawyers" are "merely heard of and never seen" (p. 178). Similarly, *The Castle*, while crowded with castle servants of varying degrees, presents no access to the castle "gentlemen"—

---

dwell God, Christ and His saints and the Chosen of the Lord. Technically the effect is achieved by covering the vaulting with hundreds of concave lenses, lined with gold foil: the whole of this covering was originally of pure gold."

[45] See the somewhat similar concept in Dante, *Inferno,* Canto V (lines 121-123).

[46] This conclusion is recounted by Max Brod from a conversation with Kafka. See Brod's postscript to the 1946 German edition of the novel, p. 415.

much less to the Count Westwest, whose name signifies the paradox of death and Resurrection,[47] the same paradox which was symbolized by the traditional western location of the Judgment Portal of a Gothic cathedral (Focillon, II, 84). When K. posts guard over the sleigh of one of the castle officials to force an encounter with him in the search for Westwest, he finds the official —Klamm—elusive if not illusory. Indeed, the villagers base their religious commonplaces upon their own interpretations of the affairs of the unseen immortals since these are incomprehensible, anyway: "We are anxious about [Klamm] and try to guard him, and so go on to infer that he's terribly sensitive. That's as it should be and it's certainly Klamm's will. But how it is in reality we don't know" (pp. 142-143).

A tale of search for such retiring authority—one character's narrative about her family's attempt to divert a curse from itself in *The Castle*—seems relevant to both Joseph K. and K. This tale-within-the-tale presents a paradigm of man's hopeless alienation from an indifferent hierarchy and also a parody of the topography traditional to God's "right hand" in Medieval Gothic iconography. The head of a condemned household is unable to contact the officials as they fly by in carriages "on the main road near the Castle" (p. 278). The redeemed Garden of Eden, which should connect with the Celestial City or castle in a complete Judgment panel, appears as the unredeemed fallen universe given over to labor and futile expiation for an unclear offense:

'Not far from the Castle entrance there's a market garden. . . . Well, there sat Father day after day; it was a wet and stormy autumn, but the weather meant nothing to him. . . . At first he used to tell us all his little adventures . . . that in one of the passing carriages he thought he had recognized this or the other official, or that this or the other coachman had recognized him again and playfully flicked him with his whip.' (pp. 280-281)

Both the man and his wife are consumed by the spiritual quest, one rather like an inverted fairy tale in which the powers, if aware at all, are not ultimately benign: "How often we found them crouching together, leaning against each other on their narrow seat, huddled up under a thin blanket that scarcely covered them, and round about them nothing but the gray of snow and mist, and far and wide for days at a time not a soul to be seen, not a carriage" (p. 282). These experiences, serving to prefigure K.'s inconclusive fate, offer simply another version of the elaborate prosecution machine of *The Trial* with its dubious "judicial hierarchy of high, indeed of the highest rank, with an indispensable and numerous retinue of servants, clerks, police, and other assistants, perhaps even hangmen" (pp. 45-46). It both recalls and subverts an earlier era's vision of a Chain of Being.

The internal tale from *The Castle* sums up Kafka's latter-day apprehension of the entire Judeo-Christian continuum in Spenglerian terms of decline.[48] In the autumn of faith, Kafka's character is grateful even for the flick of an extra-mortal whip, of possible diabolic intercession; in full winter, such as that which deepens in *The Castle* with its year of continuous snow (p. 408), man is delivered over to meaningless punishment in a blank landscape. To these

---

[47] Wilhelm Emrich, *Franz Kafka* (Bonn: Athenäum, 1958), p. 310; Politzer, *Parable and Paradox*, p. 235. See also Kafka's *Amerika* with its use of West for the name of the Hotel Occidental, symbol of decline in the direction of the sunset.

[48] Heller, p. 143, suggests affinities between Spengler and Kafka.

seasons, long past the "golden age" of either spiritual or secular society, Kafka's works are devoted.

The Castle contains several references to grotesqueries from the "other world," beings which are hardly distinguishable from those of *The Trial*. One former favorite of Klamm, for instance, produces a photograph of the "beautiful young man" who had once come "floating" to bear her to the official (p. 101). And K.'s fiancée is beset by two of Klamm's messengers who are described as fallen angels: "in appearance good, childish, merry, irresponsible youths, fallen from the sky, from the Castle" (p. 326) but also "ugly black young demons" (p. 182).[49] These episodes are only random aspects of the generally disordered milieu.

The Last Day seems heralded throughout the work, representing the seven days of Creation in a parodic form, "a cosmogony in reverse, a 'taking back' of the work performed by the Divine" (Politzer, p. 248). In the confusion of the Herrenhof—a "halfway house" between the castle and the village— K.'s seventh day of pilgrimage proceeds to the accompaniment of a "babel of voices" and a gentleman's imitation of "the crowing of a cock" (p. 356). While K. wanders aimlessly through the rooms and corridors of this inn, his recollection of his mission seems to recede into giddy, dream-like disorientation. He considers taking asylum in a basement cell among chambermaids, one of whom explicitly fears "our last hour" (p. 407). The forces of disintegration invade the world of *The Castle* utterly as the unfinished novel trails off appropriately into the silence of the fragmentary twentieth chapter.

K.'s insertion into an Apocalyptic context like that depicted in the Book of Revelation murals in Castle Karlšteyn[50] makes it entirely credible that Kafka entrusts the character with the role of "measurer" of a New Jerusalem even while his story dramatizes the fact that New Jerusalem does not materialize with its promise of impending redemption as the "old world" passes away. Certainly, it is not difficult to see something of Kafka's world in the famous cycle at Karlšteyn, with its lurid depictions of the Beast of the Apocalypse—a seven-headed dragon—pursuing the Virgin through the wilderness of the earth during the visitation of plagues and the unleashed powers of Hell appointed to the "last days." The stages of eschatology in the pictured prophecy of St. John seem analogous to seven days of reversed Creation. It is, however, definitive of Kafka's work that it does not progress beyond this reign of Satanic powers to a Millennial vision.

Heinz Politzer finds some of Kafka's dark inspiration in the occultism of Prague's seventeenth century, its confusion of materialistic and spiritual goals suggesting at least "atmospheric connection" with Kafka's fictional world (Politzer, p. 232). Also focusing upon the writer's environment, Johann Bauer asks, "How did this passionate desire for creativity take root in the isolated, dying community" of Prague's old German culture?[51] The frenetic experimentalism of the city's Gothic Baroque or Flamboyant style, verging upon an abortive Renaissance,[52] has, in fact, a continuity not suggested by

---

[49] See also Kafka's story, "The Country Doctor," for another version of demonic eroticism—one involving a groom whose supernatural horses seem representative of the dreadful "nightmare" of Incubus legend.

[50] See Dvořáková *et al.*, Plates XIV, XV; Figures 115, 138, 140-152.

[51] Johann Bauer, *Kafka and Prague* (New York: Praeger, 1971), p. 14.

[52] Erwin Panofsky, *Renaissance and Renascences in Western Art* (Stockholm: Almqvist

mere dating; and Kafka's immediacy to late Gothic art suggests that his own work may be seen more nearly as a continuation than as a revival of a Medieval mode. Maintaining a condition of spiritual fomentation, of nostalgia and conflict over a dominant past, through centuries, Prague extended its enormous fertility for Gothic Baroque synthesis to its extraordinary potential for Gothic fiction.

Thus Kafka's unique heritage serves to place Gothic aspects of culture and of art into dramatic lines of encounter and perspective which would hardly be found in combination elsewhere. The subject of the Gothic literary mode, then, is often cultural decline per se, and, led by sure intuition of affinities elsewhere in time, it is attracted to the style of an epoch's end: thus Gothic fiction rejects the symmetrical order of High Gothic Scholasticism for the late, hectic bloom of Flamboyant. It is Kafka's distinction to evoke with particular clarity—and hollowness—the iconographic formulae combining the Celestial City with the Inferno, objectified on earth in castle-and-prison by which millions of Europeans conceived of their experience and their eternal prospects for more than a thousand years. But it is always necessary to distinguish in Kafka's work both formal patterns and their inverted signification.[53] As thoroughly as Gnosticism,[54] his vision divides ideals in their purity from their actualization in the corruptible universe and modern time. At least as significant as the typicality of Kafka's work in presenting recognizable configurations from the High Gothic heritage is the fact that it is ultimately typical of the *genre noir*, as well, in its baroque revel in the fragmentation of the whole. Turning up "the hidden underside of the Middle Ages," in Focillon's phrase (II, 176), Kafka's world retains the sketch of an inaccessible City of God only to place Pandemonium in bolder relief.

---

and Wiksells, 1960), p. 34, finds the Renaissance "purely Italianate," and the Mediterranean or classical quality of the phenomenon is widely held in art history. The word is used in the text in this sense. See also Eberhard Hempel, *Baroque Art and Architecture in Central Europe,* trans. Elisabeth Hempel and Marguerite Kay (Harmondsworth: Penguin, 1965), pp. 126-139, 177-189, on graphic arts in Bohemia from sixteenth century to eighteenth century.

[53] Adrian Jaffe, *The Process of Kafka's 'Trial'* (East Lansing: Michigan State Univ. Press, 1967), bases an entire study upon the "irrelevancy" of apparent symbolism in Kafka's purely formal structures. At the other extreme, see Peter Dow Webster, " 'Dies Irae' in the Unconscious, or the Significance of Franz Kafka," *College English,* 12 (1950), 9-15, which probes psychological issues while missing entirely the formal pertinence of its title.

[54] Heller, pp. 155-181, discusses the variations upon Platonism suggested to him by Kafka's work and finds elements of Gnosticism, as well; Walter H. Sokel, *Franz Kafka—Tragik und Ironie* (Munich and Vienna: Albert Langen and Georg Müller, 1964), pp. 356-367, considers the role of the artist in relation to Platonist theory implicit in Kafka's *Trial.*

English Gothic and the French Imagination: A Calendar of Translations, 1767-1828

MAURICE LÉVY

This bibliography is a particularly venturesome enterprise for several reasons: one is the extreme scarcity of first editions—either English or French—of Gothic novels, many of which cannot be found in the British Museum or the Bibliothèque Nationale. Read to pieces, in their time, by enthusiastic subscribers to local circulating libraries, or confined, in armoried bindings, to the privacy of luxurious bookcases, these tiny *duodecimo* volumes have been eagerly sought after in the recent past and are now collectors' items which fetch terrific prices at antiquarian bookdealers, even if in barely decent condition and complete, with their naively provocative illustrations.

Very few people, indeed, can boast that they own a first (or, for that matter, any early) edition of Ann Radcliffe's first novel, *The Castles of Athlin and Dunbayne* (1789), or of the Reverend Charles Robert Maturin's last production, *The Albigenses* (1824). Probably even fewer have on their shelves a copy of the alluring, if anonymous, *Animated Skeleton* (1798), or of its French translation, *Le Château d'Albert, ou le Squelette Ambulant* (1799).

I myself, after chasing these obsolete wonders in several countries for nearly twenty years, have never been able to hold *The Mysterious Hand; or, Subterranean Horrours!* (1811) in my own, unmysterious, ones except for a few hours in the British Museum, and though I was recently lucky enough to rescue *Estelle, ou la Fugitive de la Forêt* (1803) from a sordid environment in a Parisian bookstall on the "quais," I have never in my life come across *Le Revenant de Bérézule* (1805) otherwise than draped in its French, borrowed vesture.

Had it not been for the "insane" fancy of former collectors, it would be next to impossible today to identify these forgotten best sellers issued from

MAURICE LÉVY, Professor of English at the University of Toulouse—le Mirail, is author of *Le Roman Gothique Anglais: 1764-1824* and other works. His latest book is *Images du Roman Noir*, an annotated collection of early illustrations of the Gothic novel in French translation, some of which have been reproduced in the present volume.

the prolific presses of William Lane in Leadenhall Street, or their French translations sold, among many other places, "chez Maradan, libraire, rue Pavée-André-des-Arts, n° 16," or "chez Poisson, libraire, rue de la Loi, vis-à-vis la Bibliothèque." The unique "Sadleir-Black" Collection of Gothic fiction, now in the rare book department of the University of Virginia Library, and the hardly less important "Hammond Collection," now in the New York Society Library, are today an invaluable help to such scholars as are reckless enough to investigate these futile but difficult matters. Another problem soon arises, even with the scarcest of these volumes in hand: too many titles are anonymous and remain jealously so despite the most strenuous efforts to identify the authors. Too many of them are spurious attributions and thus involve riddles often difficult to solve. As far as translations are concerned, too many of them were actually written by the alleged translators. As early as 1803, it appeared to a French critic, A. H. Dampmartin, that it was so arduous to decide which publications were genuine translations and which were frauds that probably no one, he wrote, would ever try to make the situation clear.[1] Perhaps time has come to take up Dampmartin's challenge, even though it is quite obvious that the results of such investigations can only be provisional, and doomed to rapid obsolescence.

Why the English Gothic novel was so popular in France, during the Revolutionary period and the Empire, is not easy to say, although many reasons have been suggested. If one is to believe the Marquis de Sade (himself a fine connoisseur in novels and many other things), the genre illustrated by "Monk" Lewis, Ann Radcliffe, and their innumerable followers was the logical consequence of the troubled times which Europe had endured. Everyone had suffered so many real agonies in such a short lapse of time that fiction could no longer arouse the slightest interest unless it chose to depict Hell or hellish scenes in complete harmony with the horrors of the day.[2] Whether the French Revolution had such a direct, immediate effect on novel writing is debatable; but this is not the place to discuss de Sade's statement—or its repeated echoes among the Surrealists—on the political significance of what the French call "roman noir."[3]

Perhaps a more direct reason for the popularity of English Gothic fiction among French readers of the Revolutionary period was its fierce anti-Catholicism. Georg Lukacs is right when he points out, in his *Historical Novel*, that eighteenth-century England "was already a post-revolutionary

---

[1] "Les recherches pour reconnaître les productions véritablement nées sur le sol anglais deviendraient si pénibles, si fastidieuses, qu'il n'est pas probable que personne se sente assez de patience pour les entreprendre." A. H. Dampmartin, *Des Romans* (Paris: AnX-1803), p. 49.

[2] "Il devenait le fruit indispensable des secousses révolutionnaires dont l'Europe entière se ressentait. Pour qui connaissait tous les malheurs dont les méchants peuvent accabler les hommes, le roman devenait aussi difficile à faire que monotone à lire; il n'y avait point d'individu qui n'eût éprouvé plus d'infortunes en quatre ou cinq ans que n'en pouvait peindre en un siècle le plus fameux romancier de la littérature; il fallait donc appeler l'Enfer à son secours pour se composer des titres à l'intérêt et trouver dans le pays des chimères ce qu'on savait couramment en ne fouillant que l'histoire de l'homme dans cet âge de fer." *Idée sur les Romans,* éd. O. Uzanne (Paris: Rouveyre, 1878), pp. 32-33.

[3] This point is discussed at some length in my *Le Roman Gothique Anglais* (Toulouse: Association des Publications de la Faculté des Lettres, 1968), pp. 602-615.

country."[4] It had in particular already achieved what France was then fighting for: its religious emanicipation. The English had long ago shaken off what they considered the fetters of Popish superstition and tyranny. More than two decades before writing *The Castle of Otranto*, Walpole had expressed in a juvenile piece of poetry his satisfaction at seeing Britannia's golden plains "From mitred bondage free and papal chains."[5] That his "Gothic story" had something to do with the problem of religious freedom is evinced by his suggestion, in the (anonymous) preface of the first edition, that the book was written by "an artful priest" who availed himself "of his abilities as an author to confirm the populace in their ancient errors and superstitions."[6] Obviously the Gothic novel sprang from the ambiguous attitude and divided feelings of the mid-century revivalists, who, at the same time that they celebrated the melancholy beauty of some "hallowed fane" or the picturesque effects of "yon ruin'd abbey's moss-grown piles," rejoiced at the decline and fall of the "Romish" empire over their country:

> Then from its towering height with horrid sound
> Rush'd the proud Abbey. Then the vaulted roofs,
> Torn from their walls, disclos'd the wanton scene
> Of monkish chastity! Each angry friar
> Crawl'd from his bedded strumpet, muttering low
> An ineffectual curse.

These lines, from William Shenstone's *The Ruined Abbey; or, the Effects of Superstition*,[7] written in 1764, while they are a good illustration of the feelings of the average eighteenth-century Englishman toward Roman Catholicism, might serve as an appropriate motto for M. G. Lewis's *The Monk* or many other lurid Gothic pieces.

Similar quotations might be made from dozens of minor didactic or (as some were called) "topographical" poems of the time, or from many essays and "pieces in prose" among which that on "Monastic Institutions," by Anna Laetitia Aikin, is prominent: "Ye are fallen," she emphatically wrote, "dark and gloomy mansions of mistaken zeal, where the proud priest and lazy monk fatten'd upon the riches of the land, and crept like vermin from their cells to spread their poisonous doctrines through the nation, and disturb the peace of kings!"[8] No wonder, therefore, if Ann Radcliffe's convents are described as places where rubicund friars spend their time indulging in the satisfaction of their unbridled appetites,[9] or if Father Felix, in *The Black Valley*—"a tale, from the German of Veit Weber"—is represented as "a fox-haired, red-nosed, lusty, double-chinned monk, fond of his convent but more fond of himself; punctual in the chapel, still more so in the refectory; a confirmed de-

---

[4] Georg Lukacs, *The Historical Novel*, trans. Hannah and Stanley Mitchell (Boston: Beacon Press, 1963), p. 21.

[5] "An Epistle from Florence to Thomas Ashton" [1740], *The Works of Horatio Walpole*, 5 vols. (London: G. G. & J. Robinson, 1798), I, 11.

[6] Walpole, II, 3.

[7] *The Works of the English Poets*, ed. Alexander Chalmers, 21 vols. (London, 1810), XIII, 323.

[8] J. and A. L. Aikin, *Miscellaneous Pieces in Prose* [1773], new ed. (Altenburgh: G. E. Richter, 1795), p. 63.

[9] See the scene, among many others, in *A Sicilian Romance*, Ch. 5.

bauchee, and a thorough hypocrite who could smile in a man's face while he threw poison into the cup of their greeting."[10]

No wonder, either, if what the chaste imagination of the "Enchantress of Udolpho" could only picture under the thick veils of symbols was more crudely described by less constrained novelists. W. H. Ireland's "abbess," for one, is in no way inhibited by the reputation of her sex for modesty or, for that matter, deterred by the exacting nature of her religious vows from raping one of her many nightly visitors:

> She guided his hand to her bosom. Her dress was thin; he felt the firm and beauteous breast that heaved beneath. He unconsciously threw himself on the couch where the Madre was already seated. Her ivory arm immediately encircled his neck. The Comte's head sunk, unresisting, on her snowy and palpitating bosom. The Madre was beautiful and the Comte was but a man.[11]

Of course, such scenes were read in Revolutionary France not only with the ordinary interest aroused by "curiosa," but also as the confirmation of many of the ideas that had been so far circulated only in such clandestine publications as *Les Intrigues Monastiques ou l'Amour Encapuchonné* or *Les Amours de Sainfroid et d'Eulalie, Fille Dévôte*.[12]   In fact, the French were, in 1789, one revolution late and were then discovering what had been considered as established facts in England since 1688.   While the Gothic novel in a way voiced a secular tradition of antipopery feelings, it coincided with the rise in France of a new kind of openly anticlerical literature, which only the fall of the *ancien régime* could have fostered.   Those among the French community of the time who were familiar with such plays as de Monvel's *Les Victimes Cloîtrées* (1791), Marsollier's *Camille ou le Souterrain* (1793), or *Le Couvent, ou les Voeux Forcés* by Olympe de Gouges, which went through more than eighty performances between 1790 and 1792, must have felt at ease when they read the stories of unfortunate damsels confined in dreadful convents or losing their virtue in the embrace of wanton, lecherous monks.

Of the many reasons that account for the popularity of Gothic fiction in Revolutionary France, this new identity of views regarding Roman Catholicism is probably the most important.   A craze there was, indeed, immediately after the "Terreur," for monkish crimes and mysteries, "midnight bells" and "animated skeletons," "nocturnal visits" and "solemn injunctions," nuns and abbesses of all descriptions.   What is really surprising is that, at a time when the two countries were at war with each other, so many English novels (probably far more than before 1789) should have reached Paris and been almost immediately translated into French: as though readers, on both sides of the Channel, had tried to exorcise their fears and, in some obscure way, reach a kind of reconciliation over the same imaginary terrors.

The best of the Gothic novels—the worst, too, in some cases—found eager translators: persons of the highest social rank left resourceless by the Revolution, or formerly influential members of the political circles now fallen into

---

[10] *The Black Valley,* "a Tale, from the German of Veit Weber," new ed. (Alexandria: J. V. Thomas, 1801), p. 14.

[11] *The Abbess,* a Romance, by W. H. Ireland, 4 vols. (London: Earle & Hemet, 1799), I, 167.

[12] See on that subject James R. Foster, *History of the Pre-Romantic Novel in England* (New York: MLA, 1949), p. 51.

disgrace or temporary neglect. These circumstances are probably responsible for the remarkable quality of some translations, like that of *The Mysteries of Udolpho* by the accomplished Comtesse Louise Marie Victorine Chastenay de Lanty, or those of *The Children of the Abbey, Clermont, Phedora; or, the Forest of Minski,* and *The Italian* by such a reputable member of the French Academy as the Abbé Morellet.

Other aristocratic names, like those of Vicountess de Ruolz, Count Germain Garnier, Baronness Caroline d'Aufdiener, *née* Wuiet, "agrégée à plusieurs académies étrangères"—so says the title-page of *Le Couvent de Sainte-Catherine* (1810)—and Marchais de Migneaux, also testify to the fact that translating novels was considered by the *ci-devants* as one of the few jobs not entirely unreconcilable with their exacting sense of honor.

But by far the greater number of translators were obscure "citoyens," like M. Cantwell, B. Ducos, P. L. Lebas, L. A. Marquand, R. J. Durdent, L. F. Bertin, and many others, some of them half-anonymous, like P° ° ° de C° ° ° or M. de L° ° °, some proud to inform the readers of their glorious past, like M. F. Laboissière, "ex-capitaine, membre de la Légion d'Honneur." On the whole, these "plebeian" translations, one must reluctantly admit, are poorly done, hastily written, often ungrammatical and hardly ever complete. Yet they were just as popular as the more faithful ones, from which they were not distinguished by a parodist of the time when he wrote, in the preface of a work allegedly translated "from the French into the vulgar tongue": "Mark how clever I am to declare myself translator, not author, when I am both. But I know that even the worst novel would not find a reader among you, unless you could read on the title-page the words TRANSLATED, etc. in capital letters."[13]

Indeed translations played a tremendous part in the literary life of the two or three decades that followed the Revolution. And it so happened that they were, in their vast majority, translations of *horrid* novels imported from across the Channel. The catalogues of circulating libraries—or, as the French called them, "cabinets de lecture"—had special entries like GHOST STORIES ("Ghosts, Spooks, Apparitions, Spectres and Visions, etc.etc.etc."), TALES OF MYSTERY ("Impenetrable Secrets, Mystery upon Mystery, Mysteries Elucidated, etc.etc.etc."), DARK NOVELS ("Disasters, Assassinations, Poisonings, Subterranean Passages, Prisons, Caverns, Old Castles, Elopements, Fatal Revenges, Atrocious Crimes, etc.etc.etc."), with long lists of novels obviously translated or imitated from Ann Radcliffe, Monk Lewis, Regina-Maria Roche, Francis Lathom, and several other English Gothicists.[14] Far more lively and exciting (even for the reader of today) than these bibliographical data are the prodigious adventures of Monsieur Dabaud, as related in 1799 by Bellin de la Liborlière in *La Nuit Anglaise,* probably the best *pastiche* of the Gothic genre ever written, after the ten or twelve most popular translations of the

---

[13] "Remarquez d'abord cette finesse de m'intituler *Traducteur,* et non pas auteur, tandis que je suis l'un et l'autre. Mais je sais que le plus mauvais roman ne trouverait pas un lecteur parmi vous, si vous ne lisiez au titre, en majuscules capitales, TRADUIT, etc." Louis Randol, *Un Pot sans Couvercle et rien dedans, ou les Mystères du Souterrain de la Rue de la Lune,* "Histoire Merveilleuse et Véritable, traduite du français en langue vulgaire" (Paris: B. Logerot), An VII, p. 5.

[14] A. Marc, *Dictionnaire des Romans* (Paris: A. Marc, 1819), pp. 160, 161, 164.

day.[15]   These two little volumes are a remarkably brilliant and humorous illustration of the incredible vogue for imported horrors among a nation which had just recently "supped full" on genuine ones.

Whereas the early English editions of Gothic novels were rarely, if ever, illustrated, practically all the French translations published during the first decade after the Revolution (say from "An II de la République" until 1804 or 1805) had frontispieces to each of their habitual three or four volumes. Most of them, as can be seen from the few samples illustrating this text, were tolerably good, if at times clumsy or exaggeratedly naive.   The plates drawn by Binet, Challiou, Queverdo, and engraved by Mariage, Bovinet, or De Launay are probably among the best.   They generally illustrate the most pathetic or spectacular occurrences, like murders, rapes, spectral apparitions, and prodigies of all sorts against a macabre background, with heaps of skeletons all over the place.   The decor was, not unexpectedly, the broken Gothic arches of a ruined abbey, or the appalling subterranean cells of a Medieval fortress.   Who, opening one of these fearful volumes, could long resist the temptation of knowing more about these beautiful, ardent heroines, dauntlessly facing wan, staring spectres or bony apparitions?   Even today, faded and yellowed by time as many of them are, these engravings still retain a charm of their own, not unpleasantly savoring of bygone days and long-vanished agonies.

Too frequently ridiculed by "serious" writers and critics, sometimes defamed by rigorous moralists, the "roman noir" had a lasting influence throughout the nineteenth century on the greatest French authors, even on such giants as Hugo, Balzac, and Baudelaire.   Later exalted by André Breton and the French Surrealists as a pre-Freudian manifestation of "abysmal life," the "roman noir" is now in high repute and frequently reprinted, sometimes in deluxe editions.   This new craze is perhaps just as unwise as the contempt in which the genre was held for so long.   The best way, perhaps, to approach these old-fashioned horrors is with the serene eye of a historian of literature. Few of these stories can be read today with anything like enthusiasm, even at midnight, which, according to Monsieur Dabaud, is "la plus belle heure de jour."[16]

---

[15] *La Nuit Anglaise, ou les Aventures jadis un peu extraordinaires, mais aujourd'hui toutes simples et très communes, de M. Dabaud, Marchand de la Rue Saint-Honoré à Paris; roman comme il y en a trop, traduit de l'Arabe en Iroquois, de l'Iroquois en Samoyède, du Samoyède en Hottentot, du Hottentot en Lapon et du Lapon en Français. Par le R. P. SPECTRORUINI, Moine Italien,* 2 vols., *se trouve dans les Ruines de Paluzzi, de Tivoli; dans les Caveaux de Ste Claire; dans les Abbayes de Grasville, de St. Clair; dans les Châteaux d'Udolphe, de Mortymore, de Montnoir, de Lindenberg, en un mot dans tous les endroits où il y a des Revenans, des Moines, des Ruines, des Bandits, des Souterrains et une TOUR DE L'OUEST.* (Now, unfortunately, only to be found at the Bibliothèque Municipale in Grenoble.)

[16] Id., I, 115.

A Bibliography of the English Gothic Novel in French Translation: 1767-1828

Only first editions, either English or French, have been listed. Each title has, whenever possible, been located at one or two libraries, in France, England, or the United States. The reproductions are the author's Leicagraphies.

1767

Le Château d'Otrante, Histoire Gothique, par M. Horace Walpole, traduite sur la seconde édition angloise par M. E. [Marc Antoine Eidous], 2 tomes in-12, Amsterdam & Paris (Prault), 1767   BN

The Castle of Otranto, a story, translated by William Marshal, gent., from the original Italian of Onuphrio Muralto, London (Lownds), 1765   BM/UVL
[by Horace Walpole]

1787

Le Champion de la Vertu, ou le Vieux Baron Anglois, Paris, 1787   Arsenal

The Champion of Virtue, a Gothic story, by the editor of The Phoenix, a translation of Barclay's Argenis, Colchester (W. Keymer), 1777   BM/UVL
[by Clara Reeve]

Le Vieux Baron Anglois, ou les Revenants Vengés, histoire gothique imitée de l'anglois de Mrs. Clara Reeve, par M. D.L.P.°°° [de la Place], Amsterdam & Paris (Didot), 1787   BM

The Old English Baron, a Gothic story, by Clara Reeve, London (Dilly), 1778 [same as preceding, with a different title]   BM/UVL

ABBREVIATIONS

Arsenal—Bibliothèque de l'Arsenal, Paris.

BM—British Museum, London.

BN—Bibliothèque Nationale, Paris.

BMM—Bibliothèque Municipale de Metz.

BMN—Bibliothèque Municipale de Nancy.

BMS—Bibliothèque Municipale de Strasbourg.

BMT—Bibliothèque Municipale de Toulouse.

Bodl—The Bodleian Library.

BPL—Boston Public Library.

CUL—Columbia University Library.

F—Farmington (the property of W. S. Lewis).

HCL—Harvard College Library.

Loliée—Loliée Marc, Libraire, 40 rue des Saints-Pères, Paris (7ème), Catalogue n° 79 (1952), Romans Noirs, Contes de Fées, Contes Fantastiques, le Merveilleux, Pré-Surréalistes, Esotérisme, 84 pp.

ML—The author's private collection.

Marc—Dictionnaire des Romans anciens et modernes, Paris (A. Marc), 1819, xiv+318 pp.

Monglond—La France Révolutionnaire et Impériale, 1789-1810, 8 vols., Grenoble & Paris, 1930-57.

NYSL—New York Society Library.

UPL—University of Pennsylvania Library.

UVL—University of Virginia Library.

The abbreviation fr. (frontispieces) means that the volumes are illustrated.

Le Moine, traduit de l'anglais, Paris (Maradan), An V—1797, frontispiece, tome III.

1788

L'Orpheline du Château, ou Emmeline, par Charlotte Smith, traduit de l'anglois sur la dernière édition, 4 tomes in-12, Londres & Paris (Buisson), 1788

BMN/ML

Emmeline, the Orphan of the Castle, by Charlotte Smith, 4 vols., London (Cadell) 1788
BM

1789

Alan Fitz'Osborne, roman historique traduit de l'anglais sur la 2ème édition par Mle°°° 2 tomes in-12, Amsterdam & Paris (Briand), 1789

Alan Fitz-Osborne, an historical tale, by Miss [Anne] Fuller, 2 vols., London (Robinson), 1786

1791

Le Comte de Strongbow, ou l'histoire de Richard de Clare et de la belle Geraldine, traduite de l'anglais par le traducteur d'Herfort, etc., 2 tomes in-12, Paris (Maradan), 1791, fr.
Arsenal

Earl Strongbow, or the history of Richard de Clare and the beautiful Geralda, by James White, esq., 2 vols., London (Crowden), 1789
BM

1793

Le Souterrain, ou Matilde, traduit de l'anglais sur la seconde édition, 4 tomes in-18, Hambourg [Fauche] & Paris [Lepetit], 1793, fr.
ML

The Recess; or, a tale of other times, by the author of The Chapter of Accidents [Sophia Lee], 3 vols., London (T. Cadell), 1783-5
BM/UVL

1794

La Forêt, ou l'Abbaye de Saint-Clair, traduit de l'anglais sur la seconde édition, avec figures, 4 tomes in-18, Paris (Denné), An II (1794), fr.
Loliée

The Romance of the Forest, interspersed with some pieces of poetry, by the authoress of A Sicilian Romance, etc. 3 vols., London (T. Hookham & J. Carpenter) 1797. [by Ann Radcliffe]
BM/UVL

1795

Caleb Williams, ou les Choses comme elles sont, traduit de l'anglais [par Samuel Constant], 3 tomes in-12, Genève 1795
Monglond

Things as they are; or, the Adventures of Caleb Williams, by William Godwin, London (B. Crosby), 1794
BM

1796

Les Avantures de Caleb Williams, ou les Choses comme elles sont, par Williams (sic) Godwin, traduites de l'anglais [par le comte Germain Garnier], 2 tomes in-8, Paris (H. Agasse), l'An IV de la République (1796)
BN/ML

A different translation of the above title.

1797

Les Châteaux d'Athlin et de Dunbayne, histoire arrivée dans les Montagnes d' Ecosse, par Anne Radcliffe, traduite de l'anglais, 2 tomes in-18, Paris (Tetsu & Delalain), 1797, fr.   *ML*

The Castles of Athlin and Dunbayne, a Highland story, London (T. Hook- ham), 1789   *BM/UVL*
[Ann Radcliffe's first novel]

Les Enfans de l'Abbaye, par Mme Re- gina Maria Roche, traduit de l'anglais par André Morellet, orné de gravures, 6 tomes in-12, Paris (Denné), 1797, fr.   *BN/ML*

The Children of the Abbey, a tale, by Regina Maria Roche, 4 vols., London (W. Lane, Minerva Press), 1796   *BM/UVL*

Hubert de Sévrac, ou histoire d'un émi- gré, roman du 18ème siècle, par Marie Robinson, auteur d'Angelina, de l'Amant Sicilien, de La Veuve, etc., traduit de l'anglais par M. Cantwell, 3 tomes in-12, Paris (Gide), 1797   *Monglond*

Hubert de Sevrac, a Romance of the Eighteenth Century, by Mary Robinson, author of Poems, Angelina, The Sicilian Lover, The Widow, etc., London (Hook- ham & Carpenter), 1796   *HCL*

Julia, ou les Souterrains du Château de Mazzini, traduit de l'anglais sur la sec- onde édition, 2 tomes in-12, Paris (For- get), 1797, An VI (sic)   *Loliée*

ALSO: Paris (Maradan), 1798, fr.   *BN/ML*

A Sicilian Romance, by the Authoress of The Castles of Athlin and Dunbayne, 2 vols., London (Hookham & Carpen- ter), 1790   *BM/UVL*

[Ann Radcliffe's second novel]

Isabelle et Théodore, traduit de l'anglais, avec figures, 2 tomes, Paris (Lepetit), 1797, fr.   *Loliée*

Another translation of The Castle of Otranto, q.v.

L'Italien, ou le Confessionnal des Péni- tens Noirs, traduit de l'anglais par A[ndré] M[orellet], 3 tomes in-12, Paris (Denné), 1797, fr.   *Arsenal*

The Italian; or, the Confessionnal of the Black Penitents, a Romance, by Ann Rad- cliffe, 3 vols., London (T. Cadell & W. Davies), 1797   *BM/UVL*

Eléonore de Rosalba, ou le Confession- nal des Pénitents Noirs, traduit de l'ang- lais d'Anne Radcliffe, auteur de La Forêt, ou l'Abbaye de Saint-Clair, par Mary Gay, avec figures de Queverdo, 7 tomes in-18, Paris (Lepetit) and Genève (J. J. Paschoud), 1797, fr.   *ML*

A different translation of the above title.

Le Moine, traduit de l'anglais [par J. M. Deschamps, J. B. D. Després, P. V. Beno- ist, P. B. de Lamare], 4 tomes in-18, Paris (Maradan), An V-1797, fr.   *BN*

The Monk, a Romance [by M. G. Lewis], 3 vols., London (J. Bell), 1796   *BM/UVL*

Les Mystères d'Udolphe, par Anne Rad- cliffe, traduit de l'anglais sur la troisième édition par Victorine de Chastenay, 4 tomes, Paris (Maradan), An V-1797, fr.   *BN*
(also: An VI-1798, 6 tomes in-18, fr.)   *BN/BMT*

The Mysteries of Udolpho, a Romance, interspersed with some pieces of poetry, by Ann Radcliffe, author of The Ro- mance of the Forest, etc., 4 vols., London (G. G. & J. Robinson), 1794   *BM/UVL*

1798

L'Abbaye de Grasville, traduction de l'anglais par B. Ducos, 3 tomes in-12, Paris (Maradan), An VI-1798, fr.
BM/BN

Grasville Abbey, a Romance [by George Moore], 3 vols., London (G. & J. Robinson) 1797
UVL

Le Château de Gallice, traduit de l'anglaise de Mrs. Hugill, par P. L. Lebas, 2 tomes in-12, Paris (Tavernier) An VI (1798), fr.
BM/BN

Isidora of Gallicia, a novel, by Mrs. Hugill, 2 vols., London (Lee & Hurst), 1797-8
UVL

Le Château Mystérieux, ou l'Héritier Orphelin, roman, traduit de l'anglais par P. F. Henry, avec figures, 2 tomes in-12, Paris (Denné jeune), 1798, fr.
BN

The Mystic Castle; or, Orphan Heir, a Romance, by the author of *The Wanderer of the Alps* [Mr. Singer], 2 vols., London (W. Lane, Minerva Press), 1796
UVL

Clermont, par Mme Regina-Maria Roche, traduit de l'anglais par André Morellet, 3 tomes in-12, Paris (Denné jeune), 1798
Monglond

Clermont, a Tale, by Regina Maria Roche, author of *The Children of the Abbey,* etc., London (W. Lane, Minerva Press), 1798 [One of the seven "horrid" novels mentioned in *Northanger Abbey.}*
BM/UVL

La Cloche de Minuit, traduit de l'anglais, 2 tomes in-12, Paris (Nicolle), An VI (1798), fr.
Monglond

ALSO: 3 tomes in-18, Paris (Maradan), An VII
ML

The Midnight Bell, a German Story, founded on Incidents in Real Life, 3 vols., London (H. D. Symonds), 1798
UVL

[by Francis Lathom. One of the seven "horrid" novels mentioned in *Northanger Abbey.}*

Le Fratricide, ou les Mystères du Château de Dusseldorf, traduit par F. Th. Delbare, 3 tomes in-18, Paris (Ancelle), AN VI-1798
Monglond

ALSO: *Dusseldorf, ou le Fratricide,* par Anna-Maria-Mackenzie, traduit de l'anglais par L. A. Marquand, 3 tomes in-18, Paris (Lemierre), An VII (1799), fr.
BM

Dusseldorf; or, the Fratricide, a Romance, by Anna Maria Mackenzie, 3 vols., London (W. Lane, Minerva Press), 1798
UVL

A different translation of the above title.

Eliza, ou Mémoires de la Famille Elderland, traduit de l'anglais par L. F. Bertin, 4 tomes in-12, Paris (Hautin), An VI-1798, fr.
UVL

The Castle on the Rock; or, Memoirs of the Elderland Family, London (H. D. Symonds), 1798.
ALSO: Irish edition, Dublin (John Rice), 1799
UPL
[by A. Kendall]

La Famille Napolitaine, par Mistriss Ellen d'Exeter, traduit de l'anglais par P. L. Lebas, 4 tomes in-8, Paris (Chaignieau aîné), An VI-1798, fr.
UVL

The Neapolitan; or, the Test of Integrity, a Novel, by Ellen of Exeter [pseud. for Anna Maria Mackenzie], London (W. Lane, Minerva Press), 1796
UVL

Le Prieuré de Saint Bernard, ou l'Usurpateur puni, roman traduit de l'anglais par l'auteur des *Infortunes de Maria,* [F. J. Villemain d'Abancourt], 2 tomes in-12, Paris, 1798
Monglond

St. Bernard's Priory, an old English Tale, being the first production of a young lady [Mrs. Harley], London (for the Authoress), 1786
BM

La Cloche de Minuit, traduit de l'anglais, Paris (Maradan), An VII, frontispiece, tome III.

1799

La Caverne de la Mort, traduit de l'anglais sur la troisième édition par L. F. Bertin, 1 tome in-24, Paris (H. Nicolle), An VII (1799), fr.　　　　　*BM*

ALSO: Paris (Maradan), An VIII　*BN*

The Cavern of Death, a Moral Tale, London (Bell), 1794　　　　*BM/NYSL*

Le Château d'Albert, ou le Squelette Ambulant, traduit de l'anglais par Cantwell, orné de jolies figures, 2 tomes in-18, Paris (Ancelle), An VII, fr.　*BN/BMM*

The Animated Skeleton, 2 vols., London (W. Lane, Minerva Press), 1798　*HCL*

Edgar, ou le Pouvoir du Remords, traduit de l'anglais par T. P. Bertin, 2 tomes in-12, Paris (Delalain), An VII (1799)

ALSO: Paris (Pigoreau), An IX-1801
　　　　　　　　　　　　Monglond

Edgar; or, the Phantom of the Castle, a novel, by Richard Sickelmore jun., 2 vols., London (W. Lane, Minerva Press), 1798

Edmond de la Forêt, roman historique, par l'auteur de *Cicely,* traduit de l'anglais par le traducteur de *La Forêt, ou l'Abbaye de Saint-Clair,* orné de figures, 4 tomes in-12, Paris (Langlois) An VII (1799), fr.　　　　　　　　　*BN*

Edmund of the Forest, an historical novel, by the author of *Cicely; or, the Rose of Raby,* 4 vols., London (W. Lane, Minerva Press), 1797　　　*UVL/NYSL*
[by Agnes Musgrave]

Ethelinde, ou la Recluse du Lac, traduit par M. de la Montagne, 6 tomes in-18, Paris (Maradan), An VII, fr.　*BN*

Ethelinde; or, the Recluse of the Lake, by Charlotte Smith, 5 vols., London (T. Cadell), 1789　　　　　　*BM*

Les Mystères de la Tour Noire, roman traduit de l'anglais de J. H. Palmer, célèbre acteur de Londres, par le Cen M°°°, 2 tomes in-12, Paris (Tavernier) An VII (1799), fr.　　　　　*BPL*

The Mystery of the Black Tower, a Romance, by John Palmer jun., author of *The Haunted Cavern,* 2 vols., London (W. Lane, Minerva Press), 1796　*UVL*

Phedora, ou la Forêt de Minski, par Mary Charlton, traduit de l'anglais par André Morellet, 4 tomes in-12, Paris (Denné), An VII, fr.　　　　　*ML*

Phedora; or, the Forest of Minski, a Novel by Mary Charlton, 4 vols., London (W. Lane, Minerva Press), 1798
　　　　　　　　　　　　BM/UVL

Rosalia, ou les Mystères du Château de Glawerka, traduit de l'anglais par Ch. P. Levesque　　　　　　*Monglond*

Unidentified.

Saint-Léon, Histoire du Seizième Siècle, traduit de l'anglais, 3 tomes in-12, Paris (Michel), 1799　　　　*Monglond*

St. Leon, a Tale of the Sixteenth Century, by William Godwin, 4 vols., London (G. G. & J. Robinson), 1799
　　　　　　　　　　　　BM/UVL

Le Tombeau, Ouvrage Posthume d'Anne Radcliffe, auteur de *l'Abbaye de Sainte-Claire,* des *Mystères d'Udolphe,* de l'*Italien,* etc., traduit sur le manuscrit, par Hector-Chausier, Paris (Barba), An VII (1799), fr.　　　　　　*Loliée*

ALSO: Paris (André), 1812, fr.　*ML*

A spurious attribution, probably written by the alleged "translator."

1800

Albert et Théodore, ou les Brigands, traduit de l'anglais, 2 tomes in-12, Paris (Vatar-Jouannet), An VIII (1800), fr.
BN

Unidentified.

Albert, ou le Désert de Strathnavern, avec Romances et Musiques gravées, traduit de l'anglais par Lefebvre, 3 tomes in-12, Paris, An VIII (1800), fr.

Albert; or, the Wilds of Strathnavern, by Elisabeth Helme, author of *Louisa; or, the Cottage on the Moor,* etc., 4 vols., London (Sampson Low), 1799 *UVL*

L'Eglise de Saint-Siffrid, traduit de l'anglais par L. F. Bertin, 5 tomes in-12, Paris (Maradan), An VIII (1800), fr. *ML*

The Church of St. Siffrid, 4 vols., London (G. G. & J. Robinson), 1797 *UVL* [by Mrs. Elisabeth Hervey]

ALSO: Paris (Nicolle), An VII (1799)

Roséide et Valmor, ou les Victimes de l'Orgueil, traduit de l'anglais de Sir [Sic] Horace Walpole, par F. B., 2 tomes in-12, Paris (Pigoreau), An VIII (1800), fr. *F*

A spurious attribution. Not otherwise identified.

Santa Maria, ou la Grossesse Mystérieuse, traduit de l'anglais de Fox par Madame Dufrenoy, 3 tomes in-12, Paris (Vignon), An IX [sic] 1800, fr. *BN*

Santa-Maria; or, the Mysterious Pregnancy, a Romance, by J. Fox, 3 vols., London (G. Kearsly), 1797 *UVL*

1801

L'Abbaye de Netley, histoire du Moyen Age, traduit de l'allemand (sic) par J. F. Fontallard, 2 tomes, Paris (Ledoux), An 9-1801, fr. *BN*

Netley Abbey, a Gothic Story, 2 vols., Southampton (printed for the author by T. Skelton and sold by C. Law, Ave Mary Lane, London) 1795 *BM/ML* [by the Rev. Richard Warner]

[Erroneously attributed to the German novelist J. L. Tieck by the catalogue of the BN]

Le Couvent de Saint Dominique, traduit de l'anglais par Mme de Rivarol, 3 tomes in-12, Paris (Ancelle), An IX (1801) *BN*

Unidentified.

Le Jeune Héritier, ou les Appartements Défendus, Conte traduit de l'anglais de William Linley, par Madame Dufrenoy, 2 tomes in-12, Paris (Vignon), An IX (1801), fr. *BN*

Forbidden Apartments, a Tale, by William Linley, 2 vols., London (W. Lane, Minerva Press), 1800 *HCL*

Le Pirate de Naples, traduit de l'anglais, 3 tomes in-12, Paris (Le Normant), An X (sic)-1801, fr. *BN/BMN*

The Pirate of Naples, a novel by Mary Charlton, author of *Rosella, Andronica, Phedora,* etc., 3 vols., London (W. Lane, Minerva Press), 1801 *HCL*

Maurice Lévy

Salvador, ou le Baron de Montbéliard, traduit de l'anglais de Mme Croffts, auteur du *Château d'Ankerwick,* 2 tomes in-12, Paris (J. J. Fuchs), An IX-1801, fr.   *BN*

Salvador; or, Baron de Montbeliard, by Mrs. Croffts, author of *Ankerwick Castle,* etc., 2 vols., London (W. Lane, Minerva Press), 1801   *NYSL*

La Soirée d'Eté, par M. Lewis, auteur du *Moine,* traduit de l'anglais sur la deuxième édition par D.L.M.°°°, 2 tomes in-12, Paris (Gueffier), An X-1801, fr.   *CUL*

A spurious attribution. Actually the translation of the anonymous: *Midsummer Eve; or, the Country Wake,* a Tale of the Sixteenth Century, 2 vols., London (Mawman), 1800

ALSO: *La Veille de la Saint-Jean,* traduit de l'anglais, 2 tomes in-12, Paris (Lenormant), 1801   *Monglond*
[Same novel with different title]

La Visite Nocturne, traduit de l'anglais de Maria Regina Roche, auteur des *Enfans de l'Abbaye,* par J. B. J. Breton, 6 tomes in-12, Paris (Gueffier) An IX-1801, fr.   *ML*

The Nocturnal Visit, a Tale, by Maria Regina Roche, author of *The Children of the Abbey,* etc., 4 vols., London (W. Lane, Minerva Press), 1800 *Bodl./UVL*

ALSO: 5 tomes, Paris (Michel & Le Normant), An IX-1801, fr.   *BM*
[the latter has different illustrations]

1802

L'Infernal Don Quichotte, histoire à l'ordre du jour, traduit de l'anglais, 3 tomes in-12, Paris (Le Normant), An X-1802, fr.   *BM/BMN*

The Infernal Quixote, a Tale of the Day, by Charles Lucas, 4 vols., London (W. Lane, Minerva Press), 1801   *BM/UVL*

Ethelwina, traduit de l'anglais de M. Horstley [sic] par Octave Segur, 2 tomes in-12, Paris (F. Buisson), An X-1802, fr.   *BN*

Ethelwina; or, the House of Fitz-Auburne, a Romance of Former Times, by T. J. Horsley Curites, 4 vols., London (W. Lane, Minerva Press), 1799 *NYSL*

1803

La Caverne de Sainte-Marguerite, traduit de l'anglais de Mistriss Helm [sic], auteur de *Louise, ou la Chaumière, d'Albert, ou le Désert de Strathnavern,* des *Promenades Instructives,* etc, 4 tomes in-12, Paris (Tavernier), An XI-1803, fr.   *BN*

St. Margaret's Cave; or, the Nun's Story, an Ancient Legend, by Elisabeth Helme, 4 vols., London (Earle & Hemet), 1801   *HCL/UVL*

Le Château de Néville, roman traduit de l'anglais par M. R.°°°deCh°°°[Lebrun des Charmettes], 2 tomes in-12, Paris An XII-1803, fr.   *BM/BN*

Neville Castle; or, the Generous Cambrians, a Novel, by the author of *Raynford Park,* 4 vols., London (T. Plummer & J. Cawthorne), 1802   *HCL*
[by Miss Purbeck]

Le Château de Saint-Donats, ou Histoire du Fils d'un Emigré échappé aux massacres en France, traduit de l'anglais de Charles Lucas, auteur de l'*Infernal Don Quichotte,* 3 tomes in-12, avec figures, An XI-1803, fr.   *ML*

The Castle of Saint Donats; or, the History of Jack Smith, 3 vols., London (W. Lane, Minerva Press), 1798 [by the Rev. Charles Lucas]   *UVL/HCL*

Le Château d'Albert, ou le Squelette Ambulant, traduit de l'anglais par Cantwell, orné de jolies gravures, Paris (Ancelle), An VII, frontispiece, tome II.

Estelle, ou la Fugitive de la Forêt, par Maria Lavinia Smith, traduit de l'anglais, 2 tomes in-12, Beauvais (Masson), An XI-1803   *BN/ML*

The Fugitive of the Forest, a Romance, by Maria Lavinia Smith, 2 vols., London (W. Lane, Minerva Press), 1801 *Bodl.*

Le Paysan de la Forêt des Ardennes, traduit de l'anglais de Mrs. Parsous [sic], auteur des *Anecdotes de deux familles bien connues et autres ouvrages,* 4 vols. in-8, Paris (A l'Imprimerie et Librairie Militaires), 1803, fr.   *BN*

The Peasant of Ardenne Forest, a Novel, by Mrs. Parsons, author of *Anecdotes of two well-known Families,* 4 vols., Brentford (P. Norbury), 1801   *UVL/BPL*

1805

Le Revenant de Bérézule, imité de l'anglais, par le traducteur de *La Fugitive de la Forêt,* 4 tomes in -12, Paris (Plassan), An XIII (1805)   *BN*

Unidentified.

Les Trois Espagnols, ou les Mystères du Château de Montillo, roman traduit de l'anglais par le traducteur de *Théodore et Olivia,* 4 tomes in-12, Paris (Pigoreau) An XII-1805, fr.

The Three Spaniards, a Romance, by George Walker, author of *The Vagabond,* etc., 3 vols., London (G. Walker), 1800   *UVL*

1806

Le Brigand de Venise, par M. Lewis, traduit de l'anglais par P. de C. . ., 1 tome in-12, Paris (Dentu), 1806 *BN*

The Bravo of Venice, a Romance, translated from the German by M. G. Lewis, London (J. F. Hughes), 1805
                    BM/UVL

La Cloche de Deux Heures, ou la Nuit Fatale, traduit de l'anglais par M. de L°°°, 1 tome in-12, Paris (Maison & Gervais), 1806, fr.   *BN*

Unidentified.

1807

L'Abbaye de Lusington, traduit de l'anglais par P. de C . . ., 3 tomes in-12, Paris (Dentu), 1807   *Monglond*

Lussington Abbey, by Henrietta Rouvière, 3 vols., London (Lane & Newman, Minerva Press), 1804

Le Château du Comte Roderic, ou les Tems Gothiques, roman historique, traduit de l'anglais par M. F. Laboissière, ex-capitaine, membre de la Légion d'Honneur, 2 tomes in-12, Paris (Collin), 1807   *BN*

Count Roderick's Castle; or, Gothic Times, a Tale, 2 vols., London (W. Lane, Minerva Press), 1794

ALSO: Philadelphia (Bradford), 1795
                    HCL/UVL

La Forêt de Hohenhelbe, ou Albert de Veltzlar, traduit de l'anglais par H. D., 5 tomes in-12, Paris (Dentu), 1807, fr.   *BN*

The Forest of Hohenhelbe, a Tale, by the author of *The Wanderer of the Alps* and *The Mystic Castle,* 3 vols., London (Lane, Newman & C°, Minerva Press), 1803   *NYSL*
[by Mr. Singer]

La Novice de Saint Dominique, par Lady Morgan, traduit en française par la Vtesse de Ruolz, 4 tomes in-12, Paris, 1807(?) *Monglond*

The Novice of Saint Dominique, by Miss Owenson, author of *St. Clair,* 4 vols., London (Richard Phillips), 1806 [Miss Owenson, later Lady Morgan] *BM/ML*

Le Pélerin de la Croix, par Elisabeth Helme, traduit de l'anglais par J°°° D°°°, 3 tomes in-12, Paris (Dentu), 1807 *BN*

The Pilgrims of the Cross; or, the Chronicles of Christabelle de Mowbray, an ancient Legend, by Elisabeth Helme, 4 vols., Brentford (P. Norbury), 1805 *UVL*

1808

Saint-Clair des Isles, ou les Exilés de l'Isle de Barra, roman traduit librement de l'anglais par Mme de Montolieu, 4 tomes in-12, Paris (Nicolle), 1808 *ML*

St. Clair of the Isles; or, the Outlaws of Barra, a Scottish Tradition, by Elisabeth Helme, 4 vols., London (T. N. Longman & O. Rees), 1803 *UVL*

Constance de Lindendorf, ou la Tour de Wolfenstadt, traduit de l'anglais de Sophie Frances par Mme P°°° [Julie Perin?], 4 tomes in-12, Paris (Dentu), 1808 *BN*

Constance de Lindendorf; or, the Force of Bigotry, a Tale, by Sophia Francis, author of *Vivonio,* etc., 4 vols., London (Lane, Newman & C°, Minerva Press), 1807 *UVL*

La Famille Wieland, ou les Prodiges, traduction libre d'un Manuscrit américain, par Pigault-Maubaillarcq, Membre Correspondant de la Société Philotechnique, 4 tomes in-12, Calais (Moreaux & C°), 1808, fr. *BN*

Wieland; or, the Transformation, an American Tale, 1798

ALSO: 3 vols., New York & London (H. Colburn), 1811 *UVL* [by Charles Brockden Brown]

1809

L'Epouse du Bandit, ou la Fille de Saxe, traduit de l'anglais par Mme P°°° [Julie Périn?], auteur de *Henry St. Léger; Constance de Lindendorf, La Malédiction Paternelle,* etc., 5 tomes in-12, Paris (J. Chaumerot), 1809 *Monglond*

The Bandit's Bride; or, the Maid of Saxony, a Romance, by the author of *Montbrazil Abbey,* London (Lane, Newman & C°, Minerva Press), 1807 *UVL* [by Louisa Sidney Stanhope]

La Soeur de la Miséricorde, ou la Veille de la Toussaint, par Sophie Francès, traduit de l'anglais par Mme V°°° [Viterne], 4 tomes in-12, Paris (Dentu), 1809 *BN*

The Nun of Misericordia; or, the Eve of All Saints, a Romance, by Sophia L. Frances, 4 vols., London (Lane, Newman & C°, Minerva Press), 1807 *UVL*

Les Visions du Château des Pyrénées, par Anne Radcliffe, traduit sur l'édition imprimée à Londres chez G. & J. Robinson en 1803 [par le comte Germain Garnier et Mme Zimmerman], 3 tomes in-12, Paris (Renard) 1809 *BN*

A spurious attribution. In fact, the translation of:
The Romance of the Pyrenees, 4 vols., London (G. & J. Robinson), 1803 [by Catherine Cuthbertson] *UVL*

1810

Le Couvent de Sainte Catherine, ou les Moeurs du XIIIème Siècle, roman historique d'Anne Radcliffe, traduit de l'anglais par Mme la Baronne Caroline A°°° [Aufdiener] née W°°° de°°°

A spurious attribution.

L'Abbaye de Netley, histoire du Moyen Age, traduit de l'allemand (sic) par J. F. Fontallard, Paris (Ledoux), An 9—1801.

[Wuiet], agrégée à plusieurs académies étrangères, auteur du *Phénix, d'Esope au Bal de l'Opéra,* des *Mémoires de Babiole, du Sterne du Mondego,* etc., 2 tomes in-12, Paris (Renard), 1810
BN/ML

L'Inconnu, ou la Galerie Mystérieuse, par l'auteur de *La Soeur de la Miséricorde,* traduit de l'anglais par Madame de Viterne, 5 tomes in-12, Paris (Dentu), 1810, fr.   BN

The Unknown; or, the Northern Galery, by Francis Lathom, author of *The Mysterious Freebooter, The Impenetrable Secret, Mystery,* etc., 3 vols., London (Lane, Newman & C°, Minerva Press), 1808
UVL

Le Monastère de St. Columba, ou le Chevalier des Armes Rouges, imité de l'anglais par Mme°°°, 3 tomes in-12, Paris (Dentu), 1810(?)   BN/BMS

The Monastery of St. Colomb; or, the Atonement, a Novel, by Regina Maria Roche author of *The Children of the Abbey, Houses of Osma & Almeria, Discarded Son,* etc., 5 vols., London (A. K. Newman & C°, Minerva Press), 1813
UVL

Les Orphelines de Werdenberg, par M. G. Lewis, auteur du *Brigand de Venise,* du *Moine,* etc., traduit de l'anglais par R. J. Durdent, 4 tomes in-12, Paris (Dentu), 1810   BN

Feudal Tyrants; or, the Counts of Carlsheim and Sargans, a Romance, taken from the German by M. G. Lewis, author of *The Bravo of Venice, Adelgitha, Rugantino,* etc., London (J. F. Hughes), 1806   BM/UVL

ALSO: *Elisabeth de Torrenbourg, ou les Dames de Sargans,* 4 tomes, Paris, 1810
Marc
[same novel with different title]

[translated by Lewis from *Elizabeth, Erbin von Toggenburg,* 1789, by Christiane Benedicte Naubert]

Le Tombeau Mystérieux, ou les Familles de Hénarès et d'Almanza, roman espagnol, par John Palmer, auteur des *Mystères de la Tour Noire,* de *La Caverne Habitée,* du *Monde comme il est,* etc., traduit de l'anglais par R. J. Durdent, 2 tomes in-12, Paris (Dentu), 1810
BM/BN

The Mystic Sepulchre; or, such Things have been, a Spanish Romance, by John Palmer jun., 2 vols., London (J. F. Hughes), 1807   BM

1811

Le Spectre de la Montagne de Grenade, 3 tomes, Paris, 1811   Marc

The Spectre of the Mountain of Grenada, a Romance, 3 vols., London (G. Hughes), 1811   UVL

1812

Zofloya, ou le Maure, histoire du XVème Siècle, traduit de l'anglais par Mme de Viterne, 4 tomes in-12, Paris (Barba), 1812   BN

Zofloya; or, the Moor, a Romance of the Fifteenth Century, by Charlotte Dacre, better known as Rosa Matilda, 3 vols., London (Longman, Hurst, Rees & Orme), 1806   UVL

L'Héritière de Montalde, ou le Spectre et les Mystères du Château de Bezanto, imité de l'anglais, par A. C. A. Rouargue, 4 tomes in-12, Paris (Pigoreau), 1812
BN

The Heiress Di Montalde; or, The Castle of Bezanto, by Miss Ann Ker, 2 vols., London (Kerby), 1799   BM

1813

La Forêt de Montalbano, ou le Fils Généreux, traduit de l'anglais de l'auteur des Visions du Château des Pyrénées [Ann Radcliffe], par Mme P°°° [Julie Perin?], 5 tomes in-16, Paris (Dentu), 1813
BN

A spurious attribution to Ann Radcliffe. Actually the translation of: The Forest of Montalbano, by Liss Hamilton, 4 vols., London (J. F. Hughes), 1806   UVL

L'Abbaye de St. Oṣwythe, par l'auteur d'Ethelwina, traduit de l'anglais par Mme°°° [Marèse], 2 tomes in-12, Paris (Renard), 1813   BN

Ancient Records; or, the Abbey of St. Oswythe, a Romance, by T. J. Horsley Curties, author of Ethelwina [. . .], 4 vols., London (W. Lane, Minerva Press), 1801   UVL

1815

Mathilda, ou la Tour Ténébreuse, par Sarah Lansdell, traduit de l'anglais par le traducteur de l'Abbesse, 3 tomes in-12, Paris (Pigoreau), 1815   BN

Unidentified.

1816

La Caverne d'Astolpho, histoire espagnole, traduit de l'anglais par A. J. B. D. [Auguste Jean Baptiste Defauconpret], 2 tomes in-12, Paris (Béchet), 1816(?)
BN

The Cavern of Astolpho, a Spanish Romance, 2 vols., London (Simpkin & Marshall), 1818

L'Hermite de la Tombe Mystérieuse, ou le Fantôme du Vieux Château, anecdote extraite des Annales du Treizième Siècle, par Mme Anne Radcliffe et traduite sur le manuscrit anglais par M.E.L.D.L., Baron de Langon, 3 tomes in-12, Paris (Ménard & Desenne), 1816, fr.
BN/BMS

A spurious attribution. Was in fact written by the alleged "translator," Etienne Léon Baron de Lamothe-Langon.

1817

L'Abbaye de Craigh-Melrose, ou Mémoires de la Famille de Mont-Linton, traduit de l'anglais par Jean Cohen, 4 tomes, Paris (Ledoux & Tenré), 1817   BM

Craig Melrose Abbey, by Henrietta Rouvière, 4 vols., London (Chapple), 1816

Angelo Guicciardini, ou le Bandit des Alpes, traduit de l'anglais de Mme Sophie Frances, 6 tomes, Paris (Dentu), 1817
BN

Angelo Guicciardini; or, the Alpine Bandit, by Sophia L. Francis, 4 vols., London (Lane, Newman & C°, Minerva Press), 1809   NYSL

Barozzi, ou les Sorciers Vénitiens, Chroniques du 15ème Siècle, par Mistriss Charlotte Smith [in fact, by Mrs. Catharine Smith], auteur du Bandit Calédonien, etc., 2 tomes in-12, Paris (Plancher & Delaunay), 1817   BN

Barozzi, or the Venetian Sorceress, a Romance of the Sixteenth Century, by Mrs. Smith, author of The Caledonian Bandit, etc., 2 vols., London (Newman & C°, Minerva Press), 1815   BM/UVL

Le Moine, traduit de l'anglais, Paris (Maradan), An V—1797, tome IV.

Les Mystères de Hongrie, roman historique du XVème Siècle par Edward Moore, traduit de l'anglais sur la 4ème édition par la Csse de L°°°, 4 tomes in-12, Paris (Dentu), 1817   *BN*

The Mysteries of Hungary, a Romantic Story of the Fifteenth Century, by Edward Moore, esq., author of *Sir Ralph de Bigod,* etc., 3 vols., London (A. K. Newman & C°, Minerva Press), 1817   *UVL/BM*

1818

Le Fermier de la Forêt d'Inglewood, ou les Effets de la Superstition, par Elisabeth Helme [. . .], traduit de l'anglais sur la 4ème édition par Henri V . . .n, 4 tomes in-12, Paris (Dentu), 1818   *BN*

The Farmer of Inglewood Forest, a Novel, by Elisabeth Helme, 4 vols., London (W. Lane, Minerva Press), 1796   *UVL*

L'Abbaye de Palsgrave, ou le Revenant, traduit de l'anglais de Mme Charlotte Smith, par M.D.M. Marchais de M°°° [Migneaux], 3 tomes in-12, Paris (Pigoreau), 1818   *BN/UVL*

Translated from "The Story of Edouarda" in: *Letters of a Solitary Wanderer,* containing Narratives of Various Descriptions by Charlotte Smith, 5 vols., London (Longman & C°), 1801-1802 *UVL*

1819

Les Cavernes des Montagnes Bleues, ou Orgueil et Haine, par Mme C. te Smith, traduit de l'anglais par M. Marchais de Migneaux, 5 tomes in-12, Paris (Pigoreau), 1819   *UVL*

Adapted from "The Story of Henrietta" in: *Letters of a Solitary Wanderer,* by Charlotte Smith [see above].

La Main Mystérieuse, ou les Horreurs Souterraines, par A. T. Crandolphe, traduit de l'anglais sur la troisième édition par R. J. Durdent, 3 tomes in-12, Paris (Dentu), 1819   *BN*

The Mysterious Hand; or, Subterranean Horrours! A Romance, by Augustus Jacob Crandolph, 3 vols., London (A. K. Newman & C°, Minerva Press), 1811   *BM*

Les Mystères de la Forêt, ou quel est le Meurtrier? traduit de l'anglais par l'auteur d'*Ellesmer,* Paris, 1819   *Marc*

Who's the Murderer? or, The Mystery of the Forest, a Novel by Eleanor Sleath, 4 vols., London (Lane & Newman, Minerva Press), 1802   *UVL*

Les Mystères de la Tour de Saint Jean, ou les Chevaliers du Temple, par Lewis, traduit par le Baron de L°°°, 4 tomes in-12, Paris (Corbet), 1819 *UVL/BMS/ML*

A spurious attribution. Probably by the alleged "translator," Baron de Lamothe-Langon.

1820

Alicia de Lacey, roman historique par Mistress Wrest [sic], traduit de l'anglais par Mme Elisabeth de Bon, 5 tomes in-12, Paris (Lecointe & Durey), 1820   *UVL*

Alicia de Lacy, an historical romance, by the author of *The Loyalists . . .,* 4 vols., London (Longman, Hurst, Rees, Orme & Brown), 1814   *UVL* [by Mrs. Jane West]

La Bannière Noire, ou le Siège de Clagenfurth, Paris, 1820   *Marc*

The Black Banner; or, the Siege of Clagenfurth, a Romantic Tale, by the author of *The Baron de Falkenheim, Mystery upon Mystery,* etc., London (A. K. Newman & C°, Minerva Press), 1811   *BM*

Les Mariages Nocturnes, ou Octave et la Famille Browning, par Mistress Meek, traduit de l'anglais sur la seconde édition, 4 tomes in-12, Paris (G. C. Hubert), 1820   *UVL*

Midnight Weddings, a Novel, by Mrs. Meeke, 3 vols., London (W. Lane, Minerva Press), 1802   *UVL*

Vivonio, ou l'Heure de la Rétribution, par Sophie Frances, 5 tomes in-12, Paris (Dentu), 1820   *BN*

Vivonio, or the Hour of Retribution, by a young lady [Sophia L. Francis], 4 vols., London (Lane, Newman & C°, Minerva Press), 1806   *UVL*

1821

L'Enfant de la Chaumière de Munster, traduit de l'anglais de Regina Maria Roche, par Mle G°°° deC°°° [Louise Girard de Caudemberg], 5 tomes in-12, Paris (Locard & Davi), 1821   *UVL*

The Munster Cottage Boy, a Tale, by Regina Maria Roche, 4 vols., London (A. K. Newman & C°, Minerva Press), 1820   *UVL*

L'Homme du Mystère, ou Histoire de Melmoth le Voyageur, traduit de l'anglais par Mme [Emile Bégin], 3 tomes in-12, Paris (Delaunay), 1821 *BN/BMS*

ALSO: *Melmoth, ou l'Homme Errant,* par Mathurin [sic], traduit librement de l'anglais par Jean Cohen, 6 tomes in-12, Paris (G. C. Hubert), 1821   *BN*

Melmoth the Wanderer, a Tale, by the author of *Bertram,* etc., 4 vols., Edinburgh (Constable) & London (Hurst & Robinson), 1820   *BM/UVL*

Another translation of the above title.

Le Mystère, ou il y a Quarante Ans, par l'auteur de *Calthorpe,* traduit de l'anglais par le traducteur des romans historiques de Walter Scott (A. J. B. Defauconpret), 4 tomes in-12, Paris, 1821   *BN*

Mystery; or, Forty Years Ago, 3 vols., London (Longman, Hust, Rees, Orme & Browne), 1820
[by Thomas Gaspey]

1822

Blanche et Osbright, suivi de *l'Anacondre,* traduit de l'anglais par M. de S°°°, 2 tomes in-12, Paris (Vve Renard), 1822   *BN*

Translated from: "Mistrust; or, Blanche and Osbright," a feudal Romance, and: "The Anaconda," in *Romantic Tales,* by M. G. Lewis, 4 vols., London (Longman, Hust, Rees & Orme), 1808, vol. I, pp. 3-251 & vol. II, pp. 3-114. *BM/UVL/ML*

La Famille de Montorio, ou la Fatale Vengeance, par Maturin, traduit de l'anglais par Jean Cohen, 5 tomes in-12, Paris (G. C. Hubert), 1822   *BN*

The Fatal Revenge; or the Family of Montorio, by Dennis Jasper Murphy [C. R. Maturin], 3 vols., London (Longman), 1807   *BM/UVL*

Les Ruines du Château de Dunnismoyle, ou les Malheurs de la Famille du Lord St. Kathleen, par l'auteur d'*Edmond le Rebelle,* traduit de l'anglais par M°°°, 5 tomes in-12, Paris (Corbet), 1822 *BN*

Unidentified.

La Famille Wieland, ou les Prodiges, traduction libre d'un Manuscrit américain, par Pigault-Maubaillarcq, Membre Correspondant de la Société Philotechnique, Calais (Moreaux), 1808, frontispiece, tome I.

1823

Les Brigands de l'Estramadure, ou l'Orphelin de la Forêt, librement traduit de l'anglais de W. Ireland, auteur de L'Abbesse, etc., par C. H. Des[rosiers], 3 tomes in-12, Paris (Pigoreau), 1823
BN

In fact, a spurious attribution. Written by the alleged "translator," C. H. Desrosiers, pseud. for Mme de St. Spérat.

Les Mystères Italiens, ou le Château della Torrida, par Francis Lathom, traduit de l'anglais par un des traducteurs des romans historiques de Walter Scott [J. Saladin], 4 tomes in-12, Paris (E. Garnot), 1823
BN/BMS

Italian Mysteries; or, More Secrets than one, a Romance, by Francis Lathom, 3 vols., London (A. K. Newman, Minerva Press), 1820
UVL

La Veille de Saint Pierre, ou la Vengeance, traduction libre de l'anglais par Jean Cohen, 4 tomes in-12, Paris (G. C. Hubert), 1823
BN

The Eve of San-Pietro, a Tale [by Mary Ann Neri], 3 vols., London (T. Cadell & W. Davies), 1804
UVL

1824

Le Nécromancier Irlandais, traduit de l'anglais par M.°°°, 4 tomes in-12, Paris (Boulland & C°), 1824, fr.
ML

The Irish Necromancer; or, Deer Park, a Novel [by Thomas H. Marshall], 3 vols., London (A. K. Newman), 1821

Le Spectre de Saint-Michel, ou les deux Eléonore, roman écossais, traduit de l'anglais de Mrs. C. D. Haynes, par Mme Céleste Coville, 4 tomes in-12, Paris (Pigoreau), 1824
BN

Eleanor; or, the Spectre of St. Michael's, a Romantic Tale, by Miss C. D. Haynes, 5 vols., London (A. K. Newman), 1821
BM

1825

Les Albigeois, roman historique du XIIème Siècle, par le Rév. Ch. R. Maturin, traduit de l'anglais et précédé d'une notive biographique sur le Rév. Ch. R. Maturin, 4 tomes in-12, Paris (C. Gosselin) 1825
BN/BMS

The Albingenses, a Romance, by the Author of Bertram, Woman; or, Pour et Contre, etc. [C. R. Maturin], 4 vols., London (Hurst, Robinson & C°), 1824
BM/UVL

1826

Gaston de Blondeville, ou Henri III tenant sa Cour à Kenilworth en Ardenne, roman par feu Anne Radcliffe, traduit par le traducteur des romans de Sir Walter Scott, 3 tomes in-12, Paris (Mâme & Delaunay-Vallée), 1826 BN

Gaston de Blondeville; or, the Court of Henry III keeping Festival in Ardenne, a Romance, St. Alban's Abbey, a Metrical Tale, with some Poetical Pieces by Ann Radcliffe . . . to which is prefixed a Memoir of the Author, 4 vols., London (H. Colburn), 1826
BM/UVL

1827

De Willenberg, ou le Talisman, histoire mystérieuse, traduite de l'anglaise par MM.°°°, 4 tomes in-12, Paris, 1827 BM

De Willenburgh; or, the Talisman, a Tale of Mystery, by I. M. H. Hales, esq., 4 vols., London (A. K. Newman), 1821

1828

Connal, ou les Milésiens, par Maturin, traduit de l'anglais par Mme la Comtesse°°° [Molé], 4 tomes in-12, Paris (Mâme & Delaunay-Vallée), 1828   *BN*

The Milesian Chief, a Romance, by the author of *Montorio* and *The Wild Irish Boy* [C. R. Maturin], 4 vols., London (H. Colburn), 1812   *BM/UVL*